# THE EVOLUTION OF COGNITIVE BEHAVIOR THERAPY

*The Evolution of Cognitive Behavior Therapy: A Personal and Professional Journey with Don Meichenbaum* explores the "untold story" of how Cognitive Behavior Therapy emerged and discusses the controversies encountered along the way. This volume will feature a personal account of Don Meichenbaum's contributions from his initial work on self-instructional training with schizophrenics and impulsive children, through his work on stress inoculation training, and his most recent works with traumatized individuals. These previously published papers are complemented with updated papers and accompanying commentary.

**Donald Meichenbaum, PhD**, is Distinguished Professor Emeritus, University of Waterloo, Ontario, Canada. He is currently Research Director of the Melissa Institute for Violence Prevention in Miami, Florida. He is one of the founders of Cognitive Behavior Therapy and was also voted "one of the ten most influential psychotherapists of the twentieth century." He has also received a Lifetime Achievement Award from the Clinical Division of the American Psychological Association.

# THE EVOLUTION OF COGNITIVE BEHAVIOR THERAPY

A Personal and Professional Journey with Don Meichenbaum

*Donald Meichenbaum*

Routledge
Taylor & Francis Group

NEW YORK AND LONDON

First published 2017
by Routledge
711 Third Avenue, New York, NY 10017

and by Routledge
2 Park Square, Milton Park, Abingdon, Oxon, OX14 4RN

Routledge is an imprint of the Taylor & Francis Group, an informa business.

Library of Congress Cataloging in Publication Data
A catalog entry for this book has been requested.

ISBN: 978-1-138-81221-5 (hbk)
ISBN: 978-1-138-81222-2 (pbk)
ISBN: 978-1-315-74893-1 (ebk)

Typeset in Bembo
by Cenveo Publisher Services

Visit the eResources: https://www.routledge.com/9781138812222

This book is dedicated to my beloved wife, Marianne, who has supported and encouraged me throughout this entire journey. I also want to express a heartfelt appreciation to my graduate students and colleagues at the University of Waterloo, Ontario, Canada, who helped make my professional career so rewarding.

# CONTENTS

# PROLOGUE

> Human beings are story tellers. It is human nature to make meaning of our lives by organizing what happens to us into stories. We are immersed in our stories.
>
> *(Stephen Joseph, 2011, p. 43)*

Like our clients, we are each not only homo sapiens, but also "homo narrans," or "story tellers." As psychotherapists, we get paid to listen to our clients' stories and we help them develop "healing stories," and the accompanying coping skills in order to conduct a more adaptive, self-fulfilling life.

This book is an invitation to tell my "story" of the development and evolution of Cognitive Behavior Therapy from both a personal and professional perspective. The book addresses the following three questions:

- How did I develop from being an undergraduate psychology major at City College of New York to being voted by clinicians to be "one of the ten most influential psychotherapists of the 20th century?" (Smith, 1982).

- How did the field of Behavior Therapy that initially eschewed the concept of cognition as not having any explanatory value evolve into the Association for Behavioral and Cognitive Therapies?

- How has the conceptualization of the concept of cognition changed in the field of psychotherapy and what are the implications for the ways in which interventions are implemented?

In order to answer these three challenging questions, I have been invited to select articles I have written over the course of 45 years of clinical research and practice. I am presently 75 years old and I have entered into what Erik Erikson called the

"Generativity" phase of life – "giving science away" and sharing any lessons that I have learned in seeing clients over all of these years.

In each part of this book, I have included references to updated, more recent papers that the interested reader can access. Some 20 years ago, I retired as Distinguished Professor Emeritus from the University of Waterloo in Ontario, Canada to become the Research Director of the Melissa Institute for Violence Prevention and Treatment, in Miami, Florida (see www.melissainstitute.org). In fact, the Melissa Institute's websites have had over two million hits worldwide this year. If you visit the *Homepage* and click *Resources*, and then click on *Author Index*, you can then scroll down to *Meichenbaum* and open the additional articles that I refer to in this book.

Sometimes, when a scientist dies his/her students put together a collection of writings in honor of the scholar, or what is called a Festschrift. Since I am not confident that my students would undertake such a venture, I decided to create a Festschrift to myself.

Thank you for joining me on my *journey*, but the *journey* actually continues. I have included a series of follow-up articles that you, the reader can access by visiting: https://www.routledge.com/9781138812222.

## References

Joseph, S. (2011). *What Does Not Kill Us: The New Psychology of Posttraumatic Growth*. New York: Basic Books.

Smith, D. (1982). Trends in counselling and psychotherapy. *American Psychologist*, 37: 802–9.

# THE JOURNEY CONTINUES

As mentioned, I have included a number of follow-up articles that provide an update on my work in the last decade. Throughout this book, I indicate where you, the reader, may wish to access the follow-up articles of interest listed below by visiting the web address given on page xii. Your feedback will be welcomed. You can email me at:

dhmeich@aol.com

- Ways to Implement Interventions in Schools in Order to Make Them Safer, More Inviting and Pedagogically More Effective.

- School and Community-Based Preventative Approaches: "Top Down" and "Bottom-Up" Interventions. (See also the Melissa Institute website: www. teachsafeschools.org.)

- Guidelines for Improving Generalization.

- The Emerging Neurobiology of Resilience: Implications for Psychotherapeutic Interventions.

- A Constructive Narrative Perspective of Trauma and Resilience: The Role of Cognitive and Affective Processes.

- Approaches to Bolster Resilience in Victims of Human Trafficking: Core Tasks of Intervention.

- Resilience-Building as a Means to Prevent PTSD and Adjustment Problems in Military Personnel.

- Trauma, Spirituality and Recovery: Toward a Spiritually-Integrated Psychotherapy.

- Ways to Bolster Resilience in Older Adults.
- 35 Years of Working with Suicidal Patients: Lessons Learned (An Update).
- Treatment of Individuals with Prolonged and Complicated Grief and Traumatic Bereavement.
- Child and Adolescent Depression and Suicide: Promising Hope and Facilitating Change.
- Ways to Bolster Resilience in LGBTQ (Lesbian, Gay, Bisexual, Transgender, Questioning) Youth.
- A Psychotherapist's View of Decision-Making: Implications for Peaceful Negotiations.
- How to Engage Members of the NRA in a Discussion to Change Gun Regulations.
- A Look into the Future of Psychotherapy: The Possible Role of Computer Technology.
- Self-Care for Trauma Psychotherapists and Care Givers: Individual, Social and Organizational Interventions.

# ABOUT THE AUTHOR

**Donald Meichenbaum**, PhD, is Distinguished Professor Emeritus, University of Waterloo, Waterloo, Ontario, Canada, from which he took early retirement. He is currently Research Director of the Melissa Institute for Violence Prevention in Miami, Florida. (See www.melissainstitute.org).

He is one of the founders of Cognitive Behavior Therapy and in a survey of clinicians was voted "one of the ten most influential psychotherapists of the twentieth century." He has received a Lifetime Achievement Award from the Clinical Division of the American Psychological Association. He was Honorary President of the Canadian Psychological Association and Distinguished Visiting Professor at the School of Education, University of Miami.

He received his BA from City College of New York (1962) and his PhD in clinical psychology from the University of Illinois, Champaign (1966).

He has presented in all 50 US states and internationally. He has consulted to a host of psychiatric and educational settings. He has trained clinicians who work with very varied populations including victims of natural disasters (Hurricanes Katrina and Sandy); violence such as terrorist attacks (September 11, New York City, Boston Marathon bombing), school shootings, sexual assaults, returning service members, torture victims, Native Americans, and victims of motor vehicle accidents. He has consulted at centers for the deaf, developmentally delayed, traumatic brain injury, juvenile offenders, and school systems.

He has published extensively, his most recent book being *Roadmap to Resilience* (see www.roadmaptoresilience.com).

# PART I

# Origins

## "Stories" of a Personal and Professional Journey

This part begins with an interview I gave to Dr Michael Hoyt for his 2013 book *Therapist Stories of Inspiration, Passion and Renewal*. It describes my personal journey, and where else would you expect such a story to begin? If not at my mother's kitchen table? My mother surely deserves credit, as one of the founders of cognitive behavior therapy.

The second chapter traces the changing conception of cognition and lays the groundwork for the subsequent interventions of Self-Instructional Training (Part II) and Stress Inoculation Training (Part III), and for the heuristic value of a Constructive Narrative Perspective (Parts IV and V).

The transition from a behavioral classical and operant conditioning model to a more cognitive and affective-oriented view of behavior change did not go smoothly, nor unchallenged. Consider some of the following reactions that were elicited from behavior therapists.

1. Joseph Wolpe, one of the founders of behavior therapy, wrote two articles on the "Malcontents" in the field of behavior therapy who were "bastardizing" the field (Wolpe, 1976a, 1976b).
2. A letter was circulated to have "cognitive" types kicked out of the Association for the Advancement of Behavior Therapy (AABT) and there was an effort not to allow papers on cognitive behavior therapy (CBT) to be put on the AABT conference program.
3. I had a column that appeared in the AABT newsletter that described the nascent work in cognitive behavior therapy. I was called an "oxy-moron", for trying to develop such a "hyphenated" approach to therapy. The column was taken away.

4. A leader in the development in the area of CBT, Michael Mahoney, was directly threatened professionally if he continued to advocate for a cognitive approach to psychotherapy (see Mahoney, 1974).

5. There was a meeting at the Atlanta AABT conference of so-called "cognitive" types (Michael Mahoney, Aaron Beck, Marvin Goldfried, Terry Wilson and myself) to discuss whether we should bolt from AABT and develop a parallel independent Association of Cognitive Behavior Therapy. The "wise" decision was to remain within the AABT organization and allow the data to speak for itself. Also present at that meeting was Eliot Werner who was editor of Plenum Press. This was the origin of the 1977 journal *Cognitive Therapy and Research* of which Michael Mahoney was editor and I was one of the co-editors.

6. One final observation provides some context for how the field of CBT evolved. For four years prior to the publication of the *Journal of Cognitive Therapy and Research*, I had written and distributed a newsletter, *Cognitive Behavior Therapy*. By means of this newsletter, I was able to create a so-called "invisible college." I would review some graduate student's PhD thesis and say, "Anyone working in this area should immediately contact student X." All of a sudden this student, or other similar researchers, would receive requests from around the world, consisting of some 2,000 folks who were receiving the newsletter. A sense of a collaborative research community was created. (This is before the Internet and email.) The list of 2000 names that I had collected became the subscription list for the *Journal of Cognitive Therapy and Research*. In short, I put myself out of business!

7. A zeitgeist for the development of cognitive behavior therapy was emerging that questioned the validity of learning theory (Breger and McGaugh, 1965; McKeachie, 1974), and that highlighted a constructive narrative perspective of psychotherapy (Dember, 1974; Epstein and Erskine, 1983; Shafer, 1981; and Spence, 1984). It was in this context that Michael Mahoney (1974) and Don Meichenbaum (1977) independently wrote their books on cognitive behavior therapy.

8. Finally, the field of cognitive behavior therapy would not have emerged as the "most evidence-based intervention" without the pioneering and supportive efforts of Albert Ellis who personally financed conferences of beginning cognitive behavior researchers who each went on to become leaders in the field (Phil Kendall, Steve Hollon, Marsha Linehan, Marv Goldfried, Dennis Turk, Ray Novaco, John Rush, Brian Shaw, Carol Glass, Diane Arnkoff and others). I was in charge of the invitation list and could provide an opportunity for these bright new PhDs to come together, and share ideas.

9. The second inspirational person who deserves much credit for the development of cognitive behavior therapy is Aaron Beck, the winner of the Distinguished Lasker Award (see Beck, 1970, 1974).

This brief historical description does not quite match the confrontational accounts of the Freud–Jung battles, but it does highlight the degree to which scientists, like our clients, dogmatically hold onto their beliefs.

## References

Beck, A. (1970). Cognitive therapy: nature and relation to behavior therapy. *Behavior Therapy*, 1: 184–200.

Beck, A. (1974). *Cognitive Therapy and Emotional Disorders*. New York: International University Press.

Breger, L. & McGaugh, J. (1965). Critique and reformulation of "learning theory": approaches to psychotherapy and neuroses. *Psychological Bulletin*, 63: 338–58.

Dember, W. (1974). Motivation and the cognitive revolution. *American Psychologist*, 29: 161–8.

Epstein, S. & Erskine, N. (1983). The development of personal theories of reality. In D. Magnusson & V. Allen (eds), *Human Development: An Interaction Perspective*. San Diego, CA: Academic Press, pp. 133–47.

Mckeachie, W. (1974). The decline and fall of the laws of learning. *Educational Resources*, 3: 7–11.

Mahoney, M. (1974). *Cognitive and Behavioral Modification*. Cambridge: MA: Ballinger.

Meichenbaum, D. (1977). *Cognitive Behavior Modification: An Integrative Approach*. New York: Plenum Press.

Shafer, R. (1981). Narrative in the psychoanalytic dialogue. In W. J. Mitchell (eds), *On Narrative*. Chicago: Chicago University Press, pp. 212–53.

Spence, D. (1984). *Narrative Truth and Historical Truth: Meaning and Interpretation in Psychoanalysis*. New York: Norton.

Wolpe, J. (1976a). Behavior therapy and its malcontents I. Denial of its bases and psychodynamic fusionism. *Journal of Behavioral Psychiatry*, 1: 1–5.

Wolpe, J. (1976b). Behavior therapy and its malcontents II. Multimodal electicism, cognitive exclusivism and "exposure" empiricism. *Journal of Behavior Therapy and Experimental Psychiatry*, 1: 109–16.

# 1

# AT MY MOTHER'S KITCHEN TABLE

## Who are we, but the stories we tell?

*Donald Meichenbaum*

| | |
|---|---|
| *Interviewer (Int):* | Dr Hoyt has asked me to interview you for this volume in search of any words of inspiration, passion, and renewal that can be conveyed to psychotherapists. I have been working as a psychotherapist for 25 years. I also teach and train new psychotherapists. I have been asked by these neophytes to submit questions that they would like you to address. Is that okay with you? |
| *Dr Meichenbaum:* | I am honored to be included in the present list of distinguished therapists. Your timing is quite good since I am about to celebrate my 72nd birthday and I had some occasion to reflect on my personal journey as a psychotherapist and researcher. |
| *Int:* | Let's begin with your personal journey. My students want to know how did you go from undergraduate training at City College in New York to being rated as "one of the ten most influential psychotherapists of the 20th century"? |
| *Dr M:* | You are referring to the survey of clinicians that was reported in the *American Psychologist* (Smith, 1982). Well, I entered City College in the hopes of becoming an engineer. I remember that all entering freshman had to attend a session with the Dean of Engineering, who told us to look around the room, because in four years only one in four of us would graduate the engineering program. My reaction was to immediately begin to console my three friends about how to cope with failure and disappointment. I soon learned that I was better at offering support and advice than I was at engineering. |

*Int:* So you graduated City College as a psychology major instead of as an engineer. What was the next step on your journey?

*Dr M:* Your students may be interested in what happened next. Well, I took the Graduate Record Examinations (GREs) and did *not* do well and I began to receive rejection letters from graduate schools. So I decided to write a letter to all of the remaining grad schools that I had not heard from questioning the validity of the GREs in predicting future professional success in psychology. I did a literature search and quoted Lee Cronbach (1960) who had written the textbook *Essentials of Psychological Testing* that there is always an "outlier" who scores poorly on tests, but who succeeds. I signed my letter: "The Outlier"!

*Int:* What chutzpah!

*Dr M:* Actually, the saga continues. I was accepted at the University of Illinois in Champaign in the psychology program where Cronbach had taught. Upon my arrival I was ushered into the office of the Chairman of the Psychology Department, Lloyd Humphries, who greeted individually all incoming grad students. He was a psychometrician and when he opened my application folder, he said, "There must be some mistake, we do not accept students with GRE scores like that. You have to take the GRE's again."

*Int:* Did you take them again?

*Dr M:* Yes, and my scores did not improve that much. The GREs are reliable, but I do not think they have much predictive validity. Four years later, I graduated with honors and with a PhD in clinical psychology. Once again, I found myself in Lloyd Humphrey's office, now doing an "exit" interview. I had waited four years for this moment to ask him to reopen my application folder, and now I said goodbye as the "Outlier."

*Int:* My students will get a kick out of your story of grit. But that seems to be the story of your professional career. I recall the flack you encountered, breaking the mold in the area of psychotherapy in the form of Cognitive Behavior Therapy.

*Dr M:* Well, when I left Illinois clutching my diploma, I was very fortunate to take a teaching position at the University of Waterloo in Ontario, Canada, where I taught and did research for 35 years. It was a new and vibrant university and had great young, bright faculty and graduate students. I thrived and began a research program to explore the role of cognitive and emotional factors in the behavior change process.

*Int:* Before we discuss the "flack" you encountered, can we take a moment to discuss the factors and influences that led to your developing a cognitive-behavioral approach to psychotherapy?

*Dr M:* In retrospect, it is difficult to determine how all of these influences played out. I can recall that as an undergraduate at City College, which was a hotbed of psychoanalytic thinking, they had a visiting professor give a lecture and I sat enamored of his account of people's functioning.

His name was George Kelly (1955) of Personal Construct Theory fame. At the University of Illinois, I had a chance to listen to and meet Victor Frankl, the author of *Man's Search for Meaning* (1963) and the developer of logotherapy. In fact, over the years, as a presenter at the Evolution of Psychotherapy conferences, I had several further opportunities to meet with Frankl. I arrived on the scene when the zeitgeist was filled with folks like Albert Ellis, Aaron Beck, Arnold Lazarus, Michael Mahoney, and others. I was also influenced greatly by the work of Richard Lazarus and his colleagues on the role of appraisal processes in coping, Irving Janis on decision-making, and Norman Garmezy on resilience. This is quite a "Who's Who" list, all of whom inspired and influenced me. But, when it comes down to *the* most substantial influence . . . it would be my mother.

*Int:*     So, *nu?* Doesn't it all go back to one's mother? How did she impact your career path?

*Dr M:*   When she visited me before she died, I noticed something very interesting. I would ask her how things were going in her life? She was a very good storyteller, but she had an interesting way of telling her stories. Not only would she describe the events in her life, but she would tell you what thoughts and feelings she had in the situation, and moreover, she would incorporate in her accounts an evaluation of what were good or productive thoughts versus those that were maladaptive and stress-engendering. Moreover, she would include what different thoughts, feelings and behaviors she could have engaged in to achieve a better outcome:

> So I did $X$ and felt $Y$ and I thought it is bad enough what happened and then I told myself, "Why make the situation worse?" so I changed what I said to myself – Florence Meichenbaum

It dawned on me that I ate dinner with Flo my entire childhood, through college and that this style of thinking became part of my fiber.

*Int:*     Are you suggesting that Flo was one of the founders of Cognitive Behavior Therapy?

*Dr M:*   I think she would be willing to share credit with others. Also, keep in mind that I grew up in New York City and everyone there talks to themselves, everyone has a story to tell. As the adage goes, it is a city of 10 million stories. In fact, when I went to the University of Illinois, I did my doctoral dissertation on "How to Train Schizophrenics to Talk to Themselves." I figured that they were doing this anyway, so perhaps I could influence what and how they talked to themselves.

*Int:*     So this developmental experience was the beginning of your self-talk or cognitive-behavioral therapy approach.

*Dr M:*   As I reflect back on my 35 years of research at the University of Waterloo, I essentially was teaching people in Ontario to do what New Yorkers do, and what my mother was doing all the time. I called it Cognitive Behavior Therapy and became "one of the 10 most influential psychotherapists of the 20th century." I do not understand what is the big deal. In fact, I have come to view my entire professional research career as a way of validating my socialization process.

*Int:* Actually, you are making light of the distinguished research program that you conducted. Your work on self-instructional training with a variety of child and adult clients with impulse control disorders, your work on stress-inoculation training, your work on cognitive narrative perspective of psychotherapy with traumatized clients, your current work with returning service members and their families on ways to bolster resilience, go well beyond your mother's storytelling style.

*Dr M:* That is a very gracious comment. As you know, I took early retirement some 15 years ago from the University of Waterloo and I am now a Distinguished Visiting Professor at the University of Miami in the School of Education and Research Director of the Melissa Institute for Violence Prevention which is located in Miami. Please visit our websites www.melissainstitute.org and one for educators www.teachsafeschools.org. I am very proud to report that these two Melissa Institute websites have had over two *million* hits worldwide. I am into what Erik Erikson called the "generativity phase" of life where one tries to "give science away" and leave a legacy. In fact, you can visit the Melissa Institute website and click on the Author Index on the left side and scroll down to my name and read book chapters and conference handouts that provide a description of my recent work. I welcome your feedback on these papers. You can e-mail me at dhmeich@aol.com.

*Int:* I thought you said you were "retired."

*Dr M:* You are starting to sound like my wife.

*Int:* I do couple's therapy, but we do not have time to go there. Let's pick up on the flack you received as you and others began to introduce and advocate for a cognitive-behavioral approach to psychotherapy.

*Dr M:* It may be difficult to envision what the field of psychotherapy was like back in the 1960s and 1970s, where a strict behavioral approach was dominating the field. Eysenck, Skinner, Wolpe, and many leaders of AABT (American Association of Behavior Therapy) had eschewed the notion of thoughts and feelings, or at least conceptualized them as operants and conditioned responses, subject to so-called "laws of learning," like other behaviors. Into this mix, I arrived employing a different set of metaphors that moved the field from conditioning to information processing, to a constructive narrative approach. This new stance was not welcomed. In print, I was called an "oxymoron" for trying to bridge the gap between cognition and behavior. I recall attending a Behavior Therapy conference and being told I had made "the list." My immediate reaction was that somehow I had made President Nixon's list of who should not be invited to the White House, with Eartha Kitt and others.

"No, no, you made Joseph Wolfe's list of 'malcontents' in behavior therapy." I had surely arrived! Today, Cognitive Behavior Therapy has emerged as the most evidence-based approach to psychotherapy and the organization has added a *C*, for Cognitive. They are now called the Association for Behavioral and Cognitive Therapies (ABCT).

*Int:*   Your mother would be proud of you.

*Dr M:*   But, here is the rub. While cognitive behavioral approaches have emerged as an important source of psychotherapeutic interventions, the more recent meta-analyses of cognitive behavioral therapies versus bona fide comparison groups have questioned the relative efficacy of CBT approaches. (See the recent papers by Wampold *et al.*, 1997; Wampold, 2010, listed in the Reference section.) These authors seriously challenge the mechanisms of change proposed by myself and others. Moreover, the excellent work by Michael Lambert (2010) and his colleagues highlights the critical role of the therapeutic alliance and ongoing feedback mechanisms as key to psychotherapeutic behavior change. Thus, we have come full circle in the field.

Should your students learn and master therapeutic manuals designed to treat patients with specific psychiatric disorders as advocated by some, or should they focus on the transdiagnostic commonalities across patients with varied psychiatric disorders and the common mechanisms of change? You know, there are no winners in the so-called race of which treatment procedures work best (Luborsky *et al.*, 1975). After being a psychotherapist for 40 years, and a consultant/trainer giving innumerable workshops in all 50 US states and around the world, and as a researcher for a similar period of time, I am still challenged by the question of "What makes psychotherapy work?"

*Int:*   Where does your passion for research come from?

*Dr M:*   Although it is not very fashionable at the present time, when I was in graduate school at the University of Illinois (1962–6), the clinical training program embraced the Boulder Model. We were trained to wear two professional hats – first being a contributor and critical consumer of research and the second to be a culturally sensitive practicing clinician. Each arena should inform the other. My research derived from my strong desire to test out my hypotheses and to play "detective" and to be an "honest broker" when training clinicians.

*Int:*   I am also reminded that Michael Lambert (2010) observed that in about 10% of cases patients get worse as a result of participating in psychotherapy.

*Dr M:*   Yes, that concerns me greatly, since I continue to train psychotherapists. My solution to this dilemma of negotiating between those who advocate for "evidence-based interventions" and those who highlight the role of non-specific factors (the so-called "dodo bird effect") is to highlight the role of expertise. Some therapists are "experts" in getting positive results, more so than others (interested readers may want to listen to the dialogue between myself and Scott Miller that took place at the 2009 Evolution of Psychotherapy, available at www.miltonhericksonfoundation.org).

When I present workshops on "expertise" in psychotherapy, I usually begin by asking the question: "What is the most important skill that psychotherapists need in order to achieve positive results, to have a rewarding practice and to maintain a good reputation?"

*Int:* What is that skill?

*Dr M:* An analysis of the research literature clearly indicates that the most important skill a psychotherapist needs in order to have good treatment outcomes is – get ready for this – the ability to choose one's patients carefully. Patient characteristics account for the largest portion of the variance in treatment outcome. If you could delimit your practice to what are called YAVIS – Young, Attractive, Verbal, Intelligent, and Successful – folks like yourself, then you will have positive treatment outcomes. YAVIS folks will get better with, or without, your help – so you might as well take credit for the change.

*Int:* But most of us do *not* treat patients who are YAVIS. My practice is filled with folks who have a history of victimization, present multiple comorbid problems often involving substance abuse and have high-risk unsupportive environments.

*Dr M:* That is my clientele as well. In fact, you can view various training films that I have made with such challenging clients (e.g., see my film on cognitive behavior therapy available from www.apa.org). So then, what are the various core tasks of psychotherapy that "expert" therapists engage in?

*Int:* That is *the* key question my students want an answer to.

*Dr M:* In formulating my answer, you need to know that I love doing psychotherapy or counseling. I just love it and the reason I love it so much is that I love the way I think about cases. I am totally enamored with my head. I love the "detective work," the "art of Socratic questioning," the ability to help patients "restory" their lives and develop intra- and interpersonal coping skills and bolster their resilience and build upon their strengths.

*Int:* It sounds like your inspiration, passion, and renewal come from your clients.

*Dr M:* Definitely! Most recently, working with returning service members and their family members is inspiring. Seventy percent of those who have been through horrific combat experiences, often with injuries, will evidence resilience and, in some cases, posttraumatic *growth*. They have so much to teach us. I am their student.

*Int:* But how do you help the 30% who evidence chronic disabilities, both psychological and physical?

*Dr M:* This is where the core skills of being an "expert" psychotherapist come into play. These core psychotherapeutic skills include:

1. The ability to establish, maintain and monitor a trusting, supportive, nonjudgmental *therapeutic alliance*, in a culturally and gender-sensitive manner. In addition, there is a need to address any "ruptures" in the therapeutic alliance. The quality of the therapeutic alliance is the "glue" that makes everything else work. But, from my perspective, the quality of the therapeutic alliance is a necessary, but not sufficient, condition in order to achieve psychotherapeutic success.

2. There is also a need to provide ongoing psychoeducation. I do *not* mean using a didactic lecture, but rather the art of questioning, which is your most valuable tool. It involves collaborative formulation of a Case Conceptualization Model, the dispelling of myths, and the need to assess and provide ongoing feedback. There is a need to probe for the client's "implicit theory" about his/her presenting problems and notions of what is needed to change. The "fit" between the patient's and therapist's models is critical to foster the patient's therapeutic engagement and participation. Note that ongoing assessment and session-by-session feedback is critical to outcome. Assessment and treatment are critically interlinked throughout.

3. The "expert" psychotherapist is effective in nurturing the key ingredient of *HOPE*. There are a number of ways to do this, but one of the best ways is to engage clients into collaborative goal-setting that provides "SMART" goals: Specific, Measurable, Achievable, Realistic and Time-limited goals.

   There is also the need to use the "Art of Questioning" in order to solicit the "rest of the story" of what clients have been able to achieve, to survive, *in spite of* their stressors and life experiences. There is a need to obtain multiple timelines of what they have been through, but also a timeline of what they were able to accomplish *in spite of* – namely, the signs of strengths and evidence of individual, familial, and community-cultural resilience that they possess and can call upon.

   I encourage the clinicians I train to emulate that fine inquisitor Peter Falk playing the character Detective Columbo. I encourage clinicians to "play dumb," using their befuddlement, confusion, and Socratic questioning style. For some clinicians, of course, "playing dumb" comes naturally. The trick is how to be inquisitive, without giving up your "placebo value."

4. Cognitive-behavioral techniques can be called upon to address the next psychotherapeutic goal of nurturing and teaching direct action and emotionally palliative coping skills. The expert psychotherapist does *not* merely "train and hope," but builds into treatment the technology and guidelines designed to increase the likelihood of generalization and maintenance of treatment and training effects such as relapse prevention, self-attribution training (client taking credit for change),

and putting the client into a consultative mode of teaching others, demonstrating his or her coping skills and soliciting the reasons why engaging in such behavioral acts will help them achieve their treatment goals.

In addition, for those clients with a history of victimization or current risk of revictimization, there is a need for the expert psychotherapist to ensure safety, to help clients avoid revictimization, to allow them to disclose their "story" at their own pace, and assist them to (re)consider the conclusions they draw about themselves, others and the future as a result of such life experiences. It is not that "bad" things have happened, but *what is the story that clients fashion and construct about such events that is critical*. There is a need for individuals to engage in a meaning-making mission. For some clients this may entail some form of spirituality or religious healing activities.

In short, what I am proposing is a Constructive Narrative Perspective (CNP) of psychotherapy that helps clients restory and integrate their traumatic victimization experiences into their autobiographical memories and personal accounts. Recent research highlights the value of such a CNP approach to psychotherapy that can be integrated and blended with the skills training components of cognitive-behavioral interventions. [See the Reference list for some descriptions of this research.]

*Int:*    You are suggesting that we are all storytellers and that we can live by the stories we tell.

*Dr M:*    Exactly. This book is filled with psychotherapists sharing their stories. This is exactly what our clients do. My job is to listen attentively, nonjudgmentally, and compassionately to the stories my clients have to tell and collaboratively help them develop more adaptive stories and the accompanying skills to achieve and live their more functional accounts.

*Int:*    So, renewal, inspiration, and passion are not only for the readers of this book, but for your clients, as well.

*Dr M:*    I have often asked myself, what contributed to my effectiveness as a psychotherapist? One of the answers I have come up with is that no matter how bad off are my client's presenting problems, psychiatric conditions, or life situation, I refuse, as a psychotherapist, to get depressed. No client leaves my office without my helping him or her to find some "nuggets," or signs of strength and resilience. No matter what the client does, or does not do in psychotherapy. I can help him or her view it as "buying into treatment." I can capitalize on the fact that the client's behavior can be reframed. I believe that my collaborative realistic planfulness, my efforts at joint goal-setting, my meta-communication of hopefulness are some of the key ingredients to successful treatment outcomes. As I say to my clients:

Let me explain what I do for a living. I work with folks like yourself and try to find out how things are right now in your life and how you would like them to be. How can *we* work together to help you achieve your goals?

Moreover, I would like us to be informed by what you have tried in the past. What have you tried? What worked … as evidenced by? What difficulties did you have and how did you anticipate and handle these challenges? What were you most satisfied with that we can build upon?

Moreover, if we work together, and I hope we can, how would we know if you were making progress? What would we see changed? What, if anything, would other people notice?

May I ask one last question, if I might? Can you foresee, can you envision, anything that might get in the way of your achieving your treatment goals? How can you learn to anticipate and handle those barriers should they arise?

*Int:*    Whenever I have watched you work with a client (on videotapes at conferences) I have always been struck by how present you are and how much you *care* about the person – as well as how thoughtful and constructive the questions are that you ask.

*Dr M:*    Thank you. That's the "glue" I was referring to. The therapeutic alliance is built on a foundation of caring and respect – it's not enough to just go through the motions of asking good questions.

*Int:*    I also noticed a couple of things about your client message. First, all your questions are "what" and "how" questions and you do not use "why" questions. Second, I see you bathe your social discourse with a number of "we" statements.

*Dr M:*    Yes, both of these strategies are intentional on my part. I do not find "why" questions very productive, while "what" and "how" questions pull for the process of thinking and behavior and accompanying feelings that can be addressed in treatment. The heavy emphasis on "we" statements reinforces the notion of collaboration and strengthens the therapeutic alliance. I am at my psychotherapeutic best when the clients I see are one step ahead of me, offering the advice or suggestions I would otherwise offer. Clients are more likely to implement strategies they came up with, and as a result they feel more empowered and more self-efficacious. I guard against becoming a "surrogate frontal lobe" for my clients. "Expert" psychotherapists *do not* see themselves as infallible experts, but continually ask their clients for feedback and for ways to improve the working psychotherapeutic journey.

*Int:*    There is one last question that my colleagues and students have. What do you see as the future of psychotherapy in addressing the extensive mental health needs of the general population?

*Dr M:*    As Research Director of an institute, this is something to which I have given a lot of consideration. Recently, this issue was also addressed in a thoughtful article by Al Kazdin and Stacey Blasé (2011). They asked how can psychotherapy be rebooted, using computer technology? As I mentioned, I have been consulting for the National Guard and I have recently completed a book entitled *Roadmap to Resilience* (Meichenbaum, 2012), enumerating various ways to bolster resilience in six domains (physical, interpersonal, emotional, cognitive, behavioral, and spiritual). We have been working on ways to put this information online (see www. warfighterdiaries.com), where you can download coping stories by returning service members onto your iPod, iPad, cell phone, and the like. This is a way to take "teaching stories" and turn them into modeling films.

*Int:*    Could you give an example or two of the kinds of stories soldiers (and/ or clinicians) might see?

*Dr M:*    There are now a number of resources (websites and videos) that use storytelling as a means of helping service members listen to healing accounts of other veterans who have returned from deployment. In each of these narratives, the returning service member describes some "traumatizing" event such as being injured due to an improvised explosive device, descriptions of their accompanying injuries, both physical and psychological. Most importantly, they also continue to relate the "rest of the story," of resilience and personal growth with the help of others. They relate how such events contributed to stronger interpersonal relationships, increased personal strengths, a greater appreciation of life and spiritual renewal. The interested reader can visit the following websites to listen to stories of resilience: www.warfighterdiaries.com, www. MakeTheConnection.net/stories-of-connection, and www.realwarriers.com. They should also view the HBO video *Alive Day Memories*. These are each effective demonstrations of the power of a Constructive Narrative Perspective as a psychotherapeutic tool.

*Int:*    Wow! I can imagine how having these easily available to download on your phone or computer could help someone who was discouraged or despairing.

*Dr M:*    Yes. I am also involved in a number of other computer-based training programs for clients, their family members, and for psychotherapists. Imagine that as a psychotherapist you would be able to access demonstrations of "expert" psychotherapists implementing each of the Core Skills of treatment – short vignettes illustrating ways to build and repair a therapeutic alliance, how to collaboratively establish therapy goals, how to ask useful questions, how to nurture hope, and so on. Moreover, you would be able to submit to the website your ways of implementing that psychotherapeutic skill to be shared with others, as the website goes viral.

*Int:*    Are you suggesting that what you learned at your mother's kitchen table could be given away worldwide?

*Dr M:*   I have often wondered what psychotherapy would be like if, instead of B. F. Skinner (1948), my mother had written *Walden 2*.

## References

Cronbach, L. J. (1960) *Essentials of Psychological Testing* (2nd edn). New York: Harper & Row.

Frankl, V. E. (1963) *Man's Search for Meaning: An Introduction to Logotherapy*. New York: Washington Square Press.

Kazdin, A. E. and Blasé, S. L. (2011) Rebooting psychotherapy research and practice to reduce the burden of mental illness. *Perspectives in Psychological Science*, 6, 21–37.

Kelly, G. A. (1955) *The Psychology of Personal Constructs*. New York: Norton.

Lambert, M. J. (2010) *Prevention of Treatment Failure: The Use of Measuring, Monitoring, and Feedback in Clinical Practice*. Washington DC: American Psychological Association.

Luborsky, L., Singer, B., and Luborsky, L. (1975) Comparative studies of psychotherapies: Is it true that "Everyone has won and all must have prizes"? *Archives of General Psychiatry*, 32, 995–1008.

Meichenbaum, D. (2012) *Roadmap to Resilience*. Clearwater, FL: Institute Press.

Skinner, B. F. (1948) *Walden 2*. Indianapolis, IN: Hackett.

Smith, D. (1982) Trends in counseling and psychotherapy. *American Psychologist*, 37(7), 802–9.

Wampold, B. F., Modin, G. W., Moody, M., Stah, F., Benson, K., and Ahn, H. (1997) A meta-analysis of outcome studies comparing bona fide psychotherapies: empirically, "all must have prizes." *Psychological Bulletin*, 122, 203–15.

Wampold, B. F., Imel, Z. E., Laska, K. M., and Benish, S. (2010) Determining what works in the treatment of PTSD. *Clinical Psychology Review*, 30, 923–33.

# 2

# CHANGING CONCEPTIONS OF COGNITIVE BEHAVIOR MODIFICATION

## Retrospect and prospect

### *Donald Meichenbaum*

A retrospective analysis of cognitive behavior modification reveals that three major metaphors have been offered to explain the role that cognitions play in behavior change. These metaphors include cognition as a form of conditioning, information processing, and, currently, narrative construction. The implications of using each of these metaphors are discussed.

Since its inception, cognitive behavior modification (CBM) has attempted to integrate the clinical concerns of psychodynamic and systems-oriented psychotherapists with the technology of behavior therapists. CBM has contributed to current integrative efforts in the field of psychotherapy. As in most forms of psychotherapy. CBM was the result of an evolutionary process and was part of a zeitgeist of what Dember (1974) called a "cognitive revolution."

Cognitive-behavioral therapies derived from a long tradition of semantic therapists ranging from Dubois to Kelly, and along the way were influenced by the social learning theories of Rotter, Bandura, Mischet, Kanfer, and others. The influential writings of Albert Ellis, Aaron Beck, and both Arnold and Richard Lazarus highlighted the role of cognitive and affective processes in psychopathology and in the behavior change process.

One major catalyst for the development of cognitive-behavioral therapy was the growing dissatisfaction with both the empirical and the theoretical bases of a strictly behavioral therapeutic approach. A number of authors, such as Breger and

McGaugh (1965), Brewer (1974), McKeachie (1974), Mahoney (1974), and Meichenbaum (1977), were questioning the adequacy of learning theory explanations of both psychopathology and behavioral change. A second major catalyst was the initial results of cognitive therapists such as Aaron Beck (1970) and Albert Ellis (1962) who demonstrated the promise of their interventions.

This interest in cognitive factors in psychotherapy was often not well received by "behavioral types," who called for the exclusion of "cognitive types" from such organizations as the Association for the Advancement of Behavior Therapy. Such malcontents were supposedly diluting, if not undermining, the "purity" of behavior therapy. But Pandora's box, with all of its difficulties and challenges, had been opened as cognitive behavioral practitioners struggled with questions as how best to conceptualize their clients' cognitions and how to fit such cognitive processes into the complex reciprocal interrelationships with clients' feelings, behavior, and resultant consequences, as well as with physiological and social-cultural processes. The answers to these research questions have been strongly influenced by the specific conceptualizations and metaphors used to explain clients' thought processes. I will consider three of these guiding metaphors, namely conditioning, information processing, and constructing narratives.

## Conditioning as a metaphor

Initially, cognitive behavioral therapists proposed that an individual's cognitions could be viewed as covert behaviors, subject to the same "laws of learning" as are overt behaviors. In the tradition of Skinner and conditioning theorists, cognition was viewed as covert operants, or what Homme (1965) called "coverants," supposedly responsive to both external and internal contingencies and altered by contiguous pairings, as in the case of covert sensitization (Cautela, 1973). Clients' self-statements and images were viewed as discriminative stimuli and as conditioned responses that come to guide and control overt behavior. The focus of treatment was to "decondition" and to strengthen new connections, bolster and rehearse adaptive coping skills, and the like. The technology of behavior therapy, such as modeling, mental rehearsal, and contingency manipulations, was used to alter not only clients' overt behaviors, but also their thoughts and feelings.

## Information processing as a metaphor

A different metaphor soon began to influence the development of CBM, namely that of the mind as a computer, with the accompanying language of information processing and social learning theory. It was proposed that clients' cognitions could be conceptualized as consisting of a number of processes, including decoding, encoding, retrieval, preattention and attention, attributional biases, and distortion mechanisms, the last in the form of cognitive errors. Moreover, these cognitive errors were viewed as being a consequence of the cognitive structures or beliefs, schemata, current concerns, and tacit assumptions that clients brought to situations. It was proposed that such beliefs were strengthened by the manner in which clients behaved. The operable terms to depict this sequence were *transactional, interactional,* and *bidirectional,* as described by Lazarus and Folkman, Bandura, Wachtel, and Patterson. Individuals were viewed as "architects" of their experiences, influencing the data they were creating and collecting. Rather than being passive, the information-processing perspective proposed that individuals may inadvertently, if not unwittingly and even unknowingly, behave in ways that elicited the very reactions in others (a form of data) that they could take as evidence to confirm their views of themselves and of the world.

A number of investigators (e.g., Beck, 1970, and Hollon, 1990, who studied depression; Barlow, 1988, and Clark, 1986, who studied anxiety disorders; Dodge and Coie, 1987, and Novaco, 1979, who studied aggression in children and in adults, respectively; and Marlatt and Gordon, 1985, who studied clients with addiction problems) have used an information-processing perspective to explain their clients' difficulties and to formulate an intervention plan.

From an information-processing perspective, clients are seen to be depressed because they distort reality as a result of a number of cognitive errors (e.g., dichotomous thinking, magnification, and personalization) and because they hold so-called irrational beliefs. They also hold negative views of themselves, of the past, and of the future, emitting characterological attributions of self-blame when they encounter failures and frustrations. Anxious clients who have panic attacks are seen as misinterpreting bodily cues and viewing them as personal threats given their preoccupation with physical well-being and the need to maintain a sense of personal control. Such misinterpretations or appraisals lead to "catastrophic" anxiety-engendering ideation with accompanying physiological arousal, as a vicious self-perpetuating cycle is established and maintained. Those clients who have problems with anger and who are aggressive, especially if that aggressive behavior is reactive as opposed to instrumental in nature, have been found to hold hostile attributional styles; to interpret ambiguous interpersonal cues as provocations, retrieving from memory other aggressive events; and to fail to generate and implement socially acceptable alternatives. Moreover, aggressive clients, both children and adults, behave in ways that elicit the coercive and reciprocal reactions that confirm their aggressive outlooks. Thus their expectations and self-statements become self-fulfilling prophecies.

Cognitive behavioral therapists have developed intervention programs that are designed to help clients become aware of these processes and teach them how to notice, catch, monitor, and interrupt the cognitive-affective-behavioral chains and to produce more adaptive compatible coping responses. Moreover, cognitive-behavioral therapists help clients to identify high-risk situations that they are likely to encounter and to consider ways to prepare, handle, and deal with failures if they should occur (namely, a form of relapse prevention). When positive results occur, clients are encouraged to make self-attributions for the changes that they have been able to bring about. Often, clients will require specific skills training, and treatment frequently involves significant others (spouse, family members, teachers, and peers) to increase the likelihood of generalization and maintenance.

## Constructive narrative as a metaphor

The notion that clients are architects and constructors of their environments has given rise to a third metaphor that is guiding the present development of cognitive behavioral therapies. The constructivist perspective is founded on the idea that humans actively construct their personal realities and create their own representational models of the world. This constructivist perspective finds root in the philosophical writings of Immanuel Kant, Ernst Cassirer, and Nelson Goodman, and in the psychological writings of Willhelm Wundt, Alfred Adler, George Kelly, Jean Piaget, Viktor Frankl, and Jerome Frank. More recently, the constructivist perspective has been advocated by Epstein and Erskine (1983), Mahoney and Lyddon (1988), McCann and Perlman (1990), Neimeyer and Feixas (1990), Meichenbaum (1990), and White and Epton (1990). Common to each of these proponents is the tenet that the human mind is a product of constructive symbolic activity, and that reality is a product of personal meanings that individuals create. It is not as if there is one reality and clients distort that reality, thus contributing to their problems; rather, there are multiple realities, and the task for the therapist is to help clients become aware of how they create these realities and of the consequences of such constructions. Bruner (1990), writing from a narrative psychology perspective, described how individuals make meaning or construct stories to explain their symptoms and situations. For instance, clients may use metaphors to describe their emotional experience. One client recently reported that she "always stuffed her feelings down" and then she would explode; another patient described "how he built walls between himself and others." The therapist helped these clients to appreciate the nature and impact of using such metaphors. What is the impact, what is the emotional toll, what is the price she or he pays for behaving in accord with such a metaphor of "stuffing feelings" and "building walls"? At this point, the therapist explored collaboratively and experientially the "price" they paid. "If this is not the way they would like things to be, then what could they do?" It is not a big step for clients to suggest that perhaps they should "not stuff feelings" and "not build walls." The therapist then says, "Not stuff feelings, not build walls, that is interesting. What did you have in mind?" In this manner the therapist enlists the client as a collaborator in engaging in what Shafer (1981) called "narrative repair."

The metaphor of a constructive narrative to explain clients' problems has a number of important theoretical and practical implications for the further development of CBM.

1.   The therapist is viewed as a co-constructivist helping clients to alter their stories, as Spence (1984) proposed. The therapist must first listen empathically

and reflectively to the initial story line of the patient and then collaboratively help the client to transform his or her story. A nurturant, compassionate, non-judgmental set of conditions is required for distressed clients to tell their story at their own pace. A number of clinical techniques, including reflective listening, Socratic dialogue, sensitive probes, imagery reconstruction of stressful experiences, and client self-monitoring are used to help clients relate what happened and why. Thus, the role of relationship variables is critical, as is the role of affect in the therapeutic process.

2. The therapist helps clients to cognitively reframe stressful events and to "normalize" their reactions. From this perspective, it is not the symptoms of depression, anxiety, and anger per se that interfere with functioning; rather, what clients say to themselves and others about these reactions, the stories they construct, are important to the adaptive process. The therapist not only helps to validate clients' reactions but indicates that such symptoms are normal. In fact, their emotional distress is viewed as a normal spontaneous reconstructive and natural rehabilitative adaptive process. This reconceptualization process is an attempt to formulate a "healing theory" of what happened and why (see Meichenbaum and Fitzpatrick, in press, for a fuller discussion). The therapist also helps clients relate examples of their strengths, resources, and coping abilities to convey "the rest of the story" (to use a popular metaphor). The therapist avoids holding a pathology bias, instead looking for and building on those exceptional occasions when clients coped effectively.

3. From a narrative perspective, the therapist not only helps clients to break down global stressors into behaviorally prescriptive events so they can use problem-solving and emotionally palliative coping techniques, but also helps them build new assumptive worlds and new ways to view themselves and the world (Meichenbaum, in press).

   The cognitive therapist helps clients to construct narratives that fit their particular present circumstances, that are coherent, and that are adequate in capturing and explaining their difficulties. As Shafer (1981) indicated, therapy allows clients to retell their tale "in a way that allows them to understand the origins, meanings and significance of present difficulties, and moreover to do so in a way that makes change conceivable and attainable" (p. 38). What matters most about this story telling or narrative construction is not its "historical truthfulness," as Spence (1984) observed, but its "narrative truthfulness."

4. One of the implications of adapting the constructive narrative metaphor is that it suggests that one looks at therapeutic interventions in a different fashion. Perhaps, one can even find therapeutic suggestions from the way that teachers teach narrative writing. It also suggests different types of dependent measures that individuals can use (e.g., indicators of narrative transformations).

The field of CBM has come a long way since its inception. The story continues to unfold and to change as new metaphors are adopted and new narratives constructed.

## References

Barlow, D. (1988) *Anxiety and Its Disorders: The Nature and Treatment of Anxiety and Panic.* New York: Guilford Press.

Beck, A. (1970) Cognitive therapy: nature and relation to behavior therapy. *Behavior Therapy*, 1, 184–200.

Breger, L. and McGaugh, J. (1965) Critique and reformulation of "learning theory": approaches to psychotherapy and neurosis. *Psychological Bulletin*, 63, 338–58.

Brewer, W. (1974) There is no convincing evidence for operant or classical conditioning in adult humans. In W. Weimer and D. Palermo (eds), *Cognition and the Symbolic Processes*, Vol. 1. Hillsdale, NJ: Erlbaum, pp. 1–42.

Bruner, J. (1990) *Acts of Meaning.* Cambridge, MA: Harvard University Press.

Cautela, J. (1973) Covert processes and behavior modification. *Journal of Nervous and Mental Disease*, 157, 27–35.

Clark, D. M. (1986) A cognitive approach to panic. *Behaviour Research and Therapy*, 24, 161–70.

Dember, W. (1974). Motivation and the cognitive revolution. *American Psychologist*, 29, 161–8.

Dodge, K. A. and Coie, J. D. (1987) Social information-processing factors in reactive and proactive aggression in children's peer groups. *Journal of Personality and Social Psychology*, 53, 1146–58.

Ellis, A. (1962). *Reason and Emotion in Psychotherapy.* New York: Lyle Stuart.

Epstein, S. and Erskine, N. (1983) The development of personal theories of reality. In D. Magnusson and V. Allen (eds), *Human Development: An Interactional Perspective.* San Diego, CA: Academic Press, pp. 133–47.

Hollon, S. D. (1990). Cognitive therapy and pharmacotherapy for depression. *Psychiatric Annals*, 20, 249–58.

Homme, L. (1965) Perspectives in psychology: control of coverants, the operants of the mind. *Psychological Record*, 15, 501–11.

McCann, I. L. and Perlman, L. A. (1990) *Psychological Trauma and the Adult Survivor.* New York: Brunner/Mazel.

McKeachie, W. (1974) The decline and fall of the laws of learning. *Educational Researcher*, 3, 7–11.

Mahoney, M. (1974). *Cognition and Behavior Modification.* Cambridge, MA: Ballinger.

Mahoney, M. J. and Lyddon, W. J. (1988). Recent developments in cognitive approaches to counseling and psychotherapy. *Counseling Psychologist*, 16, 190–234.

Marlatt, G. A. and Gordon, J. R. (1985) *Relapse Prevention: Maintenance Strategies in the Treatment of Addictive Behaviors.* New York: Guilford Press.

Meichenbaum, D. (1977) *Cognitive Behavior Modifications: An Integrative Approach.* New York: Plenum Press.

Meichenbaum, D. (1990) Evolution of cognitive behavior therapy: origins, tenets and clinical examples. In J. Zeig (ed.). *The Evolution of Psychotherapy: II.* New York: Brunner/ Mazel, pp. 96–115.

Meichenbaum, D. (in press) Stress inoculation training: a twenty year update. In R. L. Woolfolk and P. M. Lehrer (eds), *Principles and Practices of Stress Management*. New York: Guilford Press.

Meichenbaum, D. and Fitzpatrick, D. (in press) A constructivist narrative perspective of stress and coping: stress inoculation applications. In L. Goldberger and S. Breznitz (eds), *Handbook of Stress*. New York: Free Press.

Neimeyer, R. and Feixas, G. (1990) Constructivist contributions to psychotherapy integration. *Journal of Integrative and Eclectic Psychotherapy*, 9, 4–20.

Novaco, R. (1979) The cognitive regulation of anger and stress. In P. C. Kendall and S. D. Hollon (eds), *Cognitive Behavioral Interventions: Theory, Research and Procedures*. San Diego, CA: Academic Press, pp. 84–101.

Shafer, R. (1981) Narration in the psychoanalytic dialogue. In W. J. Mitchell (ed.), *On Narrative*. Chicago: University of Chicago Press, pp. 212–53.

Spence, D. (1984) *Narrative Truth and Historical Truth: Meaning and Interpretation in Psychoanalysis*. New York: Norton.

White, M. and Epton, D. (1990) *Narrative Means to Therapeutic Ends*. New York: Norton.

# PART II

# The Development and Implementation of Self-Instructional Training

As I mentioned, I grew up in New York City where people talk to themselves all the time; sometimes even out loud. When I began my research at the University of Illinois as a clinical intern at the local Veteran's Administration Hospital, my thesis topic was schizophrenic thought disorder. Could such psychiatric patients be taught to control pathognomonic verbalizations, emit "healthy talk," and engage in more abstract forms of thinking (Meichenbaum, 1966, 1969)? The first article in this part, conducted in collaboration with my graduate student Roy Cameron, assessed the feasibility with a schizophrenic population. Schizophrenic patients were observed often "talking to themselves," and the challenge was whether by means of direct instruction, modeling, cognitive rehearsal, and self-guidance, they could learn self-regulatory skills, attentional controls and editing processes. In 1971, the initial answer was a tentative "yes." This initial study gave impetus to the development of cognitive behavioral interventions with psychotic patients (Kingdon and Turkington, 1994; Turkington, Dudley, Warman, and Beck, 2006).

Our clinical research focus shifted to a different population, namely impulsive and hyperactive children who evidenced self-regulatory deficits and who lacked the penchant and ability to regularly "think before they act" (Meichenbaum and Goodman, 1971). In the tradition of the sociocultural approach of Vygotsky (1978) and Wertsch (1985), who highlighted that social mediation takes place by externalization and internalization, we developed a self-instructional training procedure. The trainer/teacher externalizes his/her cognitive, motivational, and emotion-regulation skills to make them accessible for the tutee who, during their learning process, internalizes those skills. Such internalization is seen as a transition from other-regulation to self-regulation. Research on socially shared regulation emerged within this perspective. In a chapter that I wrote in 1978 (Meichenbaum, 1978), I reviewed the literature on self-instructional training with children with attention deficit hyperactive disorders. This cognitive behavioral approach taught children to use performance-relevant self-statements that include:

1. problem identification, problem definition and self-interrogation;
2. focusing attention on the goals of the task;
3. specific task strategies and response guidance;
4. coping skills and error-correction options;
5. self-reinforcement for having tried, including standard setting and self-evaluation.

A number of researchers developed cognitive behavioral training programs and conducted research on self-instructional training with a variety of children who evidenced self-regulation deficits. They include many of those whom I worked with (Michael Bloomquist, Linda Braswell, Daphne Blumenthal, Ann Brown, Bonnie Camp, Ann Copeland, Virginia Douglas, Steve Graham, Karen Harris, Barbara Henker, Stephan Hinshaw, Ed Kirby, Phil Kendall, Barbara Keogh, Mary Konstantareas, Dan O'Leary, Ann Palinscar, Michael Pressley, Barbara Wasik, Carol Whalen, Bernice Wong, and Gail Zivin). Thus, a small demonstration study contributed to a zeitgeist for the development of cognitive behavioral self-instructional training interventions. The promise of employing cognitive behavioral interventions to nurture self-regulation and metacognitive skills has been demonstrated in review papers by Diamond and Lee (2011) and Piquero et al. (2010).

The next article in this part provides a discussion of ways to teach thinking and develop metacognitive skills. Metacognition is the knowledge and awareness of one's thinking processes, as well as the monitoring and control of one's thought processes. It is "thinking about thinking". In a Chapter written in 1984, I discussed how such executive cognitive skills could be taught both implicitly and explicitly in classrooms by means of teacher modeling, prompting, acknowledging, and discussing the concept of metacognition.

The need for such pedagogical interventions was highlighted by a classroom observational study conducted with a colleague, Andrew Biemiller. The next article in this part provides a basis for understanding why "smart" or high-achieving students keep getting smarter and those students who lag in the development of metacognitive skills fall further behind. The high-achieving students receive multiple opportunities to develop and exercise their frontal lobe executive cognitive capacities as a result of cooperation and collaborative social regulation with peers and teachers (Schoor, et al., 2015). In our book *Nurturing Independent Learners* (Meichenbaum and Biemiller, 1998), we discussed the pedagogical implications of this research and how metacognitive training could be used to enhance academic performance.

For example, consider the work by Karen Harris and Steven Graham who used the initial work by Meichenbaum and Goodman as a way to develop self-control strategy training in writing and math instruction (Harris and Graham, 2015). They observe:

> Meichenbaum's (1977) cognitive-behavioral intervention model (particularly his emphasis on the use of a Socratic dialogue interactive learning paradigm, modeling, scaffolding, and other self-regulation components) provided the basis for strategy instruction.

Table II.1 provides examples of six basic self-instructions that Harris and Graham (2015) collaboratively generate with students to improve their writing skills. In fact, metacognitive or executive self-guiding training has been incorporated in many school curricula and even with deaf school-age populations (Glickman, 2009, 2016; Loera and Meichenbaum, 1993).

Over the years, I have had an opportunity to work with diverse clinical populations including individuals with traumatic brain injuries (TBI). In a paper I wrote in 1993, I discussed the potential contributions of cognitive behavior modification to the rehabilitative process (Meichenbaum, 1993). Cicerone and Tupper (1990) had extended Vygotsky's concept of Zone of Proximal Developments (ZPD) to a Zone of Rehabilitation Potential (ZRP) that covers the discrepancy between a client's actual performance level as determined by independent problem-solving and the level of potential performance as determined through problem-solving under the guidance of or collaboration with others. This is the "region of sensitivity to instruction" that I proposed cognitive behavioral procedures such as self-instructional training, stress inoculation training, problem-solving and cognitive restructuring, emotional self-regulation and meta-cognitive instruction could be employed with head-injured children and adults (see Ylvisaker and Szekeres, 1989; Ylvisaker, Szekeres and Hartwick, 1991).

Such TBI clients often have associated injuries to the prefrontal parts of the brain affecting the executive system that controls everyday self-regulating functions including:

1. setting achievable goals;
2. planning, initiating, and organizing behavior to achieve these goals;
3. inhibiting behaviors that would interfere with achieving these goals;
4. monitoring and evaluating performance in relation to the goals;
5. thinking strategically and solving problems as they arise; and
6. flexibility shifting sets, plans and behaviors, as needed.

Work by Cicerone and Tupper (1990), Hogan (1999), Prigatano (2005), Sohlberg and Mateer (1998) and Ylvisaker and Feeney (1998) and the Committee on Cognitive Rehabilitation have demonstrated the value of cognitive behavioral interventions with head injured patients. Such interventions are critical given the

**TABLE II.1** Illustrations of the six basic types of self-instructions

---

**Problem definition**

Sizing up the nature and demands of the task:

*"What is it I have to do here?"*

*"What am I up to?"*

*"What is my first step?"*

*"I want to write a convincing essay."*

**Focusing of attention and planning**

Focusing on the task at hand and generating a plan:

*"I have to concentrate, be careful ... think of the steps."*

*"To do this right I have to make a plan."*

*"First I need to ... then ..."*

**Strategy**

Engaging and implementing writing or self-regulating strategies:

*"First I will write down my essay writing reminder."*

*"The first step in writing an essay is ..."*

*"My goals for this essay are ...; I will self-record on ..."*

**Self-evaluating and error correcting**

Evaluating performance, catching and correcting errors:

*"Have I used all of my story parts – let me check."*

*"Oops, I missed one; that's OK, I can revise."*

*"Am I following my plan?"*

**Coping and self-control**

Subsuming difficulties or failures and dealing with forms of arousal:

*"Don't worry, worry doesn't help."*

*"It's OK to feel a little anxious; a little anxiety can help."*

*"I'm not going to get mad; mad makes me do bad."*

*"I can handle this."*

*"I need to go slow and take my time."*

**Self-reinforcement**

Providing reward:

*"I'm getting better at this."*

*"I like this ending."*

*"Wait till my teacher reads this!"*

*"Hurray – I'm done!"*

---

Taken from Harris and Graham (2015).

high risk of suicide for individuals who have experienced TBIs (Mann, 2003; Meichenbaum, 2006; Simpson and Tate, 2001).

Finally, a common theme that cuts across each of the papers included in this part is how to meet the challenges of increasing the likelihood of both generalization (transfer across settings and tasks), and the maintenance of improvement over time in order to secure "lasting changes"? Therapists should *not* just "train and hope" for generalization and maintenance. Instead, therapists need to build into any training programs guidelines for improving generalization. There are specific intervention steps that should be implemented BEFORE, DURING and AFTER training in order to increase the likelihood of such transfer. (See my paper "Guidelines for Improving Generalization" that is on the Melissa Institute website under Author Index – Meichenbaum. This article provides a Procedural Checklist for trainers as well as a Patient Checklist. How many of these Generalization Guidelines do you include in your treatment protocols?)

In addition, in order to see how our initial work has progressed, you can Google both cognitive behavior therapy with schizophrenics and self-instructional training and metacognitive training in schools.

Additional related papers are also available to view and download from the web address given on page xii:

- Ways to Implement Interventions in Schools in Order to Make Them Safer, More Inviting and Pedagogically More Effective.
- School and Community-Based Preventative Approaches: "Top Down" and "Bottom-Up" Interventions. (See also the Melissa Institute website: www. teachsafeschools.org.)
- Guidelines for Improving Generalization.

## References

Cicerone, K. D. & Tupper, D. E. (1990). Neuropsychological rehabilitation: treatment of errors in everyday functioning. In D. E. Tupper & K. D. Cicerone (eds), *The Neuropsychology of Everyday Life: Issues in Development and Rehabilitation*. Boston, MA: Kluwer Academic.

Diamond, A. & Lee, K. (2011). Interventions shown to aid executive function development in children 4 to 12 years old. *Science*, 333: 959–94.

Glickman, N. (2009). *Cognitive-Behavioral Therapy for Deaf and Hearing Persons with Language and Learning Challenges*. New York: Routledge.

Glickman, N. (2016). *Preparing Deaf and Hearing Persons with Language and Learning Challenges for Cognitive Behavior Therapy: A Pre-therapy Workbook*. New York: Routledge.

Harris, K. R. & Graham, S. (2015). Self-regulated strategy development: theoretical bases, critical instructional elements and future research. In R. Fidelgo, K. R. Harris, & M. Braaksma (eds), *Design Principles for Teaching Effective Writing: Theoretically and Empirically Grounded Principles*. Leiden: Brill.

Hogan, B. A. (1999). Narrative therapy in rehabilitation after brain injury: a case study. *Neuroscience Rehabilitation*, 13: 21–5.

Kingdon, D. & Turkington, D. (1994). *Cognitive Behavior Therapy with Schizophrenia*. Hillsdale, NJ: Lawrence Erlbaum Associates.

Loera, P. A. & Meichenbaum, D. (1993). The "potential" contributions of cognitive behavior modification to literary training for deaf students. *American Annals of the Deaf*, 138: 87–95.

Mann, J. J. (2003). Neurobiology of suicidal behavior. *Nature Reviews/Neuroscience*, 4: 815–28.

Meichenbaum, D. (1966). The effects of social reinforcement on the level of abstraction in schizophrenics. *Journal of Abnormal Psychology*, 71: 354–60.

Meichenbaum, D. (1969). The effects of instructions and reinforcement on thinking and language behavior in schizophrenics. *Behaviour Research and Therapy*, 7: 101–17.

Meichenbaum, D. (1977). *Cognitive Behavior Modification: An Integrative Approach*. New York: Plenum Press.

Meichenbaum, D. (1978). Teaching children self control. In B. Lahey & A. Kazdin (eds), *Advances in Child Clinical Psychology*, Vol. 2. New York: Plenum Press.

Meichenbaum, D. (1993). The "potential" contributions of cognitive behavior modification to the rehabilitation of individuals with traumatic brain injury. *Seminars in Speech and Language*, 14: 18–31.

Meichenbaum, D. (2006). Trauma and suicide: a constructive narrative perspective. In T. E. Ellis (ed.) *Cognition and Suicide: Theory, Research and Therapy*. Washington, DC: American Psychological Association, pp. 333–54.

Meichenbaum, D. & Biemiller, A. (1998). *Nurturing Independent Learners: Helping Students Take Charge of Their Learning*. Cambridge, MA: Brookline Books.

Meichenbaum, D. & Goodman, J. (1971). Training impulsive children to talk to themselves: a means of developing self-control. *Journal of Abnormal Psychology*, 77: 115–26.

Piquero, A., Jennings, W., & Farrington, D. (2010). On the malleability of self-control: theoretical and policy implications regarding a general theory of crime. *Justice Quarterly*, 27: 803–34.

Prigatano, G. P. (2005). A history of cognitive rehabilitation. In P. W. Halligan and D. T. Wade (eds), *The Effectiveness of Rehabilitation for Cognitive Deficits*. New York: Oxford University Press.

Schoor, C., Narciss, S., & Korndle, H. (2015). Regulation during cooperative and collaborative learning: a theory-based review of terms and concepts. *Educational Psychologist*, 50: 97–119.

Simpson, G. & Tate, R. (2001). Suicidality after traumatic brain injury: demographic, injury and clinical correlates. *Psychological Medicine*, 32: 687–98.

Sohlberg, M. M. & Mateer, C. A. (1998). *Introduction to Cognitive Rehabilitations*. New York: Guilford Press.

Turkington, D., Dudley, B., Warman, D.M., & Beck, D. (2006). Cognitive-behavioral therapy for schizophrenia: a review. *Focus: Psychiatry and Society*, 4: 223–33.

Vygotsky, L. S. (1978). *Mind in Society*. Cambridge, MA: Harvard University Press.

Wertsch J. V. (1985). *Vygotsky and the Social Formation of Mind*. Cambridge, MA: Harvard University Press.

Ylvisaker, M. & Feeney, T. (1998). *Collaborative Brain Injury Interventions: Positive Everyday Routines*. San Diego, CA: Singular Publishing Group.

Ylvisaker, M. & Szekeres, S. F. (1989). Metacognitive and executive impairments in head-injured children and adults. *Topics in Language Disorder*, 9: 34–49.

Ylvisaker, M., Szekers, S. F., & Hartwick, P. (1991). Cognitive rehabilitation following traumatic brain injury in children. In M. Tramontana & S. Hooper (eds), *Advances in Child Neuropsychology*, Vol. 1. New York: Springer-Verlag.

# 3

# TRAINING SCHIZOPHRENICS TO TALK TO THEMSELVES

## A means of developing attentional controls

*Donald Meichenbaum and Roy Cameron*

UNIVERSITY OF WATERLOO, ONTARIO, CANADA

The efficacy of a self-instructional (SI) training procedure in altering the attention, thinking, and language behaviors of hospitalized schizophrenics was examined in two studies. Study I was an exploratory study designed to determine the feasibility of training schizophrenics to self-instruct (initially aloud and subsequently covertly) by means of cognitive modeling and cognitive rehearsal. The results of study I indicated that the SI group ($N = 5$) improved relative to practice and assessment control groups on a digit symbol substitution task and on an auditory distraction digit recall task. Study II examined the therapeutic efficacy of extended individualized SI training (viz., six hour) in changing a range of behaviors. The SI training emphasized practice in monitoring intra- and interpersonal behaviors with a view to providing the schizophrenic with cues for emitting task-relevant self-statements. The results indicated that the SI group ($N = 5$) relative to a yoked practice control group improved on a variety of measures, including amount of "healthy talk" emitted in a structured interview, level of proverb abstraction, level of perceptual integration of responses to an inkblot test, and digit recall under distraction conditions. This consistent pattern of improvement for the schizophrenics who received SI training was evident in a three-week follow-up assessment. The treatment and research implications of directly modifying schizophrenics' cognitions are discussed.

– Meichenbaum, D. and Cameron, R. (1973). Training schizophrenics to talk to themselves: a means of developing attentional controls. *Behavior Therapy*, 4, 515–34. Copyright Elsevier. 1973. Permission to reprint by Elsevier.

A general therapeutic strategy used to improve the performance of schizophrenics is the systematic manipulation of environmental events. These events include (a) the nature of the interpersonal milieu or test relationship between the schizophrenic and the examiner (e.g., Brodsky, 1963, 1968; Craig, 1971; Little, 1966); (b) the type of the contingent feedback following the schizophrenic's performance (Ayllon and Azrin, 1965; Cavanaugh, 1968; Calhoun, 1970; Meichenbaum, 1966, 1969; Wagner, 1968); (c) the nature of the task properties (Blaufarb, 1962; Chapman, 1956; Hamlin, *et al.*, 1965); and (d) the schizophrenic's motivation as influenced by instructions and time pressure (Fuhrmann, 1968; Nichols, 1964; Webb, 1955; Johannsen, 1964). These studies indicate that the schizophrenic's attentional and conceptual performance improves when the tasks involve stimulus refinement, such as reduced opportunities for distraction, or when the interpersonal conditions are perceived as non-threatening, or when the schizophrenic receives immediate contingent feedback, or has a high drive level and is motivated. However, it appears *unreasonable* to expect a therapist to be able to engineer an environment, except within the limited conditions of a laboratory, where these conditions are continually met. Therefore it is necessary to consider an alternative treatment approach in which the schizophrenic patient is explicitly trained to provide his own attentional controls, to modify his own perceptions and motivation, to provide his own contingent feedback.

Some suggestion as to how this may be accomplished was indicated by an interesting serendipitous finding in the senior author's doctoral dissertation (Meichenbaum, 1969). One of the main purposes of that investigation was to examine the problem of response generalization which follows from a laboratory operant conditioning training procedure. One group of schizophrenics had been trained to emit "healthy talk," that is, relevant coherent speech. Interestingly, a number of the schizophrenics spontaneously instructed themselves to "be coherent, be relevant, give healthy talk" on a number of the generalization tasks (such as proverbs interpretation and word association) and in an interview with a confederate patient evidence for response generalization was obtained. Specifically, schizophrenics who were trained to emit healthy talk improved on a variety of conceptual tasks, and it appeared that the spontaneous use of self-instructions mediated that generalization. The purpose of the present two studies is to determine if schizophrenics can be explicitly trained to self-instruct in order to develop attentional controls and thereby improve their performance on a variety of attentional, thinking, and language tasks. Study I represents a one-session laboratory training procedure designed to assess the feasibility of explicitly training schizophrenics to talk to themselves. The effectiveness of this one-hour training session was assessed immediately following training. Study II explores the broader therapeutic possibilities of self-instructional training. In study II the number and length of training *sessions* was extended, the range of behaviors to be assessed was enlarged, and the persistence of the treatment effects was evaluated.

## STUDY I

### *Methods and materials*

### *Subjects*

In study I an attempt was made to include a representative sample of hospitalized schizophrenics in order to *assess* the general feasibility and applicability of the self-instructional training procedures. Subjects were 15 schizophrenics (nine male and six female) from an Ontario Psychiatric Hospital, none of whom had any indication of CNS pathology, and all of whom were less than 50 years old. Average age of the sample was 38.5 years with a range of 19–47 years; average length of present hospitalization was 13.3 months with a range of 4–45 months. The subjects were selected from acute admission wards and back wards. They were all on medication, in most cases a well-stabilized maintenance dosage. Following the pretreatment assessment, subjects were assigned to one of three groups. One group comprised the cognitive self-guidance or self-instructional training group ($N = 5$). The remaining two groups included in the study were control groups. One control group met with the experimenter with the same regularity as did the cognitively trained subjects. This practice control group ($N = 5$) afforded an index of behavioral change due to factors of experimenters' presence, exposure to training materials, and any demand characteristics inherent in our measures of improvement. In addition, an assessment control group ($N = 5$) provided an index of the contribution of intercurrent life experiences and repeated testing. Assignment to these three groups was done on a random basis subject to the two constraints of (a) equating the groups on sex composition and (b) matching the groups in their pretreatment performance.

### *Procedure*

Each subject was seen for two sessions one week apart. During the first session, which took approximately 30 minutes, the schizophrenics were individually assessed on two attention performance measures. One week later, the subjects in the self-instructional training group and the practice control group received one hour of treatment, followed by a post-assessment on the two attention performance measures. The assessment control group received only the pre- and post-assessments during sessions one and two. This first pilot study had certain limitations which were overcome in study II. The post-assessment immediately followed the training session, and a follow-up assessment was not possible, and moreover, the experimenter who conducted the training also administered the pre- and post-assessments to all subjects.

### *Instruments*

Two measures of attention were included to assess the cognitive self-guidance treatment regimen with respect to its efficacy in engendering attentional controls and improving performance. The first measure used was a digit symbol test developed by Brown (1969). The second measure was an auditory distraction digit recall test developed by Chapman and McGhie (1962). Brown has developed eight parallel forms of a digit symbol task which are similar to, but longer than, the Wechsler digit symbol test. The subjects were given 30 seconds of practice to acquaint themselves with seven coded items, then two minutes to complete the remaining 120 items. One of the eight parallel digit symbol forms was administered as a pretest, and another one of the forms as the posttest. The total number correct represented the subject's performance. The performance on such a digit symbol task reflects the subject's general speed of learning an unfamiliar task with many distracting symbols, and the subject's flexibility in learning (Kitzinger and Blumberg, 1951; Lutey, 1966).

The McGhie auditory distraction task requires the subject to listen to a tape recorded female voice recite a sequence of either six digits or six letters, and to repeat each sequence aloud in the correct order immediately after delivery. There is a one-second interval between successive items in the sequence. The complete test consists of 16 sequences, each being followed by a rest interval of 10 second. In eight of the 16 sequences, the intervals between the items within a sequence are filled by an irrelevant number or letter recorded by a male voice. The subjects are instructed to ignore the male voice and to report only the information (letters or digits) spoken by the female voice. Several practice trials are first given to accustom the subject to the nature of the task. Each sequence is scored out of a total of six, one point being deducted for each error of omission, addition or order. A parallel form was used for the postassessment. McGhie et al. (1965a, 1965b) and Blum et al. (1969) have shown that in a task involving selective attention to auditory information, the performance of schizophrenic patients is markedly debilitated by both auditory and visual distractors.

## Treatments

### Self-instructional training group

The subjects in this group were seen individually for one hour of training during session two. Immediately following the training the subjects received the post-assessment. The cognitive self-guidance training technique proceeded as follows: first the experimenter modeled a task talking aloud while the subject observed; then the subject performed the same task while the experimenter instructed the subject aloud; next the subject was asked to perform the task again while instructing himself aloud; then the subject performed the task while whispering to himself (lip movements); and finally the subject performed the task covertly (without lip movements). The verbalizations which the experimenter modeled and the subject subsequently used included: (a) questions about the nature and demands of the task which were intended to encourage a general orienting preparatory set; (b) answers in the form of cognitive rehearsal and planning, designed to focus the schizophrenic's attention on relevant task requirements; (c) self-instructions in the form of self-guidance while performing the task to facilitate the maintenance of task-relevant attention and the inhibition of the schizophrenic's response to any internally or externally generated task irrelevancies; (d) coping self-statements to handle failure and frustration; and (e) self-reinforcement to maintain task perseverance, feedback, and reward.

Two tasks were used during training. The first was the digit symbol task. Six forms which were not being used for assessment were employed for training. The following is an example of the experimenter's modeled verbalizations which the subject subsequently used (initially overtly, then covertly):

> What is it I have to do? I'm supposed to fill in these numbered boxes with symbols. Now look up at the top code of symbols and numbers. Good. The first symbol I have to look for goes with number 94. It's three lines. That's it. Now quickly to the next one, number 24 has a circle with a dot in it. Just continue this way until I finish the line. I'm getting it. Let me see how many I can get. Remember, I must go quickly, but also carefully.

Thus, the experimenter modeled thinking aloud by producing a set of task-relevant self-statements which acted both as a goad and a guide for performance. Over the course of each of the six parallel forms of the digit symbols test, the experimenter behaviorally and cognitively modeled for one line of 20 digits; then the subject tried doing a line with the experimenter instructing him; and eventually the subject self-instructed while completing a line. As the training session progressed, the schizophrenic's overt self-statements were faded to the covert level.

After the subject had become quite proficient in self-instructing in a task-relevant fashion, the difficulty of the training task was increased by playing a distracting tape recording while the subject was engaged in the digit symbol test. The distracting tape included a reading of random numbers and symbols (e.g., 54 star, 32 a semicircle with a dot, etc.). The experimenter modeled the maintenance of a task relevant set so as to minimize the effect of the distraction while performing the task. The following is an example of the modeled coping verbalizations which the subject subsequently used (initially overtly, then covertly):

> That tape recorder is trying to distract me. Just pay attention to what I have to do. Number 56 gets a circle. Good. Number 12, two lines. I can disregard the distraction. Number 15, a triangle. No that's wrong. That is okay, even if I make an error I can go on carefully and quickly. Good, I'm getting it. If I make up my mind distractions won't bother me.

A second task (Halstead's (1947) Trail-Making Test) was included in the training paradigm to give the schizophrenic an opportunity to learn to use self-instructions with more than one task. The rate of progression through the treatment sequence

**TABLE 3.1** Mean pre- post-performance and change scores

| | Digit symbol substitution test | | | Digit recall task | | | | | |
| | | | | No-distraction condition | | | Distraction condition | | |
| | Pre mean SD | Post mean SD | Δ Mean SD | Pre mean SD | Post mean SD | Δ Mean SD | Pre mean SD | Post mean SD | Δ Mean SD |
|---|---|---|---|---|---|---|---|---|---|
| Self-instruction | 27.8 | 46.0 | 18.2 | 32.8 | 40.2 | 7.4 | 22.0 | 29.6 | 7.6 |
| | 5.6 | 5.1 | 6.9 | 5.5 | 3.3 | 2.5 | 2.9 | 1.2 | 2.4 |
| Practice control | 27.4 | 37.8 | 10.4 | 31.8 | 36.0 | 4.2 | 24.4 | 21.2 | −3.2 |
| | 7.9 | 7.1 | 5.4 | 6.5 | 4.4 | 2.3 | 5.5 | 2.8 | 5.8 |
| Assessment control | 28.6 | 30.2 | 1.6 | 32.0 | 32.2 | 0.2 | 23.4 | 24.4 | 1.0 |
| | 9.2 | 7.2 | 4.0 | 4.5 | 6.9 | 4.1 | 3.8 | 5.6 | 3.0 |

was individually adapted to the capabilities of the subject. Some subjects were able to use covert self-instructions quickly, while others required a slower pace with more emphasis on modeling and overt self-instructing.

## Practice control group

The schizophrenics in this untutored group spent the same amount of time with the experimenter as did the subjects in the cognitive training group. During this time these attentional control subjects were exposed to the same training materials (the digit symbol and Trail-Making tests) and engaged in the same general activities, including exposure to distracting tapes, but they did not receive any modeling or self-instructional training. An attempt was made to provide both the experimental and practice control groups with equal amounts of social reinforcement and encouragement.

## Assessment control group

This untreated control group received only the same pre- and posttreatment assessments as the cognitive treatment and practice control groups.

## Results

It is evident from both Table 3.1 and Figure 3.1, which summarize the subjects' performance measures, that the three treatment groups were equivalent in their performance on the symbol substitution and auditory distraction tasks prior to treatment. The analysis of the pre- and posttreatment digit symbols assessment

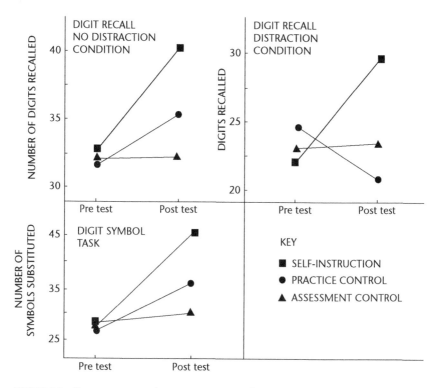

**FIGURE 3.1**  Pretreatment and posttreatment performance on digit symbol and digit recall tasks.

revealed a significant trials effect (F = 75.2, $df$ = 1/12, $p$ < .001) and a significant group by trials interaction (F = 17.2, $df$ = 2/12, $p$ < .001). The subjects who received self-instructional training improved the most on the posttest, a degree of improvement which was significant relative to the practice control subjects ($t$ = 3.95, $df$ = 8, p < .01). Both the self-instructional and practice control groups had significantly (p < .01) improved on the symbol substitution task relative to the assessment control subjects.

The results of the auditory distraction digit recall assessment provided evidence for the efficacy of cognitive training in developing attentional controls. Two scores were obtained from the recall task; namely, a recall of digits with and without distraction. The analysis of variance for digit recall for the eight trials when no distraction was present yielded a significant trials effect ($F$ = 24.7, $df$ = 1/12, $p$ < .001) and a significant group by trials interaction ($F$ = 6.92, $df$ = 2/12, p < .025). The schizophrenics who received self-instructional training showed most improvement. This degree of improvement by the self-instructionally trained schizophrenic subjects was significant ($t$ = 2.12, $df$ = 8, p < .05) relative to the subjects in the practice control group. The practice control subjects who had received practice on digit symbol and Trail-Making tests, demonstrated a significant improvement on the digit recall series without distraction relative to the assessment control subjects ($t = 1.91$, $df = 8$, p < .05).

Further evidence for the efficacy of self-instructional training came from the schizophrenics' performance on the digit recall series when distraction was included. The analysis of variance indicated that the only significant effect was the group by trials interaction ($F = 10.21$, $df = 1/12$, p < .01). Only the schizophrenics who received self-instructional training manifested a significant (p < .01) posttest improvement in recalling digits under distracting conditions. Multiple $t$ tests of the change scores among groups indicated that the self-instructional group had improved significantly relative to the practice control subjects ($t = 2.81$, $df = 8$, p < .025) and relative to the assessment control subjects ($t = 3.83$, $df = 8$, p < .01). The assessment control group showed minimal change in digit recall performance from pre- to posttest However, the practice control subjects, who had been exposed to distraction tapes during training, showed a posttest decrement in digit recall under distraction conditions. This latter result suggests that exposure to distraction conditions during training had an interfering or sensitizing effect which resulted in poorer performance. The exposure to distraction conditions without the inclusion of ways to cope and handle that distraction, such as self-instructional training, may have contributed to a deteriorated performance.

The results of the first study proved most encouraging since they suggested that a self-instructional training program can significantly alter the attentional behavior of schizophrenics. It should be noted that individuals who perform adequately on such tasks as symbol substitution do *not* actively talk to themselves. In fact, on the symbol substitution task talking to oneself aloud in the fashion, "45 is a circle with a dot, 16 two lines, etc." represents an inefficient strategy and slows down performance. However, one way to enhance attentional controls is by having schizophrenics initially talk aloud to themselves and eventually do so covertly.

The purpose of the second study was to examine the therapeutic efficacy and the durability of more extensive self-instructional training on a broad range of attentional, thinking, and language tasks.

## STUDY II

### Methods and materials

#### Subjects

Ten male hospitalized schizophrenic patients from both open and closed wards were included in study II. The mean age of the schizophrenics was 36.0 years, with a range of 23–48 years; average length of present hospitalization was 15.5 months, with a range of 9–48 months. As in study I, all subjects were receiving medication, and none had any indication of CNS pathology. An attempt was made to include a representative sample of schizophrenics; the present sample included four who had been diagnosed as paranoid schizophrenic, two as hebephrenic, and the remaining four as chronic undifferentiated. Half of the subjects could be described as relatively acute reactive schizophrenics of the paranoid type who had varying degrees of well-formulated delusional systems. The remaining subjects could be described as chronic process nonparanoid schizophrenics. The ten schizophrenics were assigned on a random basis to either a self-instructional training group or a yoked practice control group, subject to the requirements of having initially equated the groups for diagnosis, length of present hospitalization, and pretreatment performance.

## Procedure

The pretreatment assessment was carried out in two sessions, each approximately 0.5 hour in length, on two consecutive days. As in study I, the subject was told that these sessions were related to a survey which the hospital was conducting to learn more about patient's thoughts and feelings and to solicit their help in the development of new tests and training procedures to be used in the hospital. On Day 1, experimenter 1 administered a tape-recorded 10-minute structured interview and two pretreatment assessment tasks under standard conditions to all subjects. The structured interview probed the subject's attitudes toward hospitalization and his physical and mental health. The interviews gave experimenter 1 an opportunity to develop rapport with the subject and yielded a measure of "sick talk." The two pretreatment assessment tasks, which experimenter 1 administered following the interview, were Form I of the Kaufman (1960) Parallel Proverbs Test (which consists of 12 proverbs), and the auditory distraction task which was employed in study I. In session 2, experimenter 1 engaged subjects in a second tape-recorded 10-minute structured interview during which the patient's general history and current relationships were discussed. Experimenter 1 then administered 12 inkblots from Form A of the Holtzman *et al.* (1961) Inkblot Test. Following the completion of the inkblot test the subject was introduced to experimenter 2, who would next be working with the patient.

Each subject was seen for eight training sessions, each lasting 45 minutes, over a 3-week period, a total of six hours. Following the completion of the training phase experimenter 1 conducted a one-hour posttest session and three weeks later a one-hour follow-up session. The test format, which was used in both the posttest and follow-up sessions, included a structured interview and parallel forms of the proverbs, auditory distraction, and inkblot tests.

In summary, two baseline measures of the subjects' verbal behavior in a structured interview, two measures of conceptual behavior as elicited by the proverbs test and inkblot test, and two attentional measures derived from the distraction recall task were obtained. Following six-hour of training the subjects received a posttest and a three-week followup assessment. Different experimenters conducted the assessment and treatment sessions. Experimenter I, who conducted and scored the pre- post- follow-up assessments, was completely unaware of which schizophrenic subjects received self-instructional training and which had been placed in a yoked practice control group.

## Instruments

### Proverbs interpretation

Each of the parallel forms of the Proverbs Test was scored for level of abstraction according to Becker's (1956) six-point scale, ranging from absurd interpretation to high level interpretation.

### Sick talk

Ullmann *et al.* (1965) and Meichenbaum (1969) have demonstrated that sick talk (ST) scored from tape-recorded interviews can be reliably differentiated from healthy talk by naïve as well as clinically sophisticated raters, and differentially reinforced by an experimenter. The ST assessment is similar to Holtzman's (1961) classification of pathognomonic verbalizations and Piaget's (1951) concept of egocentric speech as represented by incoherent and irrelevant answers to interview questions. For purposes of statistical analysis, the basic measure was percentage sick talk (%-ST), the number of instances of sick talk divided by the number of healthy talk and sick talk. This percentage score took into account instances of both sick talk and healthy talk, was free of the direct influences of total amount of talk, and provided a single score for comparison of the experimental conditions; Meichenbaum (1969) has described the measurement procedures used to assess sick talk.

### Inkblot test

The inkblot test was included because it would give some indication of the range and "depth" of behavior change that results from explicit self-instructional training. A genetic level scoring procedure developed by Becker (1956) was used to assess changes in the degree of thought disorder. Each subject was asked to give one response per card to two sample inkblots and ten test inkblots taken from the Holtzman inkblot test. A genetic level score of 1–6 was assigned to each inkblot test response and the average determined, prorating for rejected cards.

### Auditory distraction task

The digit recall task under conditions of distraction present and absent, which had been successfully used in study I, was also included.

## Treatments

### Self-instructional training group

The first phase of SI training, which accounted for approximately three 45-minute therapy sessions, was identical to that used in study I. The purpose of this first phase of therapy was to have the schizophrenic develop a general learning set of talking to himself, i.e., he was trained to pause and think before responding, to use forced mentation. This was accomplished by having the schizophrenic perform several sensorimotor tasks (e.g., digit symbol substitution task, Trail-Making task, and Porteus Maze) while talking to himself. The rate or pace of SI training was individually adapted to each schizophrenic's capability. Some subjects required many instances of modeling followed by lengthy practice at self-instructing aloud, whereas others quickly acquired the concept of how to talk to themselves. Over the series of tasks, the modeling and overt cognitive rehearsal was faded out of the training procedures.

The training sequence was identical to that described in study I: the experimenter modeled the thinking and motor behaviors required to perform each task; he then instructed the subject as the subject performed the task; and finally the subject performed the task while talking to himself initially aloud and eventually covertly. Once the schizophrenic had developed some proficiency in performing each task, he was given the same task under the same audio tape distraction conditions as in study I. Whenever the experimenter was required to model, he demonstrated a coping style, failing on some occasions by having the distraction tape interfere with performance, but then modeling how one copes with such failure and still maintains attentional control. The specific self-statements which were emphasized were "pay attention, listen, repeat instructions, disregard distraction."

The major goals of phase II training were to extend the practice of self-instructing to more cognitively demanding interpersonally assessed tasks, and to teach the schizophrenic patients to monitor and evaluate their own behavior in order to know when to spontaneously use task relevant self-instructions. The tasks employed in the first phase of training emphasized sensorimotor tasks which readily lent themselves to the development of a sequential use of self-statements, e.g., Porteus Maze task. The tasks used in phase II of training required greater cognitive activity and emphasized interpersonal assessment. These tasks required the subjects to give abstract responses to the similarities subtest of the Wechsler intelligence tests, to give common associations to the Kent-Rosanoff word association task, to give abstract responses to proverbs, and to conduct an interview in a coherent, relevant fashion, emitting little or no sick talk.

Prior research (Meichenbaum, 1966, 1969; and Ullmann et al., 1964, 1965) has indicated that schizophrenics can be trained by means of operant procedures to emit each of these desired responses. The present study was designed to increase the efficacy of these prior treatment studies by adding self-instructional training.

It is important to note that the subjects were given explicit training on two of the four pre-post dependent measures, viz., proverb interpretation and interview behavior. The remaining two dependent measures of responses to the Holtzman inkblots and digit recall under distraction conditions were not included in training and represent an estimate of the generalizability of the treatment outcome.

Throughout training an attempt was made to have the subject develop a problem-solving strategy of assessing the demands of a task by first spontaneously repeating the task instructions. Next, the subject was to talk to himself, initially aloud and then covertly, about what he was being asked to do. He was to note whenever his responses deviated from his own expectancy or were bizarre or irrelevant.

Each subject was individually trained to first monitor and evaluate his own performance by means of self-questioning. Then, if he judged his performance to be inferior, he learned to self-instruct in a task relevant fashion in order to produce a more desirable response. The individualized training which each subject received consisted of instructions, examples, modeling, discussion, and cognitive rehearsal.

It may be instructive to illustrate by means of an example. On one of the later items of the similarities subtest the experimenter modeled the following verbalizations which the subject subsequently used (initially overtly, then covertly):

> I have to figure out how a fly and a tree are alike. A fly and a tree? (pause). A fly is small and a tree is big. I got it, the fly can carry germs to the tree ... (pause). No that doesn't make sense. That doesn't tell me how they are alike. I have to see how they are alike. Go slowly and think this one out. Don't just say the first thing that comes to mind. (Pause while the model thinks.) I want to give the best answer I can. Let me imagine in my mind the objects ... fly, tree ... out in the sunshine. They both need sunlight to live. That is it–they are both living things. Good I figured it out. If I take my time and just think about how the two objects are alike, I can do it.

Note that in this example the experimenter modeled several aspects of behavior: (a) a restatement of the task demands; (b) general instructions to perform the task slowly and to think before responding; (c) a cognitive strategy of using imagery to produce a solution; (d) self-rewarding statements; (e) an example of an inadequate response and the reason why it was inappropriate; (f) a description of how one copes and comes up with a more adequate response. This is an example of a complex, high level set of self-statements which was slowly achieved over the course of much training. The operant conditioning principles of chaining and shaping were followed to train the schizophrenics to use such complex sets of self-statements. Initially the self-statements included only components of the desired strategy. By the experimenter's modeling and the subject's self-instructional practice, additional aspects of the strategy were slowly added. The experimenter would model a specific, limited set of self-statements; then the subject would practice using these; when the subject was proficient the experimenter would introduce additional components of self-statements.[1]

Phase III of training (i.e., half of session six and sessions seven and eight) concentrated on the subject's becoming sensitive to interpersonal cues "others" emit when the subject's behavior is bizarre, incoherent, or irrelevant. The subject was trained to use others' reactions as a cue, a signal, for him to evaluate his own behavior. Cues which indicated his behavior was inappropriate became discriminative stimuli for the commencement of self-instruction.

By the end of session six the subject had been introduced to the concept of extracting information from others' reactions. At this point the subject was encouraged to observe and report on the verbal, and especially nonverbal, reactions of staff and other patients to inappropriate behavior. Session seven began with a discussion of the observations he had made. This led naturally to a discussion regarding the self-statements that the subject could employ if he noted that his behavior elicited similar reactions. Next the experimenter modeled and the subject practiced such self-statements as "be relevant, be coherent, make oneself understood" while taking a proverbs test, and in a semi-structured interview. In addition, a set of interpersonal ploys or statements was used to maintain a task relevant set and to improve performance. The interpersonal self-statements included phrases like "I' m not making myself understood"; "It's not clear, let me try again." One subject even suggested that he use the statement "I want to make this perfectly clear." Initially this phase of training seemed artificial and stilted as it required the subject to repeat the question and the self-instruction, "Give healthy talk, be coherent," before responding to interview questions. However, over the course of sessions seven and eight these self-verbalizations were emitted covertly, so that these overt self-goads and prompts gradually dropped out of the repertoire.

In summary, the self-instructional training had progressed from having the schizophrenic subjects use their private speech in an overt fashion on simple sensorimotor tasks through stages in which they learned to monitor both their own and others' behavior in order to covertly emit task relevant self-instructions. The components included in SI training were: provision of general "set" instructions, use of imagery, monitoring and evaluation of inappropriate responses, instructions in strategies to produce appropriate responses, and administration of self-reinforcement. These components were presented to the subject via a variety of procedures; namely, administration of instructions (by the experimenter and the subject, overt and covert forms), modeling, provision of examples, behavioral rehearsal, operant chaining and shaping techniques and discussion. The full clinical armamentarium was used to develop attentional controls in schizophrenics.

## Yoked practice control group (PC)

The schizophrenics in this group received the same number of sessions with the experimenter, and the same assessments as the subjects in the SI group. Each subject in the control group was yoked to an SI subject to determine the rate of his training, so that he received the same number of trials on a task. For example, on the sensorimotor tasks the control subjects received as many opportunities to perform a task such as symbol substitution with and without distraction as their yoked counterparts. During phases II and III of training the control subjects were given examples of adequate or inadequate responses, encouraged and given practice in producing instances of appropriate responses (e.g., common associations, abstract responses to similarities and proverbs test, and healthy talk in interviews). An attempt was made to provide both groups with equal amounts of social reinforcement for performance on the tasks. However, the control subjects did not receive explicit modeling or practice in self-instructing in a task-relevant fashion. The PC subjects also participated in a general discussion of how others react, but no attempt was made for them to use such behavioral cues as signals for self-instructing. An attempt was made to equate the experience of practice control and SI subjects, with the exception of the modeling and practice of self-statements which the latter received. In other words, control subjects were exposed to a therapy regimen which consisted of tutoring on a variety of tasks, training of desirable responses, and social reinforcement for adequate responses. This practice control group is essentially the same as the operantly trained social reinforcement group used by Meichenbaum (1969). Although this group had been viewed as a major treatment group in the latter study, in the present case it was included as a practice control group against which the efficacy of self-instructional training could be assessed.

## Results

The three dependent measures (%-sick talk (%-ST) emitted in an interview, level of proverb abstraction, and genetic level of inkblot responses) which were assessed during pre- post- following assessment periods, were subjected to reliability checks.[2] The methods for determining the reliability for sick-talk and proverbs were identical to those used by Meichenbaum (1969). The degree of rater reliability ranged from 0.82 (%-ST) to 0.91 (proverbs).

Tables 3.2 and 3.3 and Figure 3.2 summarize the subjects' performance on the various dependent measures. The analyses of variance and $t$ test comparisons indicate that (a) the SI and practice control (PC) groups were equivalent on the attentional, conceptual, and language tasks prior to treatment; (b) both the SI and PC groups improved significantly on the assessments over trials; and (c) the SI group showed more improvement than the PC group on all dependent measures except digit recall under conditions of no distraction.

The SI training resulted in the schizophrenic subjects (a) emitting 42% less sick talk on the postest, a level of improvement that was maintained at the 3-week follow-up assessment; (b) providing significantly more abstract interpretations to proverbs and more integrated inkblot responses, with many more instances of human movement and elaboration. In contrast, the PC subjects manifested minimal changes in level of perceptual integration of inkblot responses across the assessment periods. Differential benefit of the SI training was evident in digit recall only under the distraction condition, in which the subject must disregard a male's voice and repeat only what the female says.

**TABLE 3.2** Analyses of variance on performance measures

| Source | df | %-Sick talk | | Proverbs | | Inkblot test | | Digit recall, no distraction | | Digit recall, distraction condition | |
|---|---|---|---|---|---|---|---|---|---|---|---|
| | | MS | F | MS | F | MS | F | MS | F | MS | F |
| Treatment | 1 | 749.16 | $10.94^{.25}$ [a] | 367.49 | 2.68 | 504.32 | $3.81^{.10}$ | 5.57 | .06 | 182.53 | 2.87 |
| (a) error | 8 | 68.52 | | 137.19 | | 132.40 | | 92.58 | | 63.58 | |
| Pre- post–follow–up | 2 | 3936.05 | $154.11^{.001}$ | 549.04 | $60.21^{.001}$ | 278.45 | $51.85^{.001}$ | 157.43 | $57.88^{.100}$ | 218.04 | $14.06^{.001}$ |
| Treatment-by-trials | 2 | 175.32 | $6.86^{.01}$ | 218.01 | $23.90^{.001}$ | 86.69 | $16.14^{.001}$ | 6.46 | 2.37 | 75.44 | $4.87^{.025}$ |
| (b) error | 16 | 25.54 | | 9.12 | | 5.37 | | 2.72 | | 15.50 | |

[a] Note: Superscript numbers are p values ($p < .5, p < .01, p < .001$).

**TABLE 3.3** Mean pre- post- follow-up performance measures

| | %-Sick talk Mean SD | | | Proverbs Mean SD | | | Inkblot test Mean SD | | | Digit recall No-distraction Mean SD | | | Distraction condition Mean SD | | |
|---|---|---|---|---|---|---|---|---|---|---|---|---|---|---|---|
| | Pre | Post | Fu | Pre | Post | Fu | Pre | Post | Fu | Pre | Post | Fu | Pre | Post | Fu |
| Self-instruction | 59.8 | 17.6 | 19.0 | 2.12 | 3.81 | 3.70 | 2.26 | 3.78 | 3.54 | 30.2 | 39.0 | 36.4 | 21.4 | 34.8 | 33.6 |
| | 10.0 | 5.8 | 3.9 | .52 | .92 | .65 | .72 | .73 | .71 | 6.3 | 6.2 | 6.5 | 2.9 | 7.6 | 5.9 |
| Practice control | 60.2 | 31.4 | 34.8 | 2.20 | 2.95 | 2.70 | 2.12 | 2.62 | 2.38 | 31.0 | 38.0 | 34.0 | 22.6 | 27.6 | 24.2 |
| | 7.8 | 2.3 | 4.9 | .41 | .49 | .46 | .73 | .64 | .52 | 4.8 | 4.6 | 4.8 | 3.8 | 3.8 | 3.6 |
| t value ($df = 8$) | .071 | 4.94 | 5.64 | .282 | 1.78 | 2.79 | .305 | 2.67 | 2.95 | .213 | .289 | .663 | .558 | 1.88 | 3.04 |
| p values | us | <.005 | <.0005 | us | <.10 | <.025 | us | <.025 | <.01 | us | us | us | us | <.05 | <.01 |

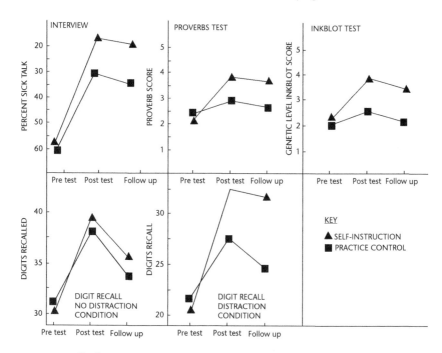

**FIGURE 3.2**   Performance measures on pretreatment, posttreatment, and follow-up assessment periods.

In summary, the results indicate a consistent picture of the efficacy of SI training in improving and maintaining the schizophrenic subject's performance on attentional, conceptual, and language tasks.

## Discussion

By now you, the reader, should be talking to yourself. The content of your private speech (hopefully task-relevant) should emphasize the fact that the results of the two studies indicate that a cognitive self-guidance program which trains schizophrenic patients to talk to themselves is effective in modifying their behavior on a variety of attentional, thinking, and language tasks. The results of study II indicate that the effects of the self-instructional treatment procedures were neither superficial nor specific to the training materials, but generalized as indicated by the performance on the inkblot test. This generalized performance improvement was maintained at a 3-week follow-up assessment. The schizophrenics were successfully taught to use their private speech for orienting, organizing, regulating, and self-rewarding functions. The consequence was greater self-control.

A major aspect of the training was to teach the schizophrenic patients when to use the task relevant self-instructions. They were trained to monitor their own behavior and thinking, as well as become sensitive to the interpersonal (facial and behavioral) cues which others emitted when the patients manifested "schizophrenic behaviors." These cues were to be signals, discriminative stimuli, for the patient to emit task-relevant self-instructions and appropriate behaviors. An attempt was made to modify how the schizophrenic perceived, labeled, and interpreted such external cues. The schizophrenic was trained to "listen to himself," to monitor his own thinking and, if his cognitions were maladaptive, to produce incompatible self-statements and behaviors. The focus of therapy shifted from manipulating external environmental consequences to directly influencing how the client perceives, evaluates, and reacts to the environment.

Our research on cognitive factors in behavior modification (Meichenbaum, 1971) has highlighted the fact that it is not the environmental consequences *per se* which are important, but what the client says to himself about those consequences. Moreover, what the client says to himself, or how he evaluates and interprets these events, is explicitly modifiable by many of the behavior therapy techniques which have been used to modify overt maladaptive behaviors.

Although in many ways the present studies should be considered exploratory, because of the limited sample size, they raise many questions concerning the nature and modification of schizophrenia. From a therapeutic point of view, one may consider adapting the self-instructional training to the specific schizophrenic subpopulation. The self-statements used in the present study were developed in a "shot-gun" fashion and future research may indicate the enhanced efficacy of tailoring self-statement packages to the needs of different types of schizophrenic patients. For instance, the cognitive strategies and tactical self-instructional maneuvers which a group of chronic process nonparanoid schizophrenics need to rehearse may be quite different from those required by a group of acute reactive paranoid schizophrenics.

## Finally, a footnote on theory

A variety of hypothetical or theoretical constructs have been proposed to explain the schizophrenic's performance deficit. A major source of such theorizing has been Broadbent's (1958) model of the human mind as an information channel of limited capacity. This model has led various investigators to hypothesize that schizophrenic behavior is a consequence of (a) a deficient attentional filter (Chapman and McGhie, 1962); (b) an input dysfunction (Venables, 1964); (c) a deterioration in channel capacity (Pishkin et al., 1962); (d) a defect in screening mechanisms (Payne et al., 1963, 1964); (e) a failure in scanning processes (Silverman, 1964); (f) a slowness of processing data in the primary channel (Yates, 1966); (g) defective programs (Callaway, 1970). The schizophrenic deficit has also been conceptualized in terms of neurological models. Thus, it has been hypothetically explained in terms of (a) a primary defect in central nervous system organization (Belmont et al., 1964); (b) a defect in the cortical regulatory system (Venables, 1963); (c) a defect in excitatory modulation (Epstein, 1970); (d) an imbalance in a dual arousal system (Claridge, 1967) and others. Such hypothetical speculation, whether derived from an information-communication model or a neurological model, seems premature and nonproductive. It is difficult to fathom from the present results if the self-instructional training has "cleaned" the schizophrenic's filter system, boosted his cortical inhibition, or reorganized his neurological structures. The point, simply, is that at present the focus of theorizing may be more productive if directed at a functional analysis of the schizophrenic's maladaptive behavior. Up to now a functional analysis of behavior has been synonymous with an examination of the environmental consequences as related to a given response repertoire. The results of the present studies and others we have conducted on the role of cognitive factors in behavior modification (see Meichenbaum, 1971) clearly indicate the additional value of including the subject's cognitions (i.e., self-statements and images) in such functional analyses. It is suggested that when a functional analysis of the client's thinking is conducted, the explanatory and therapeutic dividends derived will be quite substantial.

## Notes

1. A word of caution is in order concerning the implementation of such SI training with schizophrenics, as well as other clinical populations. It is important to ensure that the subject does not say the self-statements in a relatively mechanical, rote, or automatic fashion without the accompanying meaning and reflection. This would approximate the everyday experience of reading aloud or silently when one's mind is elsewhere. You read the paragraph aloud but cannot recall the content. What is needed instead is modeling and practice in synthesizing and internalizing the meaning of one's self-statements.
2. The authors wish to express appreciation to D. Cox, H. Marcum, L. Merei, R. Morris, S. Notar, and J. Williams who helped in the collection and scoring of the data.

## References

Ayllon, T. and Azrin, N. M. (1965) The measurement and reinforcement of behavior of psychotics. *Journal of the Experimental Analysis of Behavior*, 8, 357–83.

Becker, W. C. (1956) A genetic approach to the interpretation and evaluation of the process-reactive distinction in schizophrenia. *Journal of Abnormal and Social Psychology*, 53, 229–36.

Belmont, I., Birch, H., Klein, D., and Pollack, M. (1964) Perceptual evidence of CNS dysfunction in schizophrenia. *Archives of General Psychiatry*, 10, 395–408.

Blaufarb, H. (1962) A demonstration of verbal abstracting ability in chronic schizophrenics under enriched stimulus and instructional conditions. *Journal of Consulting Psychology*, 26, 471–5.

Blum, R., Livingston, P., and Shader, R. (1969) Changes in cognition, attention, and language in acute schizophrenia. *Diseases of the Nervous System*, 30, 31–6.

Broadbent, D. (1958) *Perception and Communication*. Oxford: Pergamon Press.

Brodsky, M. (1963) Interpersonal stimuli as interference in a sorting task. *Journal of Personality*, 31, 518–33.

Brodsky, M. (1968) Sorting decrement in schizophrenia as a function of social climate. *Journal of Clinical Psychology*, 24, 162–5.

Brown, M. (1969) A set of eight parallel forms of the digit symbol test. Unpublished set of tests, University of Waterloo, Waterloo, Ontario.

Calhoun, J. (1970) Effects of performance payoff and cues on recall by hospitalized schizophrenics. *Journal of Abnormal Psychology*, 76, 485–91.

Callaway, E. (1970) Schizophrenia and interference: an analogy with a malfunctioning computer. *Archives of General Psychiatry*, 22, 193–208.

Cavanaugh, D. (1968) Improvement in the performance of schizophrenics on concept formation tasks as a function of motivational change. *Journal of Abnormal and Social Psychology*, 57, 8–12.

Chapman, J. and McGhie, A. (1962) A comparative study of disordered attention in schizophrenia. *Journal of Mental Science*, 108, 487–500.

Chapman, L. (1956) Distractibility in the conceptual performance of schizophrenics. *Journal of Abnormal and Social Psychology*, 53, 286.

Claridge, G. (1967) *Personality and Arousal: A Psychophysiological Study of Psychiatric Disorder.* New York: Macmillan (Pergamon).

Craig, R. (1971) Overinclusive thinking and schizophenia. *Journal of Personality Assessment*, 35, 208–23.

Epstein, S. and Coleman, M. (1970) Drive theories of schizophrenia. *Psychosomatic Medicine*, 32, 113–40.

Fuhrmann, D. (1968) Effects of drive and reward upon concept formation in schizophrenia. *Proceedings of the 76th Annual Convention of the American Psychological Association*, 511–12.

Halstead, W. C. (1947) *Brain and Intelligence: A Quantitative Study of the Frontal Lobes.* Chicago: University of Chicago Press.

Hamlin, R., Haywood, H., and Folsom, A. (1965) Effects of enriched output on schizophrenic abstraction. *Journal of Abnormal Psychology*, 70, 390–4.

Holtzman, W., Thrope, J., Swartz, F., and Herron, W. (1961) *Inkblot Perception and Personality.* Austin, TX: University of Texas Press.

Johannsen, W. (1964) Motivation in schizophrenic performance: a review. *Psychological Reports*, 15, 840–70.

Kaufman, L. N. (1960) The development of a proverb scale for the measurement of thinking pathology in schizophrenia and a further investigation of the process-reactive dimension. Unpublished Master's thesis, University of Illinois.

Kitzinger, H. and Blumberg, E. (1951) Supplementary guide for administering and scoring the Wechsler-Bellevue Intelligence Scale. *Psychological Monographs*, 65 (10, Whole No. 319).

Little, L. K. (1966) Effects of the interpersonal interaction on abstract thinking performance in schizophrenics. *Journal of Consulting Psychology*, 30, 158–64.

Lutey, C. (1966) *Individual Intelligence Testing: A Manual.* Greeley, CO: Executary Press.

McGhie, A., Chapman, J., and Lawson, J. (1965a) The effect of distraction on schizophrenic performance: (1) Perception and immediate memory. *British Journal of Psychiatry*, 111, 383–390.

McGhie, A., Chapman, J., and Lawson, J. (1965b) The effect of distraction on schizophrenic performance: (2) Psychomotor ability. *British Journal of Psychiatry*, 111, 391–398.

Meichenbaum, D. (1971) *Cognitive Factors in Behavior Modification: Modifying What Clients Say to Themselves.* Paper presented at the fifth annual meeting of the Association for the Advancement of Behavior Therapy, Washington DC, September.

Meichenbaum, D. (1969) The effects of instructions and reinforcement on thinking and language behavior of schizophrenics. *Behaviour Research and Therapy*, 7, 101–14.

Meichenbaum, D. (1966) The effects of social reinforcement on the level of abstraction in schizophrenics. *Journal of Abnormal Psychology*, 71, 354–62.

Nichols, J. (1964) Overinclusion under unstructured conditions. *Journal of Clinical Psychology*, 20, 122–9.

Payne, R., Anuvich, S., and Laverty, S. (1963) Overinclusive thinking in symptom free schizophrenics. *Canadian Psychiatric Association Journal*, 8, 226–34.

Payne, R., Caird, W., and Laverty, S. (1964) Overinclusive thinking and delusions in schizophrenic patients. *Journal of Abnormal and Social Psychology*, 68, 562–6.

Piaget, J. (1951) *Play, Dreams and Imitation in Childhood*. London: Heinemann Press.

Pishkin, V., Smith, T., and Leibowitz, H. (1962) The influence of symbolic stimulus value on perceived size in chronic schizophrenia. *Journal of Consulting Psychology*, 26, 323–30.

Silverman, J. (1964) The problem of attention in research and theory in schizophrenia. *Psychological Review*, 71, 352–79.

Ullmann, L., Krasner, L., and Edinger, R. (1964) Verbal conditioning of common associations in long term schizophrenic patients. *Behaviour Research and Therapy*, 2, 15–18.

Ullmann, L., Forsman, R., Kenny, J., McInnis, T., Uniele, I., and Zeisset, R. (1965) Selective reinforcement of schizophrenics' interview responses. *Behaviour Research and Therapy*, 2, 205–12.

Venables, P. (1964) Input dysfunction in schizophrenia. In B. A. Maher (ed.), *Progress in Experimental Personality Research*, Vol. 1. New York: Academic Press, pp. 1–47.

Venables, P. (1963) Selectivity of attention, withdrawal, and cortical activation. *Archives of General Psychiatry*, 9, 74–8.

Wagner, G. (1968) The training of attending and abstracting responses in chronic schizophrenics. *Journal of Experimental Research in Personality*, 3, 77–88.

Webb, W. (1955) Conceptual ability of schizophrenics as a function of threat of failure. *Journal of Abnormal and Social Psychology*, 58, 221–4.

Yates, A. (1966) Data processing levels and thought disorder in schizophrenia. *Australian Journal of Psychology*, 18, 103–17.

# 4

# TRAINING IMPULSIVE CHILDREN TO TALK TO THEMSELVES

## A means of developing self-control

*Donald Meichenbaum and Joseph Goodman*[1]

UNIVERSITY OF WATERLOO, ONTARIO, CANADA

The efficacy of a cognitive self-instructional (SI) training procedure in altering the behavior of "impulsive" school children was examined in two studies. Study I employed an individual training procedure which required the impulsive child to talk to himself, initially overtly and then covertly, in an attempt to increase self-control. The results indicated that the SI group ($N = 5$) improved significantly relative to attentional and assessment control groups on the Porteus Maze Test, Performance IQ on the WISC, and on a measure of cognitive impulsivity. The improved performance was evident in a 1-mo. follow-up assessment. Study II examined the efficacy of the components of the cognitive treatment procedure in altering the impulsive child's performance on Kagan's measure of cognitive impulsivity. The results indicated that cognitive modeling alone was sufficient to slow down the impulsive child's response time for initial selection, but only with the addition of SI training was there a significant decrease in errors. The treatment and research implications of modifying $S$'s cognitions are discussed.

The development of the functional interaction between self-verbalization and nonverbal behavior has received much attention (Luria, 1961; Piaget, 1947; Reese, 1962; and see especially a review by Kohlberg, *et al.*, 1968). Two general research strategies have been employed to assess the influence of self-verbalizations on behavior. The first strategy is characterized by $S$'s performance on a task and $E$'s subsequent inference as to the presence or absence of specific cognitive activities. In general, this approach has used the concept of "deficiency" to explain poor performance. Reese (1962) has suggested a mediation deficiency hypothesis; Flavell and his co-workers (Flavell *et al.*, 1966; Moely *et al.*, 1969) have offered a production deficiency hypothesis, and most recently Bem (1970) has suggested a comprehension deficiency hypothesis. The developing child is characterized as going through stages during which he (*a*) does not mediate or regulate his overt behavior verbally; (*b*) does not spontaneously produce relevant mediators; and (*c*) does not comprehend the nature of the problem in order to discover what mediators to produce. Thus, problem-solving is viewed as a three-stage process of comprehension, production, and mediation, and poor performance can result from a "deficiency" at any one of these stages. The deficiency literature suggests that a training program designed to improve task performance and engender self-control should provide explicit training in the comprehension of the task, the spontaneous production of mediators, and the use of such mediators to control nonverbal behavior. The present cognitive self-guidance treatment program was designed to provide such training for a group of "impulsive" children.

The other strategy, which is designed to assess the functional role of private speech in task performance, directly manipulates the child's verbalizations and examines resulting changes in nonverbal behavior. Vygotsky (1962) has suggested that internalization of verbal commands is the critical step in the child's development of voluntary control of his behavior. Data from a wide range of studies (Bem, 1967; Klein, 1963; Kohlberg *et al.*, 1968; Lovaas, 1964; Luria, 1959, 1961; Meichenbaum & Goodman, 1969a, 1969b) provide support for the age increase in cognitive self-guiding private speech, and the increase in internalization with age. These results suggest a progression from external to internal control. Early in development, the speech of others, usually adults, mainly controls and directs a child's behavior; somewhat later, the child's own overt speech becomes an effective regulator of his behavior; and still later, the child's covert or inner speech can assume a regulatory role. The present studies were designed to examine the efficacy of a cognitive self-guidance treatment program which followed the developmental sequence by which overt verbalizations of an adult or *E*, followed by the child's overt self-verbalizations, followed by covert self-verbalization, would result in the child's own verbal control of his nonverbal behavior. By using this fading procedure, we hoped to (*a*) train impulsive *S*s to provide themselves with internally originated verbal commands or self-instructions and to respond to them appropriately; (*b*) strengthen the mediational properties of the children's inner speech in order to bring their behavior under their own verbal or discriminative control; (*c*) overcome any possible "comprehension, production, or mediational deficiencies"; and finally (*d*) encourage the children to appropriately self-reinforce their behavior. We hoped to have the child's private speech gain a new functional significance, to have the child develop a new cognitive style or "learning set" and thus to engender self-control.

Two studies are reported which apply the cognitive self-guidance treatment regimen to impulsive school children. The first study, using second-grade children who had been assigned to an "opportunity remedial class," provided four ½-hour individual training sessions over a 2-week period. The effects of training on performance measures and classroom behavior is reported. The second study examines the modification value of a particular component of the treatment regimen, namely modeling, which is designed to alter the child's impulsive cognitive style in one treatment session as assessed on Kagan's (1966) Matching Familiar Figures (MFF) Test. The impulsive Ss in the second study have been selected from kindergarten and first-grade classes as assessed by their failure to follow an instruction to "go slower" on a preassessment of the MFF test. Both studies indicate the general treatment regimen designed to train impulsive children to talk to themselves, a possible means of developing self-control.

## Study I

### Method

### Subjects

The Ss were 15 second-grade children (eight females, seven males) whose ages ranged from 7 to 9 years with a mean of 8 years, 2 months and who had been placed in an "opportunity remedial class" in a public elementary school. The children were placed into the opportunity class because of behavioral problems such as hyperactivity and poor self-control, and/or they had low IQs on one of a variety of school-administered intelligence tests. The cut-off point on the IQ measures was 85, but for several Ss the last assessment was several years prior to the present research project. The children's behavior both in class and on performance measures was measured before and after treatment as well as in a 1-month followup assessment described below. Following the pretreatment assessment, Ss were assigned to one of three groups. One group comprised the cognitive self-guidance treatment group ($N = 5$). The remaining two groups included in the study were control groups. One control group met with E with the same regularity as did the cognitively trained Ss. This attention control group ($N = 5$) afforded an index of behavioral change due to factors of attention, exposure to training materials, and any demand characteristics inherent in our measures of improvement. In addition, an assessment control group of Ss who received no treatment was included. The assessment control group ($N = 5$) provided an index of the contribution of intercurrent life experiences to any behavioral change (e.g., being a member of the opportunity remedial class). Assignment to these three groups was done randomly, subject to the two constraints of (a) equating the groups on sex composition and (b) matching the groups on their prorated WISC IQ performance scores taken prior to treatment.

## Treatments

### Cognitive training group

The Ss in this group were seen individually for four ½-hour treatment sessions over a 2-week period. The cognitive training technique proceeded as follows: First, E performed a task talking aloud while S observed (E acted as a model); then S performed the same task while E instructed S aloud; then S was asked to perform the task again while instructing himself aloud; then S performed the task while whispering to himself (lip movements); and finally S performed the task covertly (without lip movements). The verbalizations which E modeled and S subsequently used included: (a) questions about the nature and demands of the task so as to compensate for a possible comprehension deficiency; (b) answers to these questions in the form of cognitive rehearsal and planning in order to overcome any possible production deficiency; (c) self-instructions in the form of self-guidance while performing the task in order to overcome any possible mediation deficiency; and (d) self-reinforcement. The following is an example of E's modeled verbalizations which S subsequently used (initially overtly, then covertly):

> Okay, what is it I have to do? You want me to copy the picture with the different lines. I have to go slow and be careful. Okay, draw the line down, down, good; then to the right, that's it; now down some more and to the left. Good, I'm doing fine so far. Remember go slow. Now back up again. No, I was supposed to go down. That's okay. Just erase the line carefully … Good. Even if I make an error I can go on slowly and carefully. Okay, I have to go down now. Finished, I did it.

Note in this example an error in performance was included and E appropriately accommodated. In prior research with impulsive children, Meichenbaum & Goodman (1969b) observed a marked deterioration in their performance following errors. The E's verbalizations varied with the demands of each task, but the general treatment format remained the same throughout. The treatment sequence was also individually adapted to the capabilities of the S and the difficulties of the task.

A variety of tasks was employed to train the child to use self-instructions to control his nonverbal behavior. The tasks varied along a dimension from simple sensorimotor abilities to more complex problem-solving abilities. The sensorimotor tasks, such as copying line patterns and coloring figures within certain boundaries, provided S with an opportunity to produce a narrative description of his behavior, both preceding and accompanying his performance. Over the course of a training session, the child's overt self-statements on a particular task were faded to the covert level, what Luria (1961) has called "interiorization of language." The difficulty level of the training tasks was increased over the four training sessions requiring more cognitively demanding activities. Such tasks as reproducing designs and following sequential instructions taken from the Stanford–Binet intelligence test, completing pictorial series as on the Primary Mental Abilities test, and solving conceptual tasks as on the Raven's Matrices test, required $S$ to verbalize the demands of the task and problem-solving strategies. The $E$ modeled appropriate self-verbalizations for each of these tasks and then had the child follow the fading procedure. Although the present tasks assess many of the same cognitive abilities required by our dependent measures, there are significant differences between the training tasks and the performance and behavioral indexes used to assess improvement. It should be noted that the attentional control group received the same opportunities to perform on each of the training tasks, but without cognitive self-guidance training.

One can imagine a similar training sequence in the learning of a new motor skill such as driving a car. Initially the driver actively goes through a mental checklist, sometimes aloud, which includes verbal rehearsal, self-guidance, and sometimes appropriate self-reinforcement, especially when driving a stick-shift car. Only with repetition does the sequence become automatic and the cognitions become short-circuited. This sequence is also seen in the way children learn to tie shoelaces and in the development of many other skills. If this observation has any merit, then a training procedure which makes these steps explicit should facilitate the development of self-control.

In summary, the goals of the training procedure were to develop for the impulsive child a cognitive style or learning set in which the child could "size up" the demands of a task, cognitively rehearse, and then guide his performance by means of self-instructions, and, when appropriate, reinforce himself.

## Attention control group

The children in this untutored group had the same number of sessions with $E$ as did the cognitive training $Ss$. During this time, the child was exposed to identical materials and engaged in the same general activities, but did not receive any self-instructional training. For example, these attentional control $Ss$ received the same number of trials on a task as did the cognitively trained $Ss$, but they did not receive self-instructional training. An attempt was made to provide both the experimental and attention control groups with equal amounts of social reinforcement for behavioral performance on the tasks.

## Assessment control group

This untreated control group received only the same pretreatment, post-treatment, and follow-up assessments as the cognitive treatment and attention control groups.

## Instruments

Two general classes of dependent measures were used to assess the efficacy of the cognitive self-guidance treatment regimen to improve performance and engender self-control. The first class of measures involved performance on a variety of psychometric instruments which have been previously used to differentiate impulsive from nonimpulsive children. The second class of measures assessed the generalizability of the treatment effects to the classroom situation. The female *E* who performed the pretreatment, posttreatment, and follow-up assessments on the performance measures and the two female *Es* who made classroom observations during pretreatment and posttreatment periods were completely unaware of which children received which treatment.

## Performance measures

Three different psychometric tests were used to assess changes in behavioral and cognitive impulsivity during the pretreatment, posttreatment, and follow-up periods. Several investigators (Anthony, 1959; Eysenck, 1955; Foulds, 1951; Porteus, 1942) have demonstrated that the Porteus Maze test, especially the qualitative score which is based upon errors in style and quality of execution, distinguishes between individuals differing in impulsiveness. Most recently, Palkes, Stewart, and Kahana (1968) have reported that hyperactive boys significantly improved on Porteus Maze performance following training in self-directed verbal commands. Thus, the Porteus Maze performance provided one indicant of behavioral change. Because of the length of the assessment (some 45 minutes), only years 8–11 of the Porteus Maze test were used. On the posttest the Vineland Revision form of the Porteus Maze test was used.

A second measure which has been used to assess cognitive impulsivity is Kagan's (1966) MFF test. The *S*'s task on the MFF test is to select from an array of variants one picture which is identical to a standard picture. The tendency toward fast or slow decision times and the number of errors are used to identify the degree of conceptual impulsivity. Further support for the use of the MFF test in the present study comes from research by Meichenbaum and Goodman (1969a), who have reported a positive relationship between a child's relative inability to verbally control his motor behavior by means of covert self-instructions and an impulsive conceptual tempo on the MFF test. Parallel forms of the MFF test were developed by using six alternate items in the pretreatment and posttreatment assessments, with the pretreatment MFF test being readministered on the follow-up assessment.

The final set of performance measures was derived from three performance subtests of the WISC. The three subtests selected were Picture Arrangement, Block Design, and Coding. Respectively, these subtests are designed to assess (*a*) the ability to comprehend and size up a total situation requiring anticipation and planning; (*b*) the ability to analyze and form abstract designs as illustrated by *S*'s performance and approach to the problems; and (*c*) the child's motor speed and activity level (Kitzinger & Blumberg, 1957; Lutey, 1966; Wechsler, 1949). The results from the WISC subtests are reported in scaled scores and as a prorated IQ performance estimate.

In summary, the performance measures were designed to assess the range of abilities from sensorimotor, as indicated by qualitative scores on Porteus Maze and Coding tasks on the WISC, to more cognitively demanding tasks such as the MFF test, Block Design, and Picture Arrangement subtests.

## Classroom measures

Two measures were used to ascertain whether any of the expected changes would extend into the classroom. The first measure behaviorally assessed the 15 children on their appropriateness and attentiveness within the classroom setting. We used a time-sampling observational technique (10 seconds observe, 10 seconds record) which was developed by Meichenbaum et al. (1968, 1969) to rate inappropriate classroom behavior. Inappropriate classroom behavior was defined as any behavior which was not consistent with the task set forth by the teacher, that is, behavior which was not task specific. The children were observed for 2 school days 1 week before and immediately after treatment. The second measure involved a teacher's questionnaire which was designed to assess each child's behavioral self-control, activity level, cooperativeness, likeability, etc. The questionnaire consisted of ten incomplete statements, each of which was followed by three forced choice alternative completions. The teacher filled out the scale immediately prior to treatment and 3 weeks later at the conclusion of the posttreatment assessment.

## *Results*

The relative efficacy of the cognitive self-guidance treatment program was assessed by means of a Lindquist (1953) Type I analysis of variance which yields a treatment effect, trials effect (pretreatment and posttreatment assessments), and a Treatment × Trials interaction. The results from the 1 month follow-up measures were analyzed separately. Multiple $t$-test comparisons (one-tailed) were performed on the change scores for each of the dependent measures. Figure 4.1 presents the performance measures.

The analyses of the three WISC subtests revealed only a significant Group × Trials interaction on the Picture Arrangement subtest ($F = 4.56$, $df = 2/12$, $p = .033$) and a strong trend towards significance on the Coding subtest (Group × Trials $F = 2.87$, $df = 2/12$, $p = .10$). The performances on the Block Design subtest did not yield any significant groups, trials, or Group × Trials interactions. When the performances on the three WISC subtests were combined to yield a prorated IQ score, the relative efficacy of the cognitive training procedure is further revealed in a significant Group × Trials interaction ($F = 3.97$, $df = 2/12$, $p = .05$). The cognitive training group improved 8.3 IQ points ($SD = 3.8$), from an IQ of 88.4 to an IQ of 96.7. In comparison, the attention control group and the assessment control group improved, respectively, 3.4 ($SD = 4.1$) and 2.2 ($SD = 3.0$) IQ points. Multiple $t$ comparisons indicated that the cognitive training

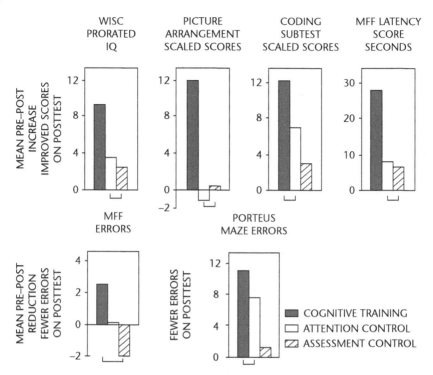

**FIGURE 4.1**  Mean change scores from pretreatment to posttreatment on performance measures. (Groups not connected by solid line are significantly different at the .05 level.)

group was significantly different ($p < .05$) from the attentional and assessment control groups on the Picture Arrangement and Coding subtests, and on the prorated IQ scores, whereas the two control groups did not significantly differ from each other on the WISC measures.

Further evidence for the efficacy of the cognitive training is derived from the measure of cognitive impulsivity, namely, the MFF test. A significant Group × Trials interaction ($F = 9.49$, $df = 2/12$, $p = .004$) was found on the initial decision time or latency score on the MFF test. The cognitive training group increased its mean total decision time for the six MFF items from pretest to posttest by 27.4 sec. ($SD = 10.3$), in comparison to the attention and assessment control groups who, respectively, increased their total post-test decision times by 7.4 sec. ($SD = 3.8$) and 6.8 sec. ($SD = 9.9$). The differential increase in response time indicates that the impulsive Ss in the cognitively trained group took significantly longer before responding on the posttest. The analyses of the error scores on the MFF test did not yield any significant differences, although the trend of the results did suggest differential effectiveness for the cognitively trained Ss. The cognitively trained Ss had a group total decrease on the posttest of eight errors in comparison to the attentional control Ss, who had a group total decrease of only two errors on the posttest, and the assessment control Ss, who had a group total increase of ten errors on the posttest. The absence of statistical significance on the error scores may be due to the relative ease of the MFF test for this age level and the use of a shortened version of the test in order to develop parallel forms (i.e., six items were used instead of the usual 12-item test). The potential usefulness of the cognitive training procedure in altering cognitive impulsivity was examined in the second study which is described below.

An analysis of the performance on the Porteus Maze test indicated a significant Group × Trials interaction ($F = 5.52$, $df = 2/12$, $p = .02$), with the cognitive training and the attentional control groups making significantly ($p < .05$) less errors on the posttest than the assessment control group. The mean change scores indicated that (a) Ss who received cognitive training improved most with 10.8 ($SD = 4.3$) less errors on the posttest; (b) Ss in the attentional control group made 7.8 ($SD = 6.8$) less errors on the posttest; and (c) the assessment control group made 1.2 ($SD = 4.7$) more errors on the posttest. Both the cognitive training group and the attentional control group decreased errors on the posttest by cutting fewer corners, crossing over fewer lines, lifting their pencils less frequently, and producing fewer irregular lines. Palkes et al. (1968) have reported a significant improvement on the Porteus Maze test for a self-directed verbal command group relative to an assessment or no-treatment control group, but they did not include an attentional control group. The present results indicated that an attentional control group which received only practice on a variety of sensorimotor and cognitive tasks also significantly improved their performance on the Proteus Maze test. The inclusion of such an attentional control group is thus necessary in order to exclude alternative hypotheses.

The analyses of the Ss' classroom behavior by means of time-sampling observations and by teachers' ratings did not yield any significant differences. The absence of a significant treatment effect in the classroom may be due to a lack of generalization because of the limited number of training sessions and/or the lack of sensitivity of the assessment measures. The analyses of the 4-week follow-up assessment revealed that the cognitive training group maintained their improved performance on the test battery, relative to the attentional and assessment control groups. The analyses of the follow-up test performances relative to the pretreatment performance indicated that on the Picture Arrangement subtest, the WISC prorated IQ score, and the decision time on the MFF, the cognitive training group was significantly different ($p < .05$) from the two control groups. The analysis of the qualitative performance on the Porteus Maze test indicated that both the cognitive training group and the attentional control group maintained their improved performance relative to the assessment control group.

The results of the first study proved most encouraging and suggested that a cognitive self-guidance training program can significantly alter behavior of impulsive children. The purpose of the second study was to examine the differential contribution of the various components of the treatment program in modifying impulsive behavior. The cognitive training procedure involved both modeling by *E* and subsequent self-instructional training by *S*. In this study a comparison is made between the relative efficacy of modeling alone versus modeling plus self-instructional training in modifying cognitive impulsivity as measured by the MFF test. Kagan (1965) has defined cognitive impulsivity as a conceptual tempo or decision-time variable representing the time *S* takes to consider alternate solutions before committing himself to one of them in a situation with high response uncertainty. Kagan and his associates (Kagan, 1965, 1966; Kagan *et al.*, 1964) have shown that performance on the MFF test has high stability and intertest generality and is related to performance on visual discrimination tasks, inductive reasoning, serial recall, and reading skills. Most recently, investigators have been interested in the modification of cognitive impulsivity. Kagan *et al.* (1966) have attempted to train, in three individual sessions, inhibition of impulsive responding by requiring the child to defer his answer for a fixed period of 10 to 15 seconds During this period the child was encouraged to study the stimuli in the task and to think about his answer, but he did *not* receive training in more efficient procedures to emit during this interval. Significant changes in latency or decision time occurred, but no corresponding significant change in errors was evident. Debus (1970) examined the usefulness of filmed modeling of reflective behavior and found a decrease only in decision time, and, like Kagan *et al.* (1966), no corresponding change in errors. The studies by Kagan *et al.* (1966) and Debus (1970) have concentrated on increasing latency times without paying sufficient attention to inducing improved cognitive and/or scanning strategies in the impulsive child. Siegelman (1969) and Drake (1970) have demonstrated that different attentional and cognitive strategies seem to underlie the performance of impulsive and reflective *S*s. The data from Siegelman and Drake indicate that the impulsive child on the MFF test (*a*) displays a greater biasing of attention both in extent of scanning and in number of alternatives ignored; (*b*) is simply in search of some variant that globally resembles the standard and is not very discriminating or analytic in his viewing. In comparison, the reflective child seems to follow a strategy designed to find explicit differences among alternatives and then to check the standard for verification. The impulsive child's approach or strategy on the MFF task results in many errors and quick decision times. The purpose of the present study was to examine the usefulness of the cognitive self-guidance training procedure in altering the attentional strategy of the impulsive child on the MFF test. The efficacy of the self-instructional training procedure in modifying cognitive impulsivity is compared with a modeling-alone procedure. An attentional control group which received exposure to the practice materials but no explicit training was included for comparative purposes.

## Study II

### Method

### Subject

The 15 impulsive children who received training were selected from a larger group of kindergarten ($N = 30$) and first-grade ($N = 30$) public school children on the basis of two behavioral criteria. All of the children were individually tested on parallel forms of six items each of the MFF test. Interspersed between the two MFF forms the instruction, "You don't have to hurry. You should go slowly and carefully," was given to all *S*s. The 15 impulsive *S*s (four male and four female kindergarteners and four male and three female first graders) were selected on the basis of the *S*'s initial performance on Form I of the MFF test and the absence of any appreciable improvement in performance on Form II of the MFF test. Thus, the selected impulsive children were initially cognitively impulsive, and they did not significantly alter their style of responding even though they were instructed to do so. The use of an instructional manipulation to select *S*s is consistent with Vygotsky's (1962) suggestion that a child's capabilities are best reflected by his response to instructions.

Following Session 1, the 15 selected impulsive *S*s were randomly assigned to one of the treatment groups (viz., modeling alone or modeling plus self-instructional training) or to the attentional control group, subject to the constraint of comparable age and sex representation in each group. One week later in a second session, each of the impulsive *S*s was individually seen by a different *E* (female), who conducted the treatment, after which *S*s were tested on a third form of the six-item MFF test by the first *E* (male) who had conducted the testing in Session 1. The *E* who administered the three forms of the MFF test was thus unaware into which group *S* had been placed. The training materials consisted of the Picture Matching subtest from the Primary Mental Abilities (PMA) test and items from the Raven's Matrices test. These materials elicit similar task abilities to the MFF test and provide a useful format for modeling reflective behaviors. The training procedure which lasted some 20 minutes. consisted of *E* performing or modeling behavior on one item of the practice material and then *S* doing an item. There were in all eight practice trials.

### Treatments

### Cognitive modeling group

The *S*s in this group ($N = 5$) initially observed the *E* who modeled a set of verbalizations and behaviors which characterized the reflective child's proposed strategy on the MFF test. The following is an example of *E*'s modeled verbalizations on the PMA Picture Matching test:

> I have to remember to go slowly to get it right. Look carefully at this one (the standard), now look at these carefully (the variants). Is this one different? Yes, it has an extra leaf. Good, I can eliminate this one. Now, let's look at this one (another variant). I think it's this one, but let me first check the others. Good, I'm going slow and carefully. Okay, I think it's this one.

The impulsive child was exposed to a model which demonstrated the strategy to search for differences that would allow him successively to eliminate as incorrect all variants but one. The *E* modeled verbal statements or a strategy to make detailed comparisons across figures, looking at all variants before offering an answer. As in the first study, *E* also modeled errors and then how to cope with errors and improve upon them. For example, following an error *E* would model the following verbalizations:

> It's okay, just be careful. I should have looked more carefully. Follow the plan to check each one. Good, I'm going slowly.

After *E* modeled on an item, *S* was given an opportunity to perform on a similar practice item. The *S* was encouraged and socially reinforced for using the strategy *E* had just modeled, but did not receive explicit practice in self-instructing. This modeling-alone group was designed to indicate the degree of behavioral change from exposure to an adult model.

## Cognitive modeling plus self-instructional training group

The *S*s in this group were exposed to the same modeling behavior by *E* as were *S*s in the modeling-alone group, but in addition they were explicitly trained to produce the self-instructions *E* emitted while performing the task. After *E* modeled on an item, *S* was instructed to perform the task while talking aloud to himself as *E* had done. Over the course of the eight practice trials, the child's self-verbalizations were faded from initially an overt level to a covert level, as in Study I.

## Attentional control groups

The *S*s in this group observed the *E* perform the task and were given an opportunity to perform on each of the practice items. The *E*'s verbalizations consisted only of general statements to "go slow, be careful, look carefully," but did not include the explicit modeling of verbalizations dealing with scanning strategies as did the two treatment groups. The *S*s were encouraged and socially reinforced to go slowly and be careful, but were not trained to self-instruct. In many ways this group approximates the methods teachers and parents use to demonstrate a task in which they make general prohibitions, but do not explicate the strategies or details involved in solving the task. This group can be considered a minimal modeling condition or an attentional control group for exposure to $E$ and practice on task materials.

An attempt was made to provide all three groups with equal amounts of social reinforcement for their performance. At the completion of the modeling session, all $Ss$ were told, "Can you remember to do just like I did whenever you play games like this? Remember to go slowly and carefully." The $E$ who conducted the training departed, and the first $E$ then administered Form III of the MFF test.

## Results

### Selection of Ss

Table 4.1 presents the performance of reflective and impulsive $Ss$ on the initial MFF test (Form I) and on the MFF test (Form II) which was administered immediately after the instructions to "go slower." Of the original 60 $Ss$ tested, 45 were classified into either the reflective or impulsive groups, based on the $S$'s response time and errors relative to the performance of the same age and sex peer group. The instructions to go more slowly resulted in a significant ($p < .05$) increase in the mean total response time on initial decisions for reflective $Ss$ (i.e., from 99.8 to 123.8 sec.), but no comparable change in errors. The latter finding may be due to a "ceiling effect" and/or a slight decrement in performance resulting from anxiety. Several reflective $Ss$ indicated that they interpreted $E$'s instruction to go more slowly as an indicant that they were not performing adequately. Ward (1968) has reported that anxiety over failure played a greater role in the performance of reflective children than it did in the performance of impulsive children. The impulsive $Ss$ demonstrated a marked variability in how their performance changed as a result of the instructional manipulation. This variability permitted selection of the 15 most impulsive $Ss$ whose performance changed

**TABLE 4.1** Impulsive and reflective $Ss$' performance on initial MFF test (Form I) and on the MFF test (Form II) administered after instructions to "go slower"

| $Ss$ | MFF performance | | | |
|---|---|---|---|---|
| | Form I | | Form II | |
| | $\bar{X}$ | SD | $\bar{X}$ | SD |
| Reflectives ($N = 20$) | | | | |
|   Total errors | 6.3 | 3.5 | 7.7 | 4.0 |
|   Total decision time | 99.8 | 6.5 | 123.8 | 10.5 |
| Impulsives ($N = 25$) | | | | |
|   Total errors | 16.4 | 3.8 | 11.4 | 7.0 |
|   Total decision time | 42.9 | 5.5 | 58.1 | 7.6 |

**TABLE 4.2** A breakdown of impulsive $Ss$' performance on Forms I and II of the MFF test

| $Ss$ | MFF performance | | | |
|---|---|---|---|---|
| | Form I | | Form II | |
| | $\bar{X}$ | SD | $\bar{X}$ | SD |
| Impulsive $Ss$ selected for treatment ($N = 15$) | | | | |
| Total errors | 15.2 | 3.5 | 12.2 | 4.6 |
| Total decision time | 42.8 | 5.3 | 51.2 | 5.9 |
| Impulsive $Ss$ *not* selected for treatment ($N = 10$) | | | | |
| Total errors | 17.6 | 4.2 | 10.5 | 5.4 |
| Total decision time | 43.0 | 6.0 | 65.0 | 8.3 |

minimally. In a second session, these impulsive $Ss$ were provided with treatment. Table 4.2 presents the performance scores for the impulsive $Ss$ who were selected for treatment and those impulsive $Ss$ who significantly improved their performance from the minimal instructional manipulation.

In summary, from a group of 60 kindergarten and first-grade children, 15 $Ss$ were selected who were most cognitively impulsive on initial testing and who minimally altered their response style when explicitly given the instruction to do so.

## Analysis of treatment efficacy

Figure 4.2 presents the performance of the modeling group, modeling plus self-instructional group, and the attentional control group for the three six-item forms of the MFF test. The analyses of the decision times and error scores on Forms I and II of the MFF test yielded no significant group, trials, or Group × Trials interaction, indicating that prior to treatment the three groups performed comparably on initial performance and in response to instructions to go more slowly. The differential efficacy of the treatment procedures is indicated in the analysis of Form III of the MFF test which was administered immediately after treatment. On the decision time measure, the two treatment groups significantly ($p < .05$) slowed down their decision time on Form III relative to their own prior performances on Forms I and II and relative to the control group's performance on Form III. The modeling plus self-instructional training group which slowed down the most was significantly different ($t = 8.10, df = 8, p < .001$) from the modeling-alone group on Form III. The analyses of the error scores indicated that *only* $Ss$ who received modeling plus self-instructional training significantly ($p < .05$) improved their performance relative to the other two groups and relative to their own prior performances.

In summary, the results indicated that the cognitive modeling plus self-instructional group was most effective in altering decision time and in reducing

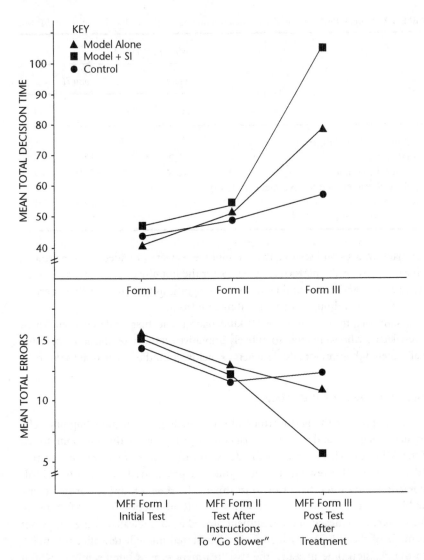

**FIGURE 4.2** MFF performances of impulsive *S*s who were in a modeling-alone group, a modeling plus self-instructional training group, and an additional control group

errors. The modeling-alone group significantly decreased decision time, but did not significantly reduce errors. The efficacy of the self-instructional component of the training procedure in fostering behavioral change is underscored by the fact that three of the five *S*s in the self-instruction group spontaneously self-verbalized on Form III of the MFF test, whereas none did so in the other two groups.

Similarly in Study I, several Ss in the self-instructional training group spontaneously self-verbalized in the posttest and follow-up sessions. It does appear that self-instructional training can bring an impulsive child's overt behavior under his own verbal discriminative control. At a macroscopic level, the impulsive children, after self-instructional training, do seem to be approaching psychometric tasks differently, taking their time, talking to themselves, and improving their performance. Research is now underway to explore the generality, persistence, and behavioral changes that result from self-instructional training.

## Discussion

The results of the two studies indicate that a cognitive self-guidance program which trains impulsive children to talk to themselves is effective in modifying their behavior on a variety of psychometric tests which assess cognitive impulsivity, Performance IQ, and motor ability. The results of Study II indicate that the addition of explicit self-instructional training to modeling procedures significantly alters the attentional strategies of the impulsive children and facilitates behavioral change. The impulsive children were taught to use their private speech for orienting, organizing, regulating, and self-rewarding functions with the consequence of greater self-control. The present self-instructional procedure seems applicable to the culturally deprived child, who has been described by Bereiter and Engelmann (1966) and Blank and Solomon (1968, 1969) as having a "central language deficit," namely, the inability to relate what he says to what he does. The deprived child does not spontaneously use language to direct his problem-solving behavior, especially when specific demands to do so are removed, nor does he exhibit normal capacities for self-control. An examination of the usefulness of the present self-instructional training procedures over a prolonged period of time with such deprived children is now underway.

The present studies indicate that the therapist can now attempt to modify not only the patient's overt behavioral response, but also the antecedent and/or accompanying cognitions. For example, cognitive self-guidance training procedures may be used to influence the attentional and cognitive strategies patients emit in a variety of situations. The possibilities of using self-instructional training procedures to alter (a) the "attentional deficit" in schizophrenics (Lang & Buss, 1965); (b) psychophysiological reactions of psychiatric patients (Grings, 1965; Schachter, 1966); and (c) cognitive styles in general (Ellis, 1962) are most promising. The application of the self-instructional procedure to operant conditioning programs with human Ss, especially children, also seems worthwhile. We suggest that having S self-verbalize, initially aloud and subsequently covertly, the contingencies of reinforcement will result in greater change and more generalization. Reinforcement can be made contingent upon not only the emission of the desired behavior, but also S's self-verbalization of what he must do to secure reinforcement. The literature on awareness (see review by Bandura,

1969) provides further support for the possible efficacy of having S learn to self-verbalize the correct reinforcement rules which influence his subsequent responding.

With the cognitive training procedure, the response chain to be modified is broadened and may thus be subjected to such modification techniques as modeling, reinforcement, and aversive consequences. We have explored in a series of studies the use of behavior modification techniques to alter the self-verbalizations of such patients as phobics, schizophrenics, smokers, speech- and test-anxious Ss, as well as impulsive children (Meichenbaum, 1970, 1971; Meichenbaum *et al.*, 1971, in press; Steffy, Meichenbaum, & Best, 1970). In each case, therapeutically attending to the patient's self-verbalizations, as well as his overt maladaptive behavior, has led to greater behavioral change, greater generalization, and greater persistence of treatment effects. In each of these therapy studies the goal has been to bring S's overt behavior under his own discriminative control, a means of developing the self-regulatory function of private speech.

In conclusion, a *heuristic* assumption underlying the present line of investigation has been that symbolic activities obey the same psychological laws as do overt behaviors and that private speech is teachable. Thus, behavior modification techniques which have been used to modify overt behaviors may be applied to cognitive processes. Only future research will indicate the validity of this assumption, but the by-products, in terms of the development of new treatment techniques, will be sizable.

## Note

1. This work was supported by the Ontario Mental Health Foundation Grant 120. The authors wish to thank Dale Willows for her assistance in the collection of the data and Richard Steffy for his many constructive comments.

## References

Anthony, A. (1959) "Normal and Neurotic Qualitative Porteus Maze Performance Under Stress and Non-stress." Unpublished PhD thesis, Columbia University.

Bandura, A. (1969) *Principles of Behavior Modification*. New York: Holt, Rinehart & Winston.

Bem, S. (1967) Verbal self-control: the establishment of effective self-instruction. *Journal of Experimental Psychology*, 74, 485–91.

Bem, S. (1970) The role of comprehension in children's problem-solving. *Developmental Psychology*, 2, 351–8.

Bereiter, C., & Engelmann, S. (1966) *Teaching Disadvantaged Children in the Preschool*. Englewood-Cliffs, NJ: Prentice-Hall.

Blank, M., & Solomon, F. (1968) A tutorial language program to develop abstract thinking in socially disadvantaged preschool children. *Child Development*, 39, 379–89.

Blank, M., & Solomon, F. (1969) How should the disadvantaged child be taught? *Child Development*, 40, 47–61.

Debus, R. L. (1970) Effects of brief observation of model behavior on conceptual tempo of impulsive children. *Developmental Psychology*, 2, 22–32.

Drake, D. M. (1970) Perceptual correlates of impulsive and reflective behavior. *Developmental Psychology*, 2, 202–14.

Ellis, A. (1962) *Reason and Emotion in Psychotherapy*. New York: Holt, Rinehart Winston.

Eysenck, A. J. (1955) A dynamic theory of anxiety and hysteria. *Journal of Mental Science*, 101, 128–51.

Flawell J. H., Beach, D. R., & Chinsky, J. M. (1966) Spontaneous verbal rehearsal in a memory task as a function of age. *Child Development*, 37, 283–99.

Foulds, G. A. (1951) Temperamental differences in maze performance. *British Journal of Psychology*, 42, 209–17.

Grings, W. W. (1965) Verbal-perceptual factors in the conditioning of autonomic responses, In W. F. Prokasy (ed.), *Classical Conditioning: A Symposium*. New York: Appleton-Century-Crofts.

Kagan, J. (1965) Impulsive and reflective children: significance of conceptual tempo. In J. D. Krumboltz (ed.), *Learning and the Educational Process*. Chicago: Rand McNally.

Kagan, J. (1966) Reflection-impulsivity: the generality and dynamics of conceptual tempo. *Journal of Abnormal Psychology*, 71, 17–24.

Kagan, J., Pearson, L., & Welch, L. (1966) The modifiability of an impulsive tempo. *Journal of Educational Psychology*, 57, 359–365.

Kagan, J., Rosman, B. L., Day, D., Albert, J., & Phillips, W. (1964) Information processing in the child: significance of analytic and reflective attitudes. *Psychological Monographs*, 78 (1, Whole No. 578).

Kitzinger, H., & Blumbero, E. (1951) Supplementary guide for administering and scoring the Wechsler-Bellevue. Intelligence Scale (Form I). *Psychological Monographs*, 65 (10, Whole No. 319).

Klein, W. L. (1963) "An Investigation of the Spontaneous Speech of Children During Problem Solving." Unpublished doctoral dissertation, University of Rochester.

Kohlberg, L., Yaeger, J., & Hjertholm, E. (1968) Private speech: four studies and a review of theories. *Child Development*, 39, 691–736.

Lang, P. J., & Buss, A. H. (1965) Psychological deficit in schizophrenia: interference activation, *Journal of Abnormal Psychology*, 70, 77–106.

Lindquist, E. F. (1953) *Design and Analysis of Experiments in Psychology and Education*. Boston: Houghton Mifflin.

Lovaas, O. I. (1964) Cue properties of words: the control of operant responding by rate and content of verbal operants. *Child Development*, 35, 245–56.

Luria, A. R. (1959) The directive function of speech in development. *Word*, 15, 341–52.

Luria, A. R. (1961) *The Role of Speech in the Regulation of Normal and Abnormal Behavior*. New York: Live-right.

Lutey, C. (1966) *Individual Intelligence Testing: A Manual*. Greeley, CO: Executary.

Meichenbaum, D. (1970) "Cognitive Factors in Behavior Modification: Modifying What People Say to Themselves." Unpublished manuscript, University of Waterloo.

Meichenbaum, D. (1971) Examination of model characteristics in reducing avoidance behavior. *Journal of Personality and Social Psychology*, 17, 298–307.

Meichenbaum, D., & Goodman, J. (1969a) The developmental control of operant motor responding by verbal operants. *Journal of Experimental Child Psychology*, 7, 553–65.

Meichenbaum, D., & Goodman, J. (1969b) Reflection-impulsivity and verbal control of motor behavior. *Child Development*, 40, 785–97.

Meichenbaum, D., Bowers, K., & Ross, R. (1968) Modification of classroom behavior of institutionalized female adolescent offenders. *Behaviour Research and Therapy*, 6, 343–53.

Meichenbaum, D., Bowers, K., & Ross, R. (1969) A behavioral analysis of teacher expectancy effect. *Journal of Personality and Social Psychology*, 13, 306–16.

Meichenbaum, D., Gilmore, J. B., & Fedoravicius, A. (1971) Group insight versus group desensitization in treating speech anxiety. *Journal of Consulting and Clinical Psychology*, in press.

Moely, B., Olson, F., Halwes, T., & Flavell, J. (1969) Production deficiency in young children's recall. *Developmental Psychology*, 1, 26–34.

Palkes, H., Stewart, W., & Kahana, B. (1968) Porteus Maze performance of hyperactive boys after training in self-directed verbal commands. *Child Development*, 39, 817–26.

Piaget, J. (1947) *The Psychology of Intelligence*. London: Routledge & Kegan Paul.

Porteus, S. E. (1942) *Qualitative Performance in the Maze Test*. Vineland, NJ: Smith.

Reese, H. W. (1962) Verbal mediation as a function of age level. *Psychological Bulletin*, 59, 502–9.

Schachter, S. (1966) The interaction of cognitive and physiological determinants of emotional state. In C. D. Speilberger (ed.), *Anxiety and Behavior*. New York: Academic Press.

Siegelman, E. (1969) Reflective and impulsive observing behavior. *Child Development*, 40, 1213–22.

Steffy, R., Meichenbaum, D., & Best, A. (1970) Aversive and cognitive factors in the modification of smoking behavior. *Behavior Research and Therapy*, 8, 115–25.

Vygotsky, L. S. (1962) *Thought and Language*. New York: Wiley.

Ward, W. C. (1968) Reflection-impulsivity in kindergarten children. *Child Development*, 39, 867–74.

Wechsler, D. (1949) *Manual: Wechsler Intelligence Scale for Children*. New York: Psychological Corporation.

# 5

# TEACHING THINKING

## A cognitive-behavioral perspective

*Donald Meichenbaum*

UNIVERSITY OF WATERLOO, ONTARIO, CANADA

Recently, Lester Mann (1979) has traced the history of the work on cognitive processes and their training. This engaging historical account provides an interesting backdrop for the present conference. Mann indicates that the preoccupation in training processes is time honored. As he notes, Socrates and Plato espoused it and Itard, Seguin, Montessori, and Binet reiterated it. Each in his or her own way was preoccupied with the question: Can one *train the mind*, or in modern terms, can one teach thinking?

Because my penchant is to put things into historical perspective, I think it is useful to trace my involvement with this question.

## Some beginnings

Let me set the stage for my interest in this issue by characterizing the zeitgeist in the late 1960s and early 1970s. A variety of different influences contributed to the development of a cognitive-behavioral training approach with children. One prominent research area evolved from social learning theory and it gave impetus to a variety of laboratory-based investigations of children's self-mediated cognitive strategies. The work of Mischel, Kanfer, and others indicated the important role of children's cognitive strategies in enhancing self-control on such tasks as delay of gratification and resistance to temptation. A related influence was the work on verbal mediation, in which learning to use task-appropriate mediators was viewed as involving the separate phases of comprehension (Bern, 1971), production (Flavell et al., 1966), and mediation (Reese, 1962). This verbal-mediational deficiency literature suggested that a training program designed to improve task performance and engender self-control should provide explicit training in the comprehension of the task, the spontaneous production of mediators, and the use of such mediators to control nonverbal behavior.

The research in the early 1970s (see Meichenbaum, 1977) on children who have self-control problems suggested that such mediational deficits play a central role in their disturbance. Children with self-control problems were viewed not as intrinsically impulsive but rather as impulsive, because they did not know how or did not desire to deal effectively with task demands. Their disruptiveness was seen as secondary to deficits in cognitive strategies. As Virginia Douglas (1972) concluded, such impulsive children fail to stop, look, and listen. More recent research as reviewed by Douglas and Peters (1979) further supports the role of a mediational (or in current terminology, a metacognitive) deficit in such impulsive children. In fact, investigators of other child populations have suggested that defective metaprocesses or deficits in executive cognitive skills contribute to poor performance in learning-disability children (McLeskey et al., 1980; Torgesen, 1977), retarded children (Borkowski & Cavanaugh, 1978; Brown et al., 1977), and children who have problems in academic performance such as in reading comprehension (Meyers & Paris, 1978; Ryan, 1981).

Another development of a related influence on the cognitive-behavior modification approach with children was the work of the Soviet psychologists Luria (1961) and Vygotsky (1962). On the basis of his work with children, Luria (1959) proposed three stages by which voluntary motor behaviors come under verbal control. During the first stage, the speech of others, usually adults, controls and directs a child's behavior. During the second stage, the child's overt speech becomes an effective mediator or regulator of his behavior. Finally, the child's covert or inner speech comes to assume a self-governing role. From this hypothetical developmental sequence, we developed a treatment paradigm to train impulsive children to talk to themselves as a means of developing self-control (Meichenbaum & Goodman, 1971).

Thus, the stage was set for us to bring together the clinical observations of those investigators who had studied impulsive children with the theoretical frameworks of social learning theory and Soviet psychology. Added to this amalgam was the increasing concern about the *inability* of behavior management procedures, such as operant conditioning programs, to foster changes that were generalizable and durable. Problems with generalization and maintenance have plagued attempts to use operant procedures to reduce children's disruptive behavior or to increase academic behavior (see Coates & Thoresen, 1982; Conway & Bucher, 1976; Emery & Margolin, 1977; Keeley et al., 1976; Wahler et al., 1979 for review and discussion). The hope when we began our cognitive-behavioral training program was that by supplementing behavior procedures with cognitive interventions, such as self-instructional training or social problem-solving, we could enhance the efficacy, generalization, and maintenance of our interventions. This hope was predicated on the assumption that if you changed the child by training self-regulatory cognitive skills, the intervention would have greater impact than a procedure that influenced the child only indirectly by controlling environmental contingencies. The goal was to train the child to regulate his or her behavior to act more effectively on the environment across situations.

Thus a strange set of bedfellows were brought together in order to give rise to a training approach.

### Cognitive-behavioral training

The training regimen we designed taught children to spontaneously generate and employ cognitive strategies and self-instructions. By self-instructions, we meant verbal statements and images to oneself that prompt, direct, or maintain behavior. More specifically the training regimen was designed to teach the child to engage in mediating responses that exemplify a general strategy for controlling behavior under various circumstances. The following procedural steps were included: (1) an adult model performed a task while talking to himself out loud (cognitive modeling); (2) the child performed the same task under the direction of the model's instructions (overt, external guidance); (3) the child performed the task while instructing himself aloud (overt self-guidance); (4) the child whispered the instructions to himself as he went through the task (faded, overt, self-guidance); and finally, (5) the child performed the task while guiding his performance via inaudible or private speech or nonverbal self-direction (covert self-instruction). Over a number of training sessions, the package of self-statements modeled by the experimenter and rehearsed by the child (initially aloud and then covertly) was enlarged by means of response chaining and successive approximation procedures. For example, in a task that required the copying of line patterns, the examiner performed the task while cognitively modeling as follows (Meichenbaum & Goodman, 1971).

> Okay, what is it I have to do? I have to copy the picture with the different lines. I have to go slowly and carefully. Okay, draw the line down, down, good; and then to the right, that's it; now down some more and to the left. Good, I'm doing fine so far. Remember, go slowly. Now back up again. No, I was supposed to go down. That's okay. Just erase the line carefully … Good. Even if I make an error I can go on slowly and carefully. I have to go down now. Finished. I did it! (p. 117)

In this thinking-out-loud phase, the model displayed several performance-relevant skills: problem definition ("What is it I have to do?"), focusing attention and response guidance ("Carefully … Draw the line down"), self-reinforcement

("Good, I'm doing fine"), and self-evaluative coping skills and error-correcting options ("That's okay ... Even if I make an error I can go on slowly").

Thus, the child was taught to generate questions about the goals of the task, answers to these questions, self-instructions that guide the execution of the task, coping thoughts and images in case of failure, and self-praise for having tried. Training evolved toward this complete set of self-instructions through successive approximations. Training was arranged so that the child received adequate practice in the use of a strategy. The focus of the training was *not* to teach the child what to think, but rather how to think.

A variety of tasks were employed to train the child to use self-instructions to control nonverbal behavior. The tasks varied from those employing simple sensorimotor abilities to those requiring more complex problem-solving abilities. The sensorimotor tasks (such as copying line patterns and coloring figures within boundaries) provided first the model, then the child, with the opportunity to produce a narrative description of the behavior, both preceding and accompanying performance. Over the course of a training session, the child's overt self-statements about a particular task were faded to the covert level. The difficulty of the training tasks was increased over the training sessions, using more cognitively demanding activities. Hence, there was a progression from tasks such as reproducing designs and following sequential instructions to completing such pictorial series as those in the Primary Mental Abilities test, to solving conceptual tasks such as Raven's Matrices. The experimenter modeled appropriate self-verbalizations for each of these tasks and then had the child follow the fading procedure.

In the initial Meichenbaum and Goodman (1971) study, the self-instructional training procedure, relative to placebo and assessment control groups, resulted in significantly improved performance on Porteus Mazes and improved IQ on the WISC, as well as showing increased cognitive reflectivity on the Matching Familiar Figures test (MFF). The improved performance was evident in a 1-month follow-up. Moreover, it was observed that 60% of the self-instructionally trained impulsive children were talking to themselves spontaneously in the posttest and followup sessions.

The cognitive-behavioral paradigm has now been used successfully to establish inner speech control over the disruptive behavior of hyperactive children (Douglas *et al.*, 1976); aggressive children (Camp *et al.*, 1977); disruptive preschoolers (Bornstein & Quevillon, 1976), cheating behavior of kindergarten and first graders (Monahan & O'Leary, 1971); Porteus Maze performance of hyperactive boys (Palkes *et al.*, 1972; Palkes *et al.*, 1968); and the conceptual tempo of emotionally disturbed boys (Finch *et al.*, 1975) as well as that of normal children (Bender, 1976; Meichenbaum & Goodman, 1971). Although these early findings have been promising, results do *not* give rise to a sense of complacency. It is becoming apparent that we are becoming more sophisticated in our understanding of cognitive-behavior modification procedures in that we are starting to understand the limitations of our procedures. Hopefully, increased understanding of the conditions under which cognitive-behavior modification procedures fail will lead us to take steps to ensure that requisite conditions for success are met before and during our training interventions.

What are some of the necessary training conditions to ensure durable generalizable results? The Douglas *et al.* (1976) study nicely illustrates the general treatment approach. The hyperactive children treated were initially exposed to a model who verbalized cognitive strategies, which the children could in turn rehearse, initially aloud and then silently. These strategies included stopping to define a problem and the various steps within it, considering and evaluating several possible solutions before acting on any one, checking one's work throughout and calmly correcting any errors, sticking with a problem until everything possible has been tried to solve it correctly, and giving oneself a pat on the back for work well done. Verbalizations modeled by the trainer to illustrate these strategies, stated by Douglas *et al.* (1976), included:

> "I must stop and think before I begin." "What plans can I try?" "How would it work out if I did that?" "What shall I try next?" "Have I got it right so far?" "See, I made a mistake there – I'll just erase it." "Now let's see, have I tried everything I can think of?" "I've done a pretty good job!" (p. 408)

The cognitive-behavioral training was applied across tasks in order to ensure that the child did *not* just develop task-specific response sets but instead developed generalizable cognitive representations. This latter point needs to be underscored. The process by which socialized (or external) speech develops into egocentric (or internal) speech and then into inner speech requires much consideration. As Vygotsky (1962) noted in *Thought and Language*, this process of internalization and abbreviation should *not* be viewed merely as a process of faded speech; instead the transformation from interpersonal speech to thought represents qualitative differences. How interpersonal instructions modeled by a therapist, teacher, or parent change into the child's own private speech and thought is a major theoretical and practical question. The answer to this question will have major implications for the potential of cognitive-behavioral training with children (see Meichenbaum, 1977, and Toulmin, 1978, for a discussion of these issues).

Elsewhere (Meichenbaum, 1977), I have described a host of clinical suggestions for conducting cognitive-behavioral self-instructional training with children. These include: (1) using the child's medium of play to initiate and model self-talk; (2) using tasks that have a high pull for the use of sequential cognitive strategies; (3) using peer teaching by having children cognitively model while performing for another child; (4) moving through the program at the child's own rate, and building up the package of self-statements to include self-talk of a problem-solving variety as well as coping and self-reinforcing elements; (5) guarding against the child's use of self-statements in a mechanical noninvolved fashion;

(6) including a trainer who is animated and responsive to the child; (7) learning to use the self-instructional training with low-intensity responses; (8) supplementing the training with imagery practice; (9) supplementing the self-instructional training with correspondence training (Rogers-Warren & Baer, 1976); and (10) supplementing the self-instructional training with operant procedures such as a response cost system (Kendall & Finch, 1976; Nelson & Eirkimer, 1978; Robertson & Keeley, 1974). A host of treatment manuals for cognitive-behavior modification in children are now available (e.g., Camp & Bash, 1981; Hinshaw *et al.*, 1979; Kendall, 1979; and Wilson *et al.*, 1978). It is important to recognize that these manuals are experimental in nature and that further critical evaluation is now under way. A number of major review papers on cognitive behavior modification with children have been written recently (Craighead *et al.*, 1978; Hobbs *et al.*, 1980; Karoly, 1977; Kendall, 1977; Mash & Dalby, 1978; Meichenbaum & Asarnow, 1979; O'Leary & Dubey, 1979; and Rosenthal, 1979, as well as an entire issue of *Exceptional Education Quarterly*, May, 1980, that was devoted to the teaching of cognitive strategies).

In general, these review articles of the cognitive-behavioral modification studies highlight the importance of instructing children in the self-management skills of goal setting, strategy planning, and self-monitoring. They indicate that, the more information a child has about his or her cognitive functioning and the ways they can be combined, the more functional will be the child's approach to new situations.

## A parallel development: metacognition

Although the work on cognitive-behavior modification arose from the efforts of clinicians to help children develop self-control by means of learning to use cognitive strategies, a parallel development was evident in the area of developmental psychology under the rubric of metacognition.

Cognition refers to the actual ongoing processes and strategies that a person uses. For example, when a child remembers something, memory processes, per se, are involved. Metacognition refers to what a person *knows* about his or her cognitions (i.e., consciously aware of the processes and being able to relate them in some way) and to the *ability to control* these cognitions (e.g., planning cognitive activities, choosing among alternatives, monitoring and changing activities). For example, Flavell (1976) uses the construct *metamemory* to refer to what a person knows about memory processes and what he or she is able to do about them.

Brown's (1978) summary of these metacognitive processes includes analyzing and characterizing the problem at hand, reflecting upon what one knows or does not know that may be necessary for a solution, devising a plan for attacking the problem, and checking or monitoring progress.

Metacognition is concerned with the nature of the *intensive intellectual commerce* of Flavell (1976), the *executive processes* of Belmont and Butterfield (1977), or what

Gagné and Briggs (1974) call *cognitive strategies:* "The internally organized skill(s) that select and guide the internal processes involved in defining and solving novel problems. In other words, it is a skill by means of which the learner manages his own thinking behavior" (p. 29). These notions of metacognition are reminiscent of Skinner's (1968) *self-management behaviors* and Miller *et al.*'s (1960) *plans*, Neisser's (1967) *executive routines*, and Atkinson and Shiffrin's (1968) *control processes* that organize and control the operations of what may be thought of as the more basic on-line learning and memory processes.

Attempts at assessing metacognition began in the area of memory (Kreutzer *et al.*, 1975); recent work has studied metacognition in relation to attentional processes (Miller & Bigi, 1979), reading comprehension (Meyers & Paris, 1978; Ryan, 1981), self-control (Mischel *et al.*, 1978), and communication (Markman, 1977). See Meichenbaum *et al.* (in press) for a discussion of the issues in assessing metacognition.

The importance of such executive processes in the area of instruction is indicated in the literature review by Belmont and Butterfield (1977). Belmont and Butterfield reviewed 114 studies on the use of cognitive instruction, none of which involved superordinate processes, *nor did any of them report generalized results*. The children who received cognitive instruction often improved on the trained tasks and exhibited improved performance immediately following training, but this improvement did *not* generalize to other tasks or across time. In contrast, Belmont *et al.* (in press) reviewed six recent studies that have produced substantial transfer, each of which focused on teaching executive cognitive skills. To quote:

> The experiments that have produced substantial transfer not only delivered specific instruction in subordinate skills, but also led the children to perform, or to see the wisdom of performing activities such as defining goals, designing appropriate plans, and monitoring the implementations and outcomes of those plans. (p. 6)

The children in these studies were taught to know when they were confronted with a problem and were encouraged to try to solve problems when they encountered them.

Both the literatures on cognitive-behavior modification and the training of metacognitive skills offer suggestions for how one can teach thinking.

## General guidelines for teaching thinking

Because the evidence that one can teach thinking is only encouraging and in no way conclusive, one can identify from both the research on cognitive behavior modification and metacognition general guidelines that should be considered. No study has included all the guidelines to be enumerated. A brief consideration of these guidelines provides a useful framework for the development of a curriculum to teach thinking.

The first suggestion is that the instructor (be it a teacher or researcher) should adopt a metacognitive perspective. The teacher needs to employ executive cognitive skills in setting up such a training program. In particular, a variety of coping-skills self-statements will be required, because inevitable failures will be encountered. Such failures should be the occasion *not* to catastrophize and conclude that the business of teaching thinking is fruitless and insurmountable, but rather such failures should be anticipated, and when they occur, should be viewed as problems to be solved. This cognitive style should permeate the entire training program, from the designers to the pupils.

A corollary of this first point is that the instructor should not only be conscious of his or her own superordinate problem-solving skills, but also of the attributions he or she is likely to emit when encountering failure. Attribution theory suggests that when the investigator or teacher encounters failure, he or she may be more disposed to attribute blame to something out there (such as the characteristics of the subjects) than to oneself or more aptly to one's training program. For example, Belmont and Butterfield (1977) argue that the poor transfer performance of subjects in the Keeney *et al.* (1976) memory training study led to the proposition that the children had a deficit (*production deficiency*). Instead, we could suggest that the experimenter suffers from a deficit. It could be argued that the experimenter has shown an instructional deficit in nurturing the processes required to ensure generalization. The results of a related training study by Asarnow and Meichenbaum (1979) indicated that altering the nature of the training can lead to success in areas where training had previously failed. These results underscore Belmont and Butterfield's point. Turnure *et al.* (1976) have offered a similar argument for an *instructional deficiency* (i.e., the trainer failed to provide the child with efficient learning cues) in contrast to attributing a production deficiency to the child.

The concern with the features of training highlight the need for the trainer to conduct a careful task analysis of the skills to be taught, which is the third guideline for teaching thinking. There is a need to carefully specify the component processes required on respective tasks. As Brown (1974) recommends, the trainer should analyze the desired target behavior into its component strategy and capacity requirements. The implication is that strategy training may have to be preceded by or accompanied by skill training, if deficits in requisite skills are discovered. Put in other words, Wood *et al.* (1976) indicate that training, or to use their term, tutoring, requires that the tutor must have at least two theoretical models: a theory of the task or problem and how it may be completed, and a theory of the performance characteristics of the tutee. Such aspects as the cognitive capacity of the pupil will obviously influence the form, content, and rate of training. Thus, it is necessary to test for the spontaneous use of task strategies to assess the pupil's capacity. In this way, the trainer can encourage pupils to use whatever skills they possess.

To teach thinking, a fourth guideline suggests that the trainer must recognize that generalization of the learned skills will not just occur and that one must develop the implicit technology to ensure such generalization. The literature indicates that pupils become welded to the specific training material and regimens. Researchers (Borkowski & Cavanaugh, 1978; Meichenbaum & Asarnow, 1979; Stokes & Baer, 1977), from quite divergent frameworks, have offered a host of suggestions as to how such generalization can be achieved. Let us consider these suggestions, and then in a later part, we can consider some of the pedagogical implications.

1. It is important to appreciate that the training of cognitive skills or the teaching of thinking will not happen quickly. Training often needs to be prolonged, in-depth, and involve feedback. The pupil requires the interplay between the adoption of a cognitive strategy and the opportunity and experience to employ that strategy. The feedback that the pupil receives should convey not only the strategy to be used, but also the purpose and usefulness of such strategies. The trainer should determine that the child can transfer or adapt the strategy to a variety of tasks before discontinuing training. In addition, the trainer should provide explicit feedback about the effectiveness with which the pupil implemented the strategy.

2. From the outset one needs the pupil to be a collaborator in the generation of the cognitive strategies. It is important to ensure that the purpose and rationale for the training is explained to the pupil as fully as possible.

3. The cognitive strategies to be taught should be general in nature and applicable across situations. But, at the same time, the cognitive training should be individualized (not predetermined) in order to ensure that the private speech trained is compatible with the style of the individual child. As Kendall & Wilcox (1980) and Schleser et al. (1981) found the use of conceptual (i.e., general) versus concrete (i.e., task specific) strategies maximized generalization and durability. It is important that the pupil does not adopt these strategies as a blind rule. In order to help achieve this, practice with the cognitive strategy should be employed across tasks and settings. A number of general problem-solving strategies have been successfully taught, including self-interrogation, self-checking, analyzing tasks and breaking the problems into manageable steps and then proceeding sequentially, scanning one's strategic repertoire to match task demands, and so forth. The pupil must not only have such strategies in his or her repertoire but must learn when and how to use such strategies and have a sense of efficacy of being able to employ them. The pupil is taught to become more aware of internal cognitive processes, to deautomatize the learning process, and to then employ the problem-solving strategies. This training approach is cognizant of the process by which a skill is acquired as described by Schiffrin and Schneider (1977). The acquisition of a skill involves a progressive shift from controlled conscious processing to automatic processing: a sequence that allows attention to be redirected

from the specific required response to the more general demands of the situation. With the development of proficiency, the explicit use of cognitive strategies is faded.

4. The use of a coping model, one who shares feelings and thoughts about performances, enhances the training regimen. The next part on the role of the affect further underscores the importance of a training regimen that anticipates and subsumes the pupil's thoughts and feelings that may interfere with performance. As Friedling & O'Leary (1979) indicate, it is important in cognitive training to identify and alter existing maladaptive and idiosyncratic self-statements rather than merely training new, and presumably adaptive, private speech. (See Meichenbaum (1975) for an example of this approach in teaching problem-solving skills to a college population.)

In the same way that cognitive-behavior modification researchers have focused on relapse prevention with adults (e.g., Marlatt & Gordon, 1980), it is possible that one can use a coping model approach with children to teach thinking. One could discuss with the pupils the conditions and factors that may interfere with their use of cognitive strategies and metacognitive skills. As we develop a technology of behavior change, these principles can be applied to the area of teaching thinking.

5. The timing of when cognitive strategies are taught and employed is important. The research suggests that it is important that component skills and experience with the task are in the pupil's repertoire before training with a cognitive strategy is undertaken. Recent reports (Higa, 1975; Robin et al. 1975; Wein & Nelson, 1975) have suggested that cognitive training may be most appropriate for children who have elemental performance skills in their repertoire, but who fail to self-regulate their behavior appropriately. It is quite likely that training self-regulatory skills will not promote improved performance unless the subskills requisite for successful execution of the target behaviors are in the child's repertoire. Meichenbaum (1977) has emphasized the importance of conducting a detailed analysis of task-related subskills before embarking on self-regulatory treatment and has provided suggestions for conducting such subskill assessments. Both Kendall (1977) and Lloyd (1980) have also commented on the importance of ensuring that performance-related subskills are in the child's repertoire before initiating cognitive training. The importance of experience in the use of cognitive training is also illustrated in the following example. Consider the novice skier who reads an instructor's manual prior to the initial attempt to ski. "Bend the knees" the manual instructs. But only after the actual experience on the slope does the instruction take on its true meaning and impact. The actual experience provides the basis for translating the instruction into a self-guiding self-instruction – "Oh, bend the knees!"[1] It is necessary for the pupil to spend a certain amount of time engaged in training activities before he or she can develop correspondence between verbalizations and the behaviors that are to be controlled by them.

6. The training tasks should be chosen to ensure a sequential gradation of difficulty. In this way, the pupil can be taught to transfer recently learned skills to

situations other than the one in which initial learning was accomplished. The pupil must recognize the new situation as one requiring transfer, must want to solve it, and must manage his or her efforts to solve it appropriately. Tasks should be chosen that have a high "pull" for the strategy that is the target of training. As Borkowski & Cavanaugh (1978) note, the instructional package should be chosen so that common elements between training and generalization contexts are evident and distractors are minimal. For example, in order to teach impulsive children to systematically scan alternatives in matching tasks, Zelniker & Oppenheimer (1976) used a Difference Familiar Figures test that required the impulsive children to search all alternatives in order to find one alternative that matched a standard stimulus. This task pulled for systematic scanning, which in turn generalized to other matching tasks. Judicious selections of tasks can be supplemented by the cognitive modeling and overt and covert rehearsal as described earlier.

7. The training tasks that are chosen should actively involve the child and require mental transformation of the strategies that are taught. The trainer must be careful not to call for rote repetition, but to require the pupil to mentally transform and extend the strategy across academic and interpersonal domains. Such active involvement and mental transformation increases the likelihood of deeper processing and the development of new cognitive structures. One can teach pupils to extend the principles underlying domain specific knowledge across areas.

8. Such active pupil involvement may be achieved as the instructor fades, prompts, and supports. In fading such supports, it is necessary to maintain the child's interest and attention and foster a positive relationship with the trainer. For example, one investigator (Weinreich, 1975), who was trying to use cognitive training with impulsive children, reported that treatment efficacy was vitiated by problems with incentives (scheduling problems and absence of contingent reinforcers).

9. Training should be conducted in multiple settings. This may involve training other agents (i.e., parents) to prompt or model cognitive strategies in natural settings. Friedling & O'Leary (1979) note that "teaching children why and when to use self-instruction, and ensuring that they do, may be as important as teaching them how to self-instruct" (p. 218). Cognitive training would be more successful if it included explicit coaching and practice in the appropriate use of the skills being trained. The trainer should explicitly encourage the child to generalize the strategy to certain types of tasks or situations. This coaching might be supplemented by having children enumerate situations where the strategy could be used and having them imagine themselves using the strategy in a variety of situations.

For example, in the teaching of a constraint-seeking strategy (as employed in a game of Twenty Questions), not only should the pupil learn this approach on academic material, but he or she should be encouraged and taught to seek use of this strategy in everyday situations (e.g., a car mechanic or a doctor making a diagnosis). The child who is learning to self-interrogate by asking "What is the problem?," "How do I know it is problem?," and so forth can do this not only on a variety of academic tasks, but also with regard to social situations as depicted in videotapes of social interactions. If we train in isolation, we will fail to achieve generalization. The pupil should be given the opportunity to use, and encouraged to become inventive in using, the newly learned cognitive skills in a variety of situations.

10. The use and compliance with such cognitive strategies should be reinforced, and a sense of self-satisfaction should be nurtured in the pupil. The naturally occurring environmental contingencies should be arranged to reinforce the use of cognitive strategies and metacognitive skills.

Surely the way in which these guidelines are implemented will vary depending upon the age and capacity of the pupil, but the intent of the program is as applicable in kindergarten as it is in graduate school. In order to appreciate that such a tutorial program should not be cold or dispassionate, the next part on the role of affect provides an important caveat.

## The role of affect

The clinical perspective of cognitive-behavior modification offers an important caveat in conducting any tutorial program for the teaching of thinking. Any training program must consider the child's feelings about both the training program and his or her own performance (e.g., sense of efficacy, helplessness, and so forth). As Piaget (1962) noted "We must agree that at no level, at no stage, even in the adult, can we find a behavior or a state which is purely cognitive without affect nor a purely affective state without a cognitive element involved. There is no such thing as a purely cognitive state" (p. 130).

In light of the intimate connections between cognition and emotion, it is surprising that the literature on cognitive psychology and cognitive training, in general, has been silent on the role of affect. As Zajonc (1980) has commented, "contemporary cognitive psychology simply ignores affect" (p. 151). The words *affect, attitude, emotion, feeling, and sentiment do not appear in the indices of any major works on cognition,* with the exception of very few works cited by Zajonc (viz., Mandler, 1975; Miller & Johnson-Laird, 1976). It should be noted that Zajonc examined ten major works on cognition and noted that in the six volumes of the *Handbook of Learning and Cognitive Processes* (Estes, 1975–78) there is only one entry for affect and only one for attitude, both of which, parenthetically, were by a social psychologist.

Miller and Johnson-Laird (1976) state: "The information-processing system that emerges is fearfully cognitive and dispassionate. It can collect information, remember it, and work toward objectives, but it would have no emotional reaction to what is collected, remembered or achieved" (p. 111).

But people have feelings as well as perceptions, memories, and intentions. These feelings have important implications for the teaching of thinking. Several examples could be offered of the role of affect in cognitive processes (see Meichenbaum & Butler, 1980). One such example has been offered by Diener and Dweck (1978, 1980). They found that so-called helpless children as identified by the Intellectual Achievement Responsibility (IAR) Scale (Crandall *et al.*, 1965), as compared to mastery-oriented children, differed in the time and occurrence of attributions when exposed to failure. The helpless children made the expected attributions for failure to lack of ability, whereas mastery-oriented children made surprisingly few attributions but instead engaged in self-monitoring and self-instructions. The helpless children focused on the cause of failure, whereas the mastery-oriented children focused on remedies of failures. The helpless children tend to attribute failures to the lack of ability and view them as insurmountable. Mastery-oriented children, in contrast, tend to emphasize motivational factors and to view failure as surmountable.

This pattern of results found in school-age children is also evident in college students who perform problem-solving tasks (Bloom & Broder, 1950; Goor & Sommerfield, 1975; Henshaw, 1978). Each of these studies used a think-aloud procedure to assess the flow of the subject's ideation while trying to solve some problems. Illustrative of the results is the work by Henshaw from our laboratory. Henshaw studied the think-aloud protocols of high- and low-creative college students while they engaged in various problem-solving tasks. He classified each unit of the subject's think-aloud protocols into one of six categories (reviewing given information, strategy units, solution units, facilitative ideation, negative inhibitive ideation, and silence). He was then able to conduct a sequential Markovian probability analysis of the sequence of verbalized thoughts.

The highly creative, good problem-solving subjects differed from the less creative or poor problem-solving subjects not only in the frequency of certain categories of thought, but also in the patterning or sequence of their thoughts. Following every major category of verbal behavior, highly creative subjects were significantly more likely than less creative subjects to emit facilitative cognitive ideation and expressions of positive affect ("What else can I do?" "Just try to think of possibilities." "Hey, I'm pretty good at this."), and less likely to become silent. In contrast, the less creative individuals produced significantly more inhibitive ideation, reflecting a negative feeling about their own personality or abilities, their task strategy or solution, the task itself, or the experiment as a whole. Expressions of negative affect were manifested in terms of negative self-referent self-statements reflecting frustration, anger and/or boredom, for example: "I don't think I ever could do this." "How would Mary do this? She is always better than me. I'm not a very good problem solver." "I'm dumb!"

Interestingly, facilitative positive ideation functioned similarly in both the high- and low-scoring creative groups, especially during the first five minutes of a ten-minute problem-solving task, whereas inhibitive negative ideation functioned differently over time in the two groups. Both the high- and low-scoring creative individuals came up with good responses at the outset of the task, but over the course of the task, both affect and cognitions changed in a negative direction for the less creative individuals. It is as if one's cognitions became self-fulfilling prophecies that merely reconfirm one's negative beliefs; thus the cycle is self-perpetuating. One can well imagine how poor performance could lead to affective disturbance and negative self-statements and, in turn, to further poor performance as the cycle continues.

Such an affectively tied internal dialogue tends: (a) to be self-oriented rather than task oriented, which serves to deflect attention from the task at hand; (b) to have a basic orientation that is negative (often catastrophizing) rather than positive and coping, which serves to deflate motivation; and (c) to have an automatic, stereotyped, run-on character, which has the effect of escalating rather than controlling anxiety. Meichenbaum *et al.* (1982) have suggested that a common pattern of ideation contributes to poor performance in diverse achievement or stressful situations. The *absence* of a problem-solving set (i.e., viewing a task, social situation or stressor as a problem to be solved) leads to inadequate performance.

Any training program that is designed to teach thinking must take into consideration the important role of the child's feelings and the accompanying images, self-statements, attributions, appraisals, and expectations.

*Pedagogical Implications.* For the last several months, we have been conducting observations in grade school classrooms in order to identify the opportunities that are available to teach cognitive strategies and metacognitive skills. Because any specific training program competes for time with other instructional content and usually results in teacher and administrative resistance, our approach has been to consider how cognitive training could become part of the entire curriculum. Could one imbue the entire school curriculum and environment with the possibility of nurturing metacognitive skills? Our hope (or delusion) is to eventually develop a program to teach cognitive and metacognitive skills from kindergarten to graduate school. We see our approach as supplementing the already existing school curriculum, which we would use as the basis for training cognitive and metacognitive skills.

Because those who have delusions often like to enlist others (i.e., a kind of *folie à deux* or *trois*) into their delusional system, let me challenge you to imagine what a curriculum would look like that was designed to teach mental processes, to teach thinking? How can you incorporate the guidelines we have just reviewed into the daily curriculum? Could one affect the metacognitive style of teachers? Could one make cognitive coping modeling films to teach both children and teachers to use cognitive strategies? How could one use peer teaching?

Some attempts along these lines have recently begun by cognitive behavior modification investigators who are employing problem-solving techniques in the classrooms (see Meichenbaum, 1978 for a review of this literature). The focus of the problem-solving approach has been on teaching children to become sensitive to both academic and interpersonal problems, to develop the ability to generate alternative solutions, to understand means–end relationships, and the effect of one's social acts on others. Children are taught the distinction between facts, choices, and solutions. A variety of teaching aids such as verbal and behavioral videotapes, cartoon-workbooks, poster-pictorial cards, and activities are used to teach children to identify problems, generate alternatives, collect information, recognize personal values, make a decision, and then review that decision at a later time. Modeling procedures, behavioral rehearsal, role playing, and other procedures seem to provide useful ways of teaching such metaprocesses.

We can conceive of academic tasks where the teacher provided the children with a set of tasks, both academic and interpersonal, and the child's job was to identify across the variety of tasks what the problem is, how he or she will go about solving the task, where the likely pitfalls are, etc. In short, we would suggest that training should be focused on the production and evaluation of metacognitive skills. Children could be presented with a variety of tasks that require the production of plans to produce plans. Teachers could give assignments and ask children to describe in detail how they are going to go about performing the assignment. Discussion could center on the process, not only the product, of the assignment. In short, the entire study-skill process could become the focus of education.

No less of a challenge was put forth by Plato and Socrates, Itard, and Seguin. If you are going to have a delusion, you should be in good company.

## Acknowledgments

This chapter was written while the author was on sabbatical leave supported by a grant from the Social Science Research Council of Canada.

## Note

1. The author is grateful to Marvin Goldfried for this example.

## References

Asarnow, J., & Meichenbaum, D. (1979) Verbal rehearsal and serial recall: the mediational training of kindergarten children. *Child Development*, 50, 1173–7.

Atkinson, R., & Shiffrin, R. (1968) Human memory: a proposed system and its control processes. In K. Spence & J. Spence (eds), *The Psychology of Learning and Motivation* (Vol. 2). New York: Academic Press.

Belmont, J., & Butterfield, E. (1977) The instructional approval to developmental cognitive research. In R. Keil & J. Hagan (eds), *Perspectives on the Development of Memory and Cognition*. Hillsdale, NJ: Lawrence Erlbaum Associates.

Belmont, J., Butterfield, E., & Ferretti, R. (in press) To secure transfer of training, instruct self-management skills. *Intelligence*.

Bem, S. (1971) The role of comprehension in children's problem solving. *Developmental Psychology*, 2, 351–4.

Bender, N. (1976) Self-verbalization versus tutor verbalization in modifying impulsivity. *Journal of Educational Psychology*, 68, 347–54.

Bloom, B., & Broder, L. (1950) *The Problem-Solving Processes of College Students*. Chicago: University of Chicago Press.

Borkowski, J., & Cavanaugh, J. (1978) Maintenance and generalization of skills and strategies by the retarded. In N. Ellis (ed.), *Handbook of Mental Deficiency: Psychological Theory and Research* (2nd edn). Hillsdale, NJ: Lawrence Erlbaum Associates.

Bornstein, P., & Quevillon, R. (1976) The effects of a self-instructional package on overactive preschool boys. *Journal of Applied Behavior Analysis*, 9, 176–88.

Brown, A. (1978) Knowing when, where, and how to remember: a problem of metacognition. In R. Glaser (ed.), *Advances in Instructional Psychology*. Hillsdale, NJ: Lawrence Erlbaum Associates.

Brown, J. (1974) The role of strategic behavior in retardate memory. In N. Ellis (ed.), *International Review of Research in Mental Retardation* (Vol. 7). New York: Academic Press.

Brown, A., Campione, J., & Murphy, M. (1977) Maintenance and generalization of trained meta-mnemonic awareness of educable retarded children. *Journal of Experimental Child Psychology*, 24, 191–211.

Camp, E., & Bash, M. (1981) *Think Aloud*. Champaign, IL: Research Press.

Camp, E., Blom, G., Herbert, P., &.Van Doorninck, W. (1977) "Think aloud": a program for developing self-control in young aggressive boys. *Journal of Abnormal Child Psychology*, 8, 157–69.

Coates, T., & Thoresen, C. (1982) Self-control and educational practice or do we really need self-control? In D. Berlinger (ed.), *Review of Research in Education*. Ithaca, NY: Praeger.

Conway, J., & Bucher, E. (1976) Transfer and maintenance of behavior changes in children: a review and suggestions. In E. Mash & C. Handy (eds), *Behavior Modification and Families*. New York: Brunner/Nazel.

Craighead, E., Craighead-Wilcoxon. L., & Meyers, A. (1978) New directions in behavior modification with children. In M. Hersen, R. Eiseler, & P. Miller (eds), *Progress in Behavior Modification* (Vol. 6). New York: Academic Press.

Crandall, V., Katkovky, W., & Crandall, U. (1965) Children's belief in their own control of reinforcements in intellectual academic achievement situations. *Child Development*, 36, 91–109.

Diener, C., & Dweck, C. (1978) Analysis of learned helplessness: continuous changes in performance, strategy, and achievement cognitions following failure. *Journal of Personality and Social Psychology*, 36, 461–82.

Diener, C., & Dweck, C. (1980) An analysis of learned helplessness, II: the processing of success. *Journal of Personality and Social Psychology*, 39, 940–52.

Douglas, V. (1972) Stop, look and listen! The problem of sustained attention and impulse control in hyperactive and normal children. *Canadian Journal of Behavioral Science*, 4, 259–76.

Douglas, V., & Peters, K. (1979) Toward a clearer definition of the attentional deficit of hyperactive children. In C. Hale & M. Lewis (eds), *Attention and the Development of Cognitive Skills*. New York: Plenum Press.

Douglas, V., Parry, P., Martin, P., & Garson, C. (1976) Assessment of a cognitive training program for hyperactive children. *Journal of Abnormal Child Psychology*, 4, 389–410.

Emery, R., & Margolin, D. (1977) An applied behavior analysis of delinquency: the irrelevancy of relevant behavior. *American Psychologist*, 32, 860–73.

Estes, W. (ed.) (1975–8) *Handbook of Learning and Cognitive Processes* (Vols 1–6). Hillsdale, NJ: Lawrence Erlbaum Associates.

Finch, A., Wilkinson, M., Nelson, W., & Montgomery, L. (1975) Modification of an impulsive cognitive tempo in emotionally disturbed boys. *Journal of Abnormal Child Psychology*, 3, 49–52.

Flavell, J. (1976) Metacognitive aspects of problem solving. In L. Resnick (ed.), *The Nature of Intelligence*. Hillsdale, NJ: Lawerence Erlbaum Associates.

Flavell, J., Beach, D., & Chinsky, J. (1966) Spontaneous verbal rehearsal in a memory task as a function of age. *Child Development*, 37, 283–99.

Friedling, C., & O'Leary, S. (1979) Effects of self-instructional training on second- and third-grade hyperactive children: a failure to replicate. *Journal of Applied Behavior Analysis*, 12, 211–19.

Gagné, R., & Briggs, L. (1974) *Principles of Instructional Design*. New York: Holt, Rinehart, & Winston.

Goor, A., & Sommerfeld, R. (1975) A comparison of problem-solving processes of creative students and noncreative students. *Journal of Educational Psychology*, 67, 495–505.

Henshaw, D. (1978) "A Cognitive Analysis of Creative Problem Solving." Unpublished doctoral dissertation, University of Waterloo, Ontario.

Higa, W. (1975) "Self-Instructional Versus Direct Training in Modifying Children's Impulsive Behavior." Unpublished doctoral dissertation. University of Hawaii.

Hinshaw, S., Alkus, S., Whalen, C., & Henker, B. (1979) *STAR Training Program: A Cognitive Behavior Modification Training Manual)*. Unpublished manuscript. University of California at Los Angeles.

Hobbs, S., Maguin, L., Tyroler, M., & Lahey, B. (1980) Cognitive behavior therapy with children: has clinical utility been demonstrated? *Psychological Bulletin*, 87, 147–65.

Karoly, P. (1977) Behavioral self-management in children: concepts, methods, issues and directions. In M. Hersen, R. Eisler, & P. Miller (eds), *Progress in Behavior Modification* (Vol. 5). New York: Academic Press.

Keeley, S., Shenberg, K., & Carbonell, J. (1976) Operant clinical intervention: behavior management or beyond? Where are the data? *Behavior Therapy*, 7, 292–305.

Keeney, T., Cannizzo, S., & Flavell, J. (1976) Spontaneous and induced verbal rehearsal in a recall task. *Child Development*, 38, 953–66.

Kendall, P. (1977) On the efficacious use of verbal self-instructional procedures with children. *Cognitive Therapy and Research*, 1, 331–41.

Kendall, P. (1979) "Developing Self-Control in Children: A Manual of Cognitive-Behavioral Strategies." Unpublished manuscript, University of Minnesota.

Kendall, P., & Finch, A. (1976) A cognitive-behavioral treatment for impulsivity: a group comparison study. *Journal of Consulting and Clinical Psychology*, 46, 110–18.

Kendall, P., & Wilcox, I. (1980) Cognitive-behavioral treatment for impulsivity: concrete versus conceptual training in nonself-controlled problem children. *Journal of Consulting and Clinical Behavior*, 48, 80–91.

Kreutzer, M., Leonard, C., & Flavell, J. (1975) An interview study of children's knowledge about memory. *Monographs of the Society for Research in Child Development*, 40 (1, Serial No. 159)

Lloyd, J. (1980) Academic instruction and cognitive techniques: the need for attack strategy training. *Exceptional Education*, 1, 53–64.

Luria, A. (1959) The directive function of speech in development. *Word*, 15, 341–52.

Luria, A. (1961) *The Role of Speech in the Regulation of Normal and Abnormal Behaviors*. New York: Liveright.

McLeskey, J., Reith, H., & Polsgrove, L. (1980) The implications of response generalization for improving the effectiveness of programs for learning disabled children. *Journal of Learning Disabilities*, 13, 59–62.

Mandler, G. (1975) *Mind and Emotion.* New York: Wiley.

Mann, L. (1979) *On the Trail of Progress: A Historical Perspective on Cognitive Processes and Task Training.* New York: Grune & Stratton.

Markman, E. (1977) Realizing that you don't understand: a preliminary investigation. *Child Development,* 43, 986–92.

Marlatt, A., & Gordon, J. (1980) Determinants of relapse: implications for the maintenance of behavior change. In P. Davidson (ed.), *Behavioral Medicine: Changing Health Lifestyles.* New York: Brunner Mazel.

Mash, E., & Dalby, J. (1978) Behavioral interventions for hyperactivity. In R. Trites (ed.), *Hyper-activity in Children: Etiology, Measurement and Treatment Implications.* Baltimore, MD: University Park Press.

Meichenbaum, D. (1975) Enhancing creativity by modifying what subjects say to themselves. *American Educational Research Journal,* 12, 129–45.

Meichenbaum, D. (1977) *Cognitive-Behavior Modification: An Integrative Approach.* Teaching children self-control. In B. Lahey, & A. Kazdin (eds), *Advances in Child Clinical Psychology* (Vol. 2). New York: Plenum Press.

Meichenbaum, D. (1978) Teaching children self-control. In B. Lahey, & A. Kazdin (eds), *Advances in Child Clinical Psychology* (Vol. 2). New York: Plenum Press.

Meichenbaum, D., & Asarnow, J. (1979) Cognitive-behavior modification and metacognitive development: implications for the classroom. In P. Kendall, & S. Hollon (eds), *Cognitive Behavioral Interventions: Theory Research and Procedures.* New York: Academic Press.

Meichenbaum, D., & Butler, L. (1980) Cognitive ethology: assessing the streams of cognition and emotion. In K. Blankstein, P. Pliner, & J. Polivy (eds), *Advances in the Study of Communication and Affect: Assessment and Modification of Emotional Behavior* (Vol. 6). New York: Plenum Press.

Meichenbaum, D., & Goodman, J. (1971) Training impulsive children to talk to themselves: a means of developing self-control. *Journal of Abnormal Psychology,* 77, 115–26.

Meichenbaum, D., Henshaw, D., & Himel, N. (1982) Coping with stress as a problem-solving process. In W. Krohne, & L. Daux (eds), *Achievement, Stress and Anxiety.* Washington, DC: Hemisphere.

Meichenbaum, D., Burland, S., Gruson, L., & Cameron, R. (in press) Metacognitive assessment. In S. Yussen (ed.), *Growth of Insight.* New York: Academic Press.

Meyers, M., & Paris, S. (1978) Children's metacognitive knowledge about reading. *Journal of Educational Psychology,* 70, 680–90.

Miller, G., & Johnson-Laird, P. (1976) *Language and perception.* Cambridge, MA: Harvard University Press.

Miller, G., Galanter, E., & Pribram, K. (1960) *Plans and Structure of Behavior.* New York: Holt, Reinhart, & Winston.

Miller, P., & Bigi, L. (1979) The development of children's understanding of attention. *Merill-Palmer Quarterly,* 25, 235–50.

Mischel, W., Mischel, H., & Hood, S. (1978) "The Development of Effective Ideation to Delay Gratification." Unpublished manuscript, Stanford University.

Monahan, J., & O'Leary, D. (1971) Effects of self-instruction on rule-breaking behavior. *Psychological Reports,* 29, 1059–66.

Neisser, U. (1967) *Cognitive Psychology.* Englewood, NJ: Prentice-Hall.

Nelson, W., & Eirkimer, J. (1978) Role of self-instruction and self-reinforcement in the modification of impulsivity. *Journal of Consulting and Clinical Psychology,* 46, 183.

O'Leary, S., & Dubey, D. (1979) Applications of self-control procedures by children: a review. *Journal of Applied Behavior Analysis*, 12, 449–65.

Palkes, H., Stewart, M., & Freedman, J. (1972) Improvement in maze performance on hyperactive boys as a function of verbal training procedures. *Journal of Special Education*, 5, 237–42.

Palkes, H., Stewart, M., & Kahana, B. (1968) Porteus maze performance after training in self-directed verbal commands. *Child Development*, 39, 817–26.

Piaget, J. (1962) The relation of affectivity to intelligence in the mental development of the child. *Bulletin of Menninger Clinic*, 26, 129–37.

Reese, H. (1962) Verbal mediation as a function of age. *Psychological Bulletin*, 59, 502–9.

Robertson, D., & Keeley, S. (1974, August) *Evaluation of a Mediational Training Program for Impulsive Children by a Multiple Case Study Design*. Paper presented at the meeting of the American Psychological Association, New Orleans.

Robin, A., Amel, S., & O'Leary, D. (1975) The effects of self-instruction on writing deficiency. *Behavior Therapy*, 6, 178–87.

Rogers-Warren, A., & Baer, D. (1976) Correspondence between saying and doing: teaching children to share and praise. *Journal of Applied Behavior Analysis*, 9, 335–54.

Rosenthal, T. (1979) Applying a cognitive behavioral view to clinical and social problems. In G. Whitehurst & B. Zimmerman (eds), *The Functions of Languages and Cognition*. New York: Academic Press.

Ryan, E. (1981) Identifying and remediating factors in reading comprehension: toward an instructional approach for poor comprehenders. In E. Mackinnon & T. Waller (eds), *Advances in Reading Research* (Vol. 3). New York: Academic Press.

Schiffrin, R., & Schneider, W. (1977) Controlled and automatic human information processing, II: perceptual, learning, automatic attending and a general theory. *Psychological Review*, 84, 127–90.

Schleser, R., Meyers, A., & Cohen, R. (1981) Generalization of self-instructions: effects of general versus specific content, active rehearsal and cognitive level. *Child Development*, 52, 335–40.

Skinner, B. F. (1968) *The Technology of Teaching*. New York: Appleton-Century-Crofts.

Stokes, T., & Baer, D. (1977) An implicit technology of generalization. *Journal of Applied Behavior Analysis*, 10, 349–67.

Torgesen, J. (1977) The role of nonspecific factors in the task performance of learning disabled children: a theoretical assessment. *Journal of Learning Disabilities*, 10, 27–34.

Toulmin, S. (1978) The Mozart of psychology. *New York Review of Books*, 25, 50–6.

Turnure, J., Buium, N., & Thurlow, M. (1976) The effectiveness of interrogatives for prompting verbal elaboration productivity in young children. *Child Development*, 47, 851–5.

Vygotsky, L. (1962) *Thought and Language*. New York: Wiley.

Wahler, R., Eerland, R., & Coe, T. (1979) Generalization processes in child behavior change. In B. Lahey, & A. Kazdin (eds), *Advances in Clinical Child Psychology* (Vol. 2). New York: Plenum.

Wein, K., & Nelson, R. (1975) "The Effect of Self-Instructional Training in Arithmetic Problem-Solving Skills." Unpublished manuscript, University of North Carolina.

Weinreich, R. (1975) "Inducing Reflective Thinking in Impulsive, Emotionally Disturbed Children." Unpublished thesis, Virginia Commonwealth University.

Wilson, C., Hall, D., & Watson, D. (1978) "Teaching Educationally Handicapped Children Self-Control: Three Teacher's Manuals Grades 1 to 9." Unpublished manuscripts, San Diego County School Board.

Wood, D., Bruner, J., & Ross, G. (1976) The role of tutoring in problem-solving. *Journal of Child Psychology and Psychiatry*, 17, 89–100.

Zajonc, E. (1980) Feeling and thinking: preferences need no inferences. *American Psychologist*, 35, 151–75.

Zelniker, T., & Oppenheimer, I. (1976) Effect of different training methods on perceptual learning in impulsive children. *Child Development*, 47, 492–7.

# 6

# THE NATURE AND NURTURE OF THE SELF-DIRECTED LEARNER

*Andrew Biemiller and Donald Meichenbaum*

By observing how children approach tasks, giving them appropriate tasks, and resisting the urge to "think for" less self-directed learners, teachers can help each individual attain mastery and expertise.

Seven-year-old Rita talks to herself regularly, but it's not just chatter. Engaged in a painting project, she thinks out loud and encourages herself with such statements as, "I know what I'll do. I'll mix this white and the red and get pink." When the color is still not to her liking, she tells herself, "That's OK. I'll just add some more white."

Rita can be called a self-regulated learner. Her confidence leads her to increasing competence at all kinds of tasks.

Research conducted in the last ten years suggests that one source of the differences between the highest- and lowest-achieving children is the degree to which they become self-regulators of their own learning. High-achieving students engage in a number of helpful strategic skills, including goal setting, planning, self-interrogating, self-monitoring (checking answers), asking for help, using aids, and using memory strategies (Pressley *et al.* 1990, Zimmerman and Shunk 1989, Meichenbaum 1984). In addition, more competent students bring a greater knowledge to school tasks. Self-regulated learners behave in ways that often characterize adult experts (Bereiter and Scardamalia 1986). Their "budding expertise" is evident in: the complexity of their skills; the amount and structure of their knowledge; the strategic nature of their behavior; and the motivated effort they make, especially in response to failure (Dweck 1986).

− Biemiller, A. & Meichenbaum, D. (1992). The nature and nurture of the self-directed learner. Educational Leadership, 50, 75–80.

How do such differences in academic expertise develop? Moreover, how do these differences in self-regulation express themselves in classroom activities? And what can be done to help children who are less likely to engage in such self-regulatory behaviors to begin to do so? These are the questions we have tried to answer during the past three years as we developed and tested ways of observing self-regulation and expertise as they occur naturally in classrooms.

## Observing expertise in elementary classrooms

In 1989, we asked 15 teachers in grades 1–6 to nominate their most "self-directed" students (those who "know what to do and do it without having to be told"). Over the course of our study, we observed more than 70 of these children, as well as 70 of their low-self-directed counterparts. Literally, we put ourselves in these children's "back pockets," recording everything they did; what they said to themselves, to their peers, to their teacher; and in turn, what their peers and teachers said to them.[1] As a result of this preliminary work, we developed a sensitive and reliable coding system for the children's discourse about tasks.

We discovered that what children say about their work to others and to themselves can help us to infer the nature of their cognitive and metacognitive self-regulatory activities. The children's task-related speech, whether directed to others or to themselves, provides a "window" on their cognitive processes. As Piaget (1964) observed, in the process of relaying thoughts to others, we also relay them to ourselves. For instance, while in a conversation with teachers, the self-directed children often answered their own questions – "It's OK, I know what to do now." In the process of formulating thoughts into communicative acts, thoughts become the object of reflection.

## A transactional view of expertise

Our analysis of children's task-directive speech and the contexts in which it occurs has led us to develop a transactional view of the development of expertise. While the range of achievement is great, the range of academic demands placed upon children is not as varied. For example, fractions are generally introduced in the 3rd grade, ready or not. Children whose level of cognitive development exceeds the complexity of tasks they are being taught have "surplus mental capacity" permitting them to "think" (self-dialogue) about what they are doing.[2] Cognitively advanced children acquire new skills from a position of strength – they have the needed cognitive capacity, plus prerequisite skills, to learn the basics of new skills relatively easily.

These "elementary experts" apply their surplus capacity to think about what they are doing while consolidating skills during independent work periods. As they work, they talk to themselves and others about the task and associated skills. As a result of these dialogues, they come to understand the task, and to be able to call upon the associated skills (in a literal, verbal sense) when new situations occur in which the skills are relevant.

This tendency to think about what they are doing is rehearsed and reinforced by teachers and peers. Teachers and peers are more likely to ask these advanced elementary experts to verbally review tasks and to help others. Advanced children also do these things spontaneously.

When less cognitively advanced children are given the same task, they approach it with less well-established prerequisite skills. The sequence of steps to be considered in the new task creates "overload," or at least occupies the student's full attention.[3] Little or no capacity is left for verbal thought processes while conducting the task. In short, the less self-directed children are less likely to *do* the task and *think* about it at the same time. As these children try to consolidate the task through practice, they may go through the motions, carrying out some or all of the steps of the task. However, they are less likely to carry on a dialogue with themselves or others about the task (think about it). If they do initiate talk to others about the task, it is more likely to be in the form of a question about how to do the task or a spontaneous comment about their own lack of ability ("I can't do this!"). In this case, they are thinking about the task but *not* doing it! Thus, while children who are rich in self-regulatory skills get richer, others get poorer.

## Using teachers as crutches

Teachers and more advanced peers sometimes "think for" less self-directed children. We suggest that teachers and peers act as "mental crutches" for these children by doing defining, planning, and monitoring activities for them. This is a self-maintaining cycle. As less self-directed children become expert at gaining assistance, they continue to be in need of help rather than learn to regulate their own tasks. Others continue to help them, and thus the cycle continues.

While less advanced children may in time master the steps of the task, they are infrequently put in the position of talking about it to others. By the time they have mastered the task, the teacher has moved on to new, more complex tasks. As a result, less self-directed children are not often asked to review the task verbally. Others rarely turn to them for assistance. Consequently, less advanced children make less use of language to plan and monitor tasks. Development of elementary expertise reflects a fit between the demands of the task and the ability of the child that allows for the development of self-directed social and self-discourse.

## What teachers can do

To help low achievers, teachers should strive to systematically monitor their students' social and self-discourse in order to infer the children's level of knowledge, strategies, and motivation. How children monitor their own performance and that of others, how they convey plans, and how they respond to failure – each provides important clues to the level of their competence and expertise. Teachers need to become more astute observers of, and listeners to, their students' spontaneous task-directive speech.

Second, teachers could also become more aware of the effects of their interaction with students. Since those students who are more expert have the ability to nurture their own self-regulatory skills, teachers may unintentionally strengthen the more expert children's skills at the expense of the less competent students. Out of a desire to help, they provide planning and monitoring information. Thus, they may not provide the less competent child with the same opportunities or tasks to practice to develop his or her self-regulatory competence.

The level of task difficulty or task complexity also influences this transactional pattern. Thus, an important implication of our work is that expertise is not a function of the child's ability alone; rather, it is a joint product of the student's ability (knowledge, strategies, motivation) and the level of task difficulty. In order to build students' self-regulatory skills, teachers must present them with tasks *that just* exceed their current level of expertise. When tasks are too easy or too difficult, the students have minimal opportunity or motivation to practice and consolidate their self-regulatory skills.

An analogy illustrates this important point. When someone learning to ski is taken to either the easiest or the most difficult slope, he or she will have little opportunity to employ self-regulatory skills (planning, monitoring, elaboration). Either boredom or fear may interfere with the use of self-regulatory activities. The ski slope that is optimum for the development of the student's skiing expertise is just beyond the student's current level of competence. The classroom teacher needs to be a careful and astute engineer of classroom tasks, varying and matching tasks to each child's competence level. In the same way that the expert ski instructor would alter the nature of assignments, instructions, and supports to suit the novice skier's abilities, the classroom teacher should alter task demands, instruction, and assistance to each child's level of skill.

The challenge for the teacher is further complicated because students vary in the areas in which they have expertise. Our observations indicate that some children who use self-regulatory language in one subject (art) do not show a similar pattern in another (math). We suspect that these differences reflect different degrees of fit between children's abilities and task demands. Most children have the capacity to use metacognitive behavior and demonstrate expertise when provided with the right settings and tasks.

Another implication of our work is that teachers can use a broad array of instructional techniques to nurture elementary expertise. These include teacher think-alouds, labeling of student metacognitive behavior, explicit cognitive instruction with feedback and evaluative discussions, reciprocal teaching, scaffolding, and cooperative learning. We believe our observational tools can be used to assess the benefits that follow from the cognitive strategy interventions such as those described by Brown and Palincsar (1989), Meichenbaum (1984), Meichenbaum and Asarnow (1979), and Pressley and associates (1990).

## LISTENING IN ON SELF-DIRECTED LEARNERS

To study the development of expertise in the classroom, we observed 70 1st–6th grade students nominated by their teachers as "most self-directed" and 70 nominated as "low self-directed." Our observation system focused on children's statements and questions to peers, teachers, and selves, while a narrative account of each child's behavior provided the background for interpreting what was said. An observer who followed the child about the classroom recorded everything the child said, along with accompanying behaviors.

Each sentence was coded for *dialogue features, task functions,* and *emotional tone.* The dialogue features describe the social context in which the sentence occurred. The task functions describe the metacognitive or task-regulatory function of each sentence. (Dialogue features and task functions are illustrated below.) Finally, in order to tap the emotions that accompany performance, each verbal unit was coded for emotional tone (*positive, neutral,* or *negative*). We did not code instances of social talk concerning non-task-related events (such as, "Do you know how the Toronto Blue Jays did last night?") and "verbal products" (reading, counting, or spelling aloud). Thus, only task-directive language was coded.

Each sentence the child uttered was coded for five dialogue features, for a specific task function, and for emotional tone. (We coded language directed *to* the child in the same way.) The promise of the coding system in explicating the nature of self-regulatory behavior is evident from a preliminary analysis of observations of 14 "highly self-directed" and 14 "less self-directed" children as nominated by their teachers in several different schools (grade 1 to grade 6). A second study concerned repeated observations of two highly self-directed and two less self-directed children in a 3rd grade. Major findings from these studies included the following:

## Categories of task directive speech:

### Dialogue features

1. *Initiation:* Whether a child initiated the sentence spontaneously or whether the sentence was in response to a teacher or peer.
2. *Direction:* To whom the sentence was directed (to a specific peer, group of peers, teacher, or self).
3. *Mode:* Whether the verbalization was a statement or a question.
4. *Ownership:* Whether the task being discussed belonged to the child or a peer, or was shared.
5. *Context:* Whether the context conveyed by the verbalization was strictly current (referring only to the immediate situation), or whether it was elaborated to include reference to other settings ("This *is like* what we did at recess") or to categories ("Some people would call this editing.").

**Task functions**

1. *Defining:* Statement or question labels and notes features of tasks, procedures, and objects ("It's John's game." "That's red paint.").
2. *Planning:* Statement or question about what will or should happen next ("Can I do X?" "Mix some soap in the paint." "Where are the sparkles?" "I need ...").
3. *Conditional planning:* Statement or question relates a plan to a condition or specifies the basis for choosing between alternative plans ("If we make noise, then we won't have recess.").
4. *Monitoring* (ongoing task): Statement or question notes progress, or lack thereof, on the task ("You're going too fast." "Slow down.").
5. *Evaluating* (completed or aborted task): Statement or question concerns conclusions on ending the task – regarding the product, the child's ability, or the experience of doing the task. ("This is my best one so far!" "I can't do it!" "The math squares are fun!").

## Attending to mastery

Our position is consistent with the observations offered by John Carroll (1989), who argued that attempting to achieve equal outcomes for all children at the same time is educationally counterproductive if we want maximum possible outcomes for each child. Teachers should be more concerned about achieving reasonable levels of independent mastery of what each child *can* do, as opposed to being concerned with covering an arbitrarily established curriculum. This proposal is not new; it is just not done very often.

- Highly self-directed children spontaneously initiated more than twice as many statements about tasks per hour (22) as the less self-directed children (11).
- Most of the higher rate of the self-directed children's spontaneous statements about tasks was accounted for by *planning* (what next), *conditional planning* (if, then; choosing between alternative plans), and *monitoring* (checking own or others' progress) statements. Both groups had similar rates of defining and evaluating statements. We suggest that spontaneous planning and monitoring statements are crucial indicators of the degree to which a child is functioning with expertise in a specific situation.
- When expressing emotion about their own tasks, the highly self-directed children were mostly positive, while the less self-directed children's emotions were about half negative.

- While both groups asked similar numbers of questions, highly self-directed children questioned peers about half the time, while the less self-directed children mostly asked questions of teachers.
- Data from our second study indicate that less self-directed children received an average of 17 task-directive sentences per hour from their teacher. In contrast, the highly self-directed children received an average of just two sentences per hour from their teacher. This suggests that teachers and peers often "think for" less self-directed children.
- Teacher language directed toward the less self-directed children shows that the teacher is planning, monitoring, and the like *for* the children (see below). These children elicit more task-directive support from their teacher than from themselves.

## Examples of children's verbal exchanges:

### Less self-directed children

*Teacher to child*
What are you doing?
What do you have to do first?
Did you check your assignment?
You will have to clean up your desk after you're finished.

*Peer to child*
You forgot to loop again.
You can't have two the same.
Did you ask three people yet?
You have already done that.
If you do *X*, then *Y* will happen.

*Child to peer*
Can you help me?
What do they mean by ...?
Do you know what I'm supposed to do here?
My card is missing.

### Highly self-directed children

*Teacher to child*
You did research about Terry Fox.
This is just like that.
Look it up in your book. You can find the answer.
Tell me how you solved that.

*Peer to child*
What are we supposed to do?
Should I ...?
How did you do that?

*Child to peer*
You don't cut each one individually.
You cut the whole thing.
That glue goes this way.
You've done that already, haven't you?

In contrast, highly self-directed children received many opportunities to nurture and practice their metacognitive skills. They were often asked by teachers to help other children and were also asked to share procedural information with the class. Thus, highly self-directed children seem to create a learning environment in which they can develop their self-regulatory skills.

The Laidlaw Foundation and the Izaak Killam Research Fellowship provided support for this research.

          – Andrew Biemiller and Donald Meichenbaum

If we could attend more carefully to mastery and expertise and less to grade level curriculum and norms, the level of effective school skills would rise noticeably. We would wind up with a substantially larger group of literate and numerate graduates. Students might be exposed to fewer subjects but would be truly able to use what skills they have for purposes they value.

## Notes

1. Details of this preliminary work are described in D. Meichenbaum and A. Biemiller, "In Search of Student Expertise in the Classroom: A Metacognitive Analysis," in *Promoting Academic Competence and Literacy in School*, edited by M. Pressley, K. Harris, and J. Guthrie (1992). San Diego, CA: Academic Press.
2. This analysis follows from Case's (1985) model of intellectual development, Fischer and Pipp's (1984) analysis of the interaction of intellectual development and skill acquisition, and Vygotsky's (1978) discussion of the implications of the "zone of proximal development" for education.
3. We conceive of tasks roughly as lists of steps to be carried out to achieve a goal. "Capacity" refers to the number of steps that can be successfully coordinated (Case, 1985).

## References

Bereiter, C., and M. Scardamalia (1986) "Educational Relevance of the Study of Expertise." *Interchange* 17: 10–19.
Brown, A., and A. M. Palincsar (1989) "Guided, Cooperative Learning and Individual Knowledge Acquisition." In *Knowing, Learning, and Instruction*, edited by L. B. Resnick, pp. 393–452. Hillsdale, NJ: Erlbaum.

Carroll, J. (January/February 1989) "The Carroll Model: A 25-Year Retrospective and Prospective View." *Educational Researcher* 18: 26–31.

Case, R. (1985) *Intellectual Development from Birth to Adulthood.* New York: Academic Press.

Dweck, C. S. (1986) "Motivational Processes Affecting Learning." *American Psychologist* 41: 1040–1048.

Fischer, K. W., and S. L. Pipp (1984) "Processes of Cognitive Development: Optimal Level and Skill Acquisition." In *Mechanisms of Cognitive Development*, edited by R. J. Sternberg. Prospect Heights, IL: Waveland Press.

Meichenbaum, D. (1984) "Teaching Thinking: A Cognitive-Behavioral Perspective." In *Thinking and Learning Skills*, Vol. 2, edited by J. Segal, S. Chipman, and R. Glaser. Hillsdale, NJ: Erlbaum.

Meichenbaum, D., and J. Asarnow (1979) "Cognitive Behavior Modification and Metacognitive Development." In *Cognitive-Behavioral Interventions,* edited by P. Kendall and S. Hollon. New York: Academic Press.

Piaget, J. (1964) "Development and Learning." In *Piaget Rediscovered*, edited by T. R. Ripple and V. Rockcastle. Ithaca, NY: Cornell University Press.

Pressley, M., V. Woloshyn, L. M. Lysynchuk, V. Martin, E. Wood, and T. Willoughby (1990) "A Primer of Research on Cognitive Strategy Instruction: The Important Issues and How to Address Them." *Educational Psychology Review* 2: 1–58.

Vygotsky, L. S. (1978) *Mind in Society: The Development of Higher Psychological Processes.* Cambridge, MA: Harvard University Press.

Zimmerman, B. J., and D. Shunk (eds) (1989) *Self-Regulated Learning and Academic Achievement.* New York: Springer-Verlag.

# PART III

# The Development and Application of Stress Inoculation Training

Another evidence-based cognitive-behavioral intervention that was developed in the clinical lab at the University of Waterloo is Stress Inoculation Training (SIT) (Meichenbaum, 1977, 1985; Meichenbaum & Deffenbacher, 1988; Meichenbaum & Fitzpatrick, 1993). Like the concepts of medical inoculation and attitude inoculation, individuals are exposed to graduated levels of stressors that approximate the real life stressful situations that they are likely to encounter (a form of scenario training). Such exposure training opportunities follow initial psycho-educational and skill acquisition and consolidation phases.

The most appealing qualities of SIT include its applicability to a wide variety of populations, settings and problems; the clinical flexibility it offers practitioners to match intervention strategies with identified individual clinical needs and specific deficits; and the format for programming generalization (see Meichenbaum & Jaremko, 1989; Israelshvili, 1998; Sheely & Horan, 2004).

Results from a meta-analysis conducted by Saunders *et al.* (1996), based on 37 studies with 1,837 participants, showed that SIT was effective in reducing performance anxiety and state anxiety and on enhancing performance under stress. SIT has also been successfully applied to children, adolescents, as well as adults (Maag & Kotlash, 1994). (See Feindler & Fremouw, 1989; Hains, 1992; and Szabo & Marian, 2012, for application of SIT with adolescents.)

The three chapters in this part illustrate the broad application of SIT to a variety of stressors. Ray Novaco (1975, 1977a, 1977b) in the area of anger control and Dennis Turk (Turk *et al.*, 1983) in the area of pain management were pioneers in applying SIT. The two additional articles in this part illustrate the application of SIT in these two areas. For further examples of SIT, please Google "stress inoculation training" and see the YouTube applications in military settings, as documented by John Morgan in what he calls "hyper-realistic training." Other examples from *www.psychalive.org* are also available online. Note that when you type stress inoculation training into a Google search, the word "inoculation" only has one n, *not* two – in*n*oculation. I was once going to write an article – "Stress inoculation training: an N = 1."

## References

Feindler, E. & Fremouw, W. J. (1989). Stress inoculation training for adolescent anger. In D. Meichenbaum & M. Jaremko (eds), *Stress Reduction and Management*. New York: Springer, pp. 451–85.

Hains, A. A. (1992). A stress inoculation training program for adolescents in a high school: a multiple baseline approach. *Journal of Adolescence*, 15: 163–75.

Israelshvili, M. (1998). Preventative school counseling: a stress inoculation perspective. *Professional School Counseling*, 1: 25–31.

Maag, J. W. & Kotlash, J. (1994). Review of stress inoculation training with children and adolescents: issues and recommendations. *Behavior Modification*, 18: 443–69.

Meichenbaum, D. (1977). *Cognitive Behavior Modification: An Integrative Approach*. New York: Plenum Press.

Meichenbaum, D. (1985). *Stress Inoculation Training*. New York: Pergamon.

Meichenbaum, D. & Deffenbacher, R. (1988). Stress inoculation training. *Counseling Psychologist*, 16: 69–90.

Meichenbaum, D. & Fitzpatrick, D. (1993). A constructivist narrative perspective on stress and coping: stress inoculation applications. In I. Goldberger & S. Breznitz (eds), *Handbook of Stress*. New York: Free Press, pp. 373–406.

Meichenbaum, D. & Jaremko, M. (eds) (1989). *Stress Reduction and Prevention*. New York: Springer.

Novaco, R. (1975). *Anger Control: The Development and Evaluation of an Experimental Treatment*. Lexington, MA: Hech.

Novaco, R. (1977a). Stress inoculation: a cognitive therapy for anger and its application to a case of depression. *Journal of Consulting and Clinical Psychology*, 45: 600–8.

Novaco, R. (1977b). Stress inoculation approach to anger management in the training of law enforcement officers. *American Journal of Community Psychology*, 5: 327–46.

Saunders, T., Driskell, J. E., Johnson, J. H. & Salas, E. (1996). The effects of stress inoculation training on anxiety and performance. *Journal of Occupational Health Psychology*, 1: 170–86.

Sheely, R. & Horan, J. J. (2004). Effects of stress inoculation training for 1st year law students. *International Journal of Stress Management*, 11: 41–55.

Szabo, Z. & Marian, M. (2012). Stress inoculation training in adolescents: classroom intervention benefits. *Journal of Evidence-Based Psychotherapists*, 12: 175–88.

Tan, S. Y. (1982). Cognitive and cognitive-behavioral methods for pain control: a selective review. *Pain*, 12: 201–28.

Turk, D. C., Meichenbaum, D., & Genest, M. (1983). *Pain and Behavioral Medicine: A Cognitive Behavioral Perspective*. New York: Guilford Press.

# 7

# STRESS INOCULATION TRAINING

## A preventative and treatment approach

*Donald Meichenbaum*

Clinicians who seek to provide help to stressed individuals, either on a treatment or on a preventative basis, are confronted with a major challenge. As Elliott & Eisdorfer (1982) observed, stressful events come in diverse forms that include exposure to:

1. *Acute time-limited stressors*, including such events as preparing for specific medical procedures (e.g., surgery, dental examination) or for invasive medical examinations (e.g., biopsies, cardiac catherization) or having to confront specific evaluations (e.g., a PhD defense).
2. *A sequence of stressful events* that may follow from the exposure to traumatic events, such as a terrorist attack, a rape, a natural disaster that results in a major loss of resources, or exposure to stressors that require *transitional adjustments* due to major losses (e.g., death of a loved one, becoming unemployed), each of which gives rise to a series of related challenges.
3. *Chronic intermittent stressors* that entail repeated exposures to stressors such as repetitive evaluations and ongoing competitive performances (e.g., musical or athletic competitions), recurrent medical tests or treatments, or episodic physical disorders such as recurrent headaches, as well as the exposure to intermittent stress that accompanies certain occupational roles, such as military combat.
4. *Chronic continual stressors* such as debilitating medical or psychiatric illnesses, physical disabilities resulting from exposure to traumatic events (e.g., burns, spinal cord injuries, traumatic brain injuries), or exposure to prolonged distress, including marital or familial discord, urban violence, poverty, and racism,

– Reproduced by permission of Guilford Press. Meichenbaum, D. (2007). Stress inoculation training: a preventative and treatment approach. In P. M. Lehrer, R. L. Woolfolk, & W. E. Sime (eds). *Principles and Practice of Stress Management* (3rd edn). New York: Guilford Press (pp. 497–518).

as well as exposure to persistent occupational dangers and stressors in professions such as police work, nursing, and teaching.

These varied stressful events may range from those that are time-limited and require situational adjustments to those chronic stressful events that are persistent and that require long-term adaptation. Stressors may also differ between those that are potentially controllable (i.e., can be lessened, avoided, or eliminated by engaging in certain behaviors) and those judged to be uncontrollable (i.e., an incurable illness, exposure to ongoing threats of violence, caring for a spouse with severe dementia) and whether they are predictable or unpredictable; of short duration (i.e., an examination) or chronic (i.e., living in a racist society, being exposed to poverty, having a stressful job); intermittent or recurrent; current or distant in the past. Distant stressors are traumatic experiences that occurred in the distant past yet have the potential to continually affect one's well-being and even modify the individual's immune system because of the long-lasting emotional, cognitive, and behavioral sequelae (Segerstrom & Miller, 2004).

In some instances, individuals are exposed to multiple features of such stressful events. As an example, I was asked to consult in the possible application of cognitive-behavioral stress inoculation techniques for a highly distressed population. In July 2002 the Canadian government established a treatment team to address the clinical needs of a native Inuit people in the newest Canadian province of Nunavit. The Inuit people had been dislocated, being forced to shift from a nomadic existence to confined resettlements with accompanying economic deprivations (substandard living conditions, overcrowding, poverty) and disruptions to traditional roles and relationships. On top of having to cope with all of these chronic stressors, a subset of young male Inuit youths experienced a prolonged period of victimization. Over a period of six years in the early 1980s, in three native Inuit communities, a self-confessed male paedophile schoolteacher, who was appointed by the government, sexually abused 85 male Inuit youths. The aftermath of this exposure to multiple stressors has been a high rate of depression, substance abuse, and domestic violence. Most telling is the high suicide rate among the Inuit, who are twice as likely to commit suicide as other native populations and four times as likely to engage in self-destructive behaviors. They also have the highest completion rate of suicide attempts (some 38% of attempters; Brody, 2000; Meichenbaum, 2005).

What clinical tools exist to help individuals and communities cope with the diversity of such stressors (acute, sequential, and chronic)? What empirically based stress management procedures exist that can be used in a culturally sensitive fashion to aid individuals in their adaptation processes? How can clinicians help individuals prepare for and prevent maladaptive responses to stressors and help them build on the strengths and resilience that they bring to such challenging situations?

For the past 30 years, I have been involved in the development of stress prevention and reduction procedures to address these challenging questions, under the label of *stress inoculation training* (SIT; Meichenbaum, 1975, 1976, 1977, 1985,

1993, 1996, 2001; Meichenbaum & Deffenbacher, 1988; Meichenbaum & Fitzpatrick, 1993; Meichenbaum & Fong, 1993; Meichenbaum & Jaremko, 1993; Meichenbaum & Novaco, 1978; Meichenbaum & Turk, 1976, 1987; Turk *et al.*, 1983).

In this chapter, I bring together these clinical experiences and research from this 30-year journey, highlighting the work of other clinical researchers who have adapted SIT or who have developed related cognitive-behavioral stress management interventions. In lieu of the multiple ongoing stressors that society now confronts, including possible terrorist attacks, wars, AIDS, increasing poverty, and urban and family violence, the need for effective empirically based interventions is all the more pressing. This need is more evident to me since I retired from the University of Waterloo in Ontario, Canada, and became the research director of the Melissa Institute for Violence Prevention and Treatment of Victims of Violence in Miami, Florida (see *www.melissainstitute.org*).

The discussion of stress reduction interventions begins with a consideration of the concept of inoculation that gave rise to the SIT treatment approach. I then consider the theoretical underpinnings of SIT and provide a detailed description of the clinical procedural steps involved in conducting SIT. Illustrative applications of how SIT has been applied on both a treatment and a preventative basis are offered. For a detailed summary of the empirical status and meta-analytical review of SIT, the interested reader is directed to reviews by Maag and Kotlash (1994), who examined SIT with children and adolescents; by Saunders *et al.* (1966), who reviewed patients with anxiety; by Meichenbaum (1993), who provided a 20-year update of some 200 SIT case studies, demonstration projects, and clinical research outcome studies; and by Meichenbaum (1996, 2001), who offered a review of SIT with adults with posttraumatic stress disorder (PTSD) and adults with anger-control problems and aggressive behaviors.

The primary focus of this chapter is on the "clinical wisdom" that has been garnered over 30 years of applying SIT on both a treatment and a preventive basis.

## The concept of inoculation

A central concept underlying SIT is that of *inoculation*, which has been used both in medicine and in social-psychological research on attitude change. In 1796 Edward Jenner noted that inoculation of humans with cowpox conferred immunity against the more deadly smallpox virus. In medicine, vaccinations often involve exposure to weaker forms of a disease so as to ward off more severe reactions. In such cases, the earlier exposure is generally to a more moderate form of the stress or disease to be guarded against. Such exposure produces antibodies and physically prepares the body for future attacks.

Consistent with the concept of inoculation, Aldwin & Levenson (2004) highlight an area of biology called *hormesis* that studies the *positive* results that derive from exposure to small amounts of toxins that in larger amounts might prove lethal. A series of studies on animals indicated that small and brief exposure to stressors can contribute to the development of repair mechanisms that protect against the impact of subsequent, more intense stressors (Calabrese & Baldwin, 2002). In a comparable fashion SIT, which is designed to intervene with humans at the psychosocial level, provides individuals with experience with minor stressors that fosters psychological preparedness and promotes resilience.

Similarly, in the area of attitude change, McGuire (1964) has observed that prior exposure to attitudinal information can protect or "inoculate" individuals from subsequent, more intense efforts at persuasion. Such prior exposure to persuasive efforts mobilizes counter-attitudinal strategies that can be used in subsequent conversion efforts. In both medical and attitudinal inoculations, a person's resistance is enhanced by exposure to a stimulus strong enough to arouse defenses and coping processes without being so powerful that it overwhelms the individual. SIT is based on the notion that exposing clients to milder forms of stress can bolster both coping mechanisms and the individual's (group's, community's) confidence in using his or her coping repertoire. SIT is designed to bolster an individual's preparedness and develop a sense of mastery.

## Theoretical underpinnings

SIT adopts a transactional view of stress and coping as espoused by Lazarus and Folkman (1984). Their model proposed that stress occurs whenever the perceived demands of a situation tax or exceed the perceived resources of the system (individual, family, group, or community) to meet those demands, especially when the system's well-being is judged or perceived as being at stake. This relational process-oriented view of stress emphasizes the critical role of cognitive-affective appraisal processes and coping activities. According to the transactional perspective, stress is neither a characteristic of the environment alone nor a characteristic of the person alone. Instead, stress is defined as a particular type of transactional, bidirectional, dynamic relationship between the person and the environment in which the individual or group perceives the adaptive demands as taxing or exceeding their perceived available coping resources to meet those demands. Like beauty, stress is in large part "in the eye of the beholder."

Another related literature that has influenced the development of SIT is that deriving from a *constructive narrative perspective* (CNP). The CNP views individuals, groups, and communities as *storytelling entities* who construct narratives about themselves, others, the world, and the future. The nature and content of the "stories" that individuals tell themselves and others play a critical role in influencing the coping processes. A growing literature on the roles that cognitions and emotions play in the maintenance of stress reactions, especially in the case of persistent PTSD, has highlighted the potential usefulness of a CNP (Brewin & Holmes, 2003; Ehlers & Clark, 2000; Harvey, 2000; Howard, 1991; Janoff-Bulman, 1990; McAdams *et al.*, 2001; Neimeyer, 2001; Smucker *et al.*, 2003). At both the personal and cultural levels, the narratives are organized around identifiable episodes, including intelligible plots and characters, and they convey goals and themes. In the case of traumatic stressful events, the narratives often highlight the perceived "defining moments" of the life stories. Meichenbaum (2005) has summarized the features of clients' narratives and behaviors that contribute to persistent stress reactions. These elements are enumerated in Table 7.1.

**TABLE 7.1** Summary of behaviors and cognitions that lead to persistent PTSD and prolonged stress responses: a constructive narrative perspective

A. *Self-focused cognitions* that have a "victim" theme
   1. Seeing oneself as being continually *vulnerable*
   2. Seeing oneself as being *mentally defeated*
   3. Dwelling on negative *implications*
   4. Being preoccupied with *others'* views
   5. Imagining and ruminating about *what might have happened* ("near-miss experience")

B. *Beliefs*
   1. Changes are *permanent*
   2. The world is unsafe, unpredictable, untrustworthy
   3. The *future* will be negative
   4. Life has *lost its meaning*

C. *Blame*
   1. Blaming *others,* with accompanying anger
   2. Blaming *oneself,* with accompanying guilt, shame, and humiliation

D. *Comparisons*
   1. Oneself with others
   2. Before with now
   3. Now with what might have been

E. *Actions taken*
   1. Being continually *hypervigilant*
   2. Being *avoidant* – *cognitive level* (suppressing unwanted thoughts, dissociating, engaging in "undoing" behaviors)
   3. Being *avoidant* – *behavioral level* (avoiding reminders, using substances, withdrawing, abandoning normal routines, engaging in avoidant safety behaviors)
   4. *Ruminating* and engaging in *contrafactual* thinking ("Only if")
   5. *Delaying* change behaviors
   6. Failing to *resolve* and *share* trauma story (keeping secrets)
   7. Putting oneself at risk for *revictimization*

F. Actions *not taken*
   1. *Believing* that anything *positive* could result from trauma experience
   2. Retrieving and accepting data of *positive self-identity*
   3. *Seeking social supports*
   4. Protecting oneself from *negative, unsupportive stress-engendering environments*
   5. Using *faith* and *religion* as a means of coping

How distressed individuals and communities try to make sense of and transform their emotional pain can influence their coping processes. The more individuals and communities engage in the cognitions and behaviors enumerated in Table 7.1, the greater the likelihood that they will have persistent stressful reactions. SIT can be viewed as an engaging way to help clients become aware of the impact of their narratives and maladaptive stress-engendering behaviors (e.g., avoidance, rumination and brooding, catastrophizing, safety-seeking behaviors, absence of self-disclosure, and failure to access and employ social supports). SIT helps distressed individuals become aware of how they can engage in behaviors that maintain and exacerbate their distress. SIT helps clients construct a more adaptive narrative, find "meaning," and engage in more adaptive direct-action problem-solving and palliative, emotional-regulation, accepting, and coping skills. SIT trainers are *not only* in the business of teaching coping skills and enhancing the clients' confidence and sense of efficacy in applying these coping skills; the SIT trainer is also in the business of helping clients construct new life stories that move them from perceiving themselves as "victims" to becoming "survivors," if not indeed "thrivers." How does SIT help clients achieve these challenging and laudable goals?

## What is SIT?

SIT is a flexible, individually tailored, multifaceted form of cognitive-behavioral therapy. Given the wide array of stressors that individuals, families, and communities experience, SIT provides a set of general principles and clinical guidelines for treating distressed individuals, rather than a specific treatment formula or a set of "canned" interventions. SIT is *not* a panacea, and it is often used as a supplemental tool to other forms of interventions, such as prolonged exposure with traumatized patients or environmental and community supports with individuals confronting chronic stressors, as described later.

SIT consists of three interlocking and overlapping phases:

1. A conceptual educational phase.
2. A skills acquisition and skills consolidation phase.
3. An application and follow-through phase.

The ways that these SIT phases are implemented will vary depending on both (1) the nature of the stressors (e.g., acute time-limited stressors, such as a medical procedure, vs. prolonged ongoing repetitive stressors, such as working in a highly stressed occupation or living in a high-risk violent environment); and (2) the resources and coping abilities of the clients.

The treatment goals of SIT are to bolster the clients' coping repertoire (intra- and interpersonal skills), as well as their confidence in being able to apply their coping skills in a flexible fashion that meets their appraised demands of the stressful situations. Some stressors lend themselves to change and can be altered or avoided, whereas other stressors are *not* changeable (e.g., irreversible loss, incurable illness). Thus some stressful situations do not lend themselves to direct-action problem-solving coping efforts, because resolutions are not always attainable. In such instances, an emotionally palliative and accepting set of coping responses are most appropriate (e.g., mindfulness training, reframing, attention diversion, adaptive engaging in spiritual rituals, adaptive affective expression, and humor). SIT demonstrates that there is no one "correct" way to cope with the diversity of stressors. What coping efforts may work in one situation or at one time may not be applicable at other times or in other situations.

In the *initial conceptual education phase of SIT*, a collaborative working relationship and therapeutic alliance are established between the clients and the trainer. This relationship provides the basis, or the "glue," that allows and encourages clients to confront stressors and implement the variety of coping skills, both within the training sessions and *in vivo*, that constitute the needed "inoculation" exposure trials. Norcross (2004) has underscored the critical importance of therapy relationship factors that contribute to the change processes. Besides working on the formulation and maintenance of a therapeutic alliance, the second objective of this initial phase of SIT is to enhance the clients' understanding and awareness of the nature and impact of their stress and coping resources. A variety of clinical techniques are used to nurture this educational process. This informational exchange is not a didactic lecture by the trainer/therapist but rather a by-product of a discovery-oriented inductive Socratic exchange (i.e., the SIT trainer uses "curious" questions to promote the clients' processing). Moreover, this educational process is ongoing throughout the course of SIT training. Although at the outset of SIT, the focus may be on possible warning signs or triggers and on the chain analyses of clients' accounts, later on in SIT training the education process may focus on relapse prevention and self-attributional processes (i.e., how to ensure that clients take "personal credit" for changes they have brought about).

A variety of clinical techniques, including Socratic discovery-based interviewing; psychological testing with constructive feedback about deficits, styles of responding, and "strengths" or signs of resilience; self-monitoring activities; bibliotherapy; and exposure to modeling films are used to foster the clients' increased awareness and sense of personal control and mastery. Table 7.2 provides an enumeration of the informational content that is covered over the course of various phases of SIT.

In a collaborative fashion, a more facilitative reconceptualization of the clients' stressful experiences and reactions is formulated. Rather than conceiving their stressors as being overwhelming, uncontrollable, unpredictable, debilitating, and hopeless, the SIT trainer helps clients develop a sense of "learned resourcefulness."

The *second phase* of SIT, which follows naturally from the reconceptualization process, focuses on helping clients *acquire coping skills*, and on *consolidation of those coping skills* that they already possess, and on removing any intra- and interpersonal and systemic barriers that may exist. The intra- and interpersonal coping skills are taught and practiced in the clinical or training setting and then gradually practiced *in vivo*. A major focus of this skills-training phase is the emphasis placed on following guidelines

**TABLE 7.2** Ongoing educational components of SIT

SIT helps clients ...

1. Appreciate that the stress they experience is *not* abnormal and *not* a sign that they are "going crazy" or "losing their minds." Rather, their distressing reactions may be a "normal" reaction to a difficult and challenging stressful situation.
2. Appreciate that many of their reactions may be the "wisdom of the body," or "nature's way" of coping with overwhelming stressors. For example, intrusive ideation may be a way of trying to make sense of what has happened; denial may be a way to "dose oneself" in order to handle so much stress at a given time. (In fact, each of the symptoms of PTSD could be reframed as a coping effort; see Meichenbaum, 1996.)
3. View their current coping efforts as a reflection of being "stuck," namely using (or overusing) a coping pattern such as dissociation that at one time was adaptive (e.g., when being repeatedly raped in an incestuous situation) or being hypervigilant (i.e., continually being on "sentry duty" even when it is no longer required). The problem is that clients are "stuck" (not "crazy," or "inadequate," or "weak") using coping efforts that at one time were adaptive but are now being overemployed.
4. Recognize how they may inadvertently and perhaps even unknowingly employ intrapersonal coping efforts (avoidance, suppression, rumination and brooding, contrafactual thinking, and safety behaviors) that make the stressful situation worse; educate clients about the transactional nature of stress.
5. Appreciate that their stress reactions are made up of different components (biopsychological perspective, physiological arousal, plus cognitive appraisals) and that these reactions go through different phases (namely, the phase of preparing for a stressor, the phase of confronting the stressor, the phase of being truly tested or overwhelmed, and the phase of reflecting on how they handled or did not handle the stressor). In this way, their stress reactions are differentiated into several phases that are made up of different components. Patients are educated about how each phase can trigger appropriate coping efforts.
6. Notice the "cycle" by which internal and external triggering events (12 o'clock on an imaginary clock) elicit primary and secondary emotions (3 o'clock) and accompanying thoughts (automatic thoughts, thinking processes and schemas or beliefs; (6 o'clock), which, in turn, lead to specific behaviors and resultant consequences (9 o'clock). Clients can be asked to self-monitor if, indeed, they engage in such "vicious" (stress–engendering) cycles. Moreover, if they do, clients can be asked, "What is the impact, what is the toll, what is the price of engaging in such a cyclical pattern? Moreover, what can be done to break the cycle?" The various coping efforts follow naturally from such probes.
7. Appreciate the distinction between the changeable and unchangeable aspects of stressful situations and to match either problem-focused or emotion-focused coping efforts to meet the perceived demands of the stress-engendering situation.
8. Break down or disaggregate global stressors into specific short-term, intermediate, and long-term coping goals. Such goal-directed thinking nurtures a sense of hopefulness.
9. Debunk any myths held by the client or significant others concerning their presenting problems (e.g., myths concerning rape, sexual abuse) and challenge so-called stage models of reactions to stress. Also address any myths concerning stress and coping, such as: (1) people need to go through uniform emotional stages of reactions in response to stress; (2) there is a "right" way to cope; (3) distressed people cannot experience positive emotions in the aftermath of traumatic stress; and (4) people should *not* expect to *experience* stressful reactions well after stressful life events occur.

to achieve generalization and maintenance of the treatment effects. Therapists cannot merely "train and hope" for generalization. SIT trainers need to explicitly build the technology of generalization training into the treatment protocol, as is later noted.

The *final application and follow-through phase* of SIT includes opportunities for clients to *apply the variety of coping skills* on a graduated basis across increasingly demanding levels of stressors (that is, following the "inoculation" concept). Such techniques as imagery and behavioral rehearsal, modeling, role playing, and graded *in vivo* exposure are employed. A central feature of this application phase is the use of relapse prevention procedures (Marlatt & Gordon, 1988; Witkiewitz & Marlatt, 2004). The SIT trainer explores with clients the variety of possible high-risk stressful situations that they may reexperience (e.g., reminders, anniversary effects, dysphoric emotions, interpersonal conflicts and criticisms, and social pressures). Then the clients rehearse and practice in a collaborative fashion with the trainer (and with other clients in a group setting or with significant others) the various intra- and interpersonal coping techniques that might be employed. As part of the relapse prevention intervention, clients are taught how to view any lapses, should they occur, as "learning opportunities" rather than as occasions to "catastrophize" and relapse. The follow-through features of SIT are designed to extend training into the future by including booster training sessions, active case management, engagement of significant others, and environmental manipulations.

Consistent with a transactional model of stress that SIT embraces, and consistent with the recognition that the stress clients experience may be endemic, societal, institutional and unavoidable, *SIT often goes beyond the clients* to involve significant others. For example, in preparing patients for stressful medical examinations, the SIT trainer can focus on teaching coping skills to distressed medical patients but can also attempt to work with hospital staff in order to reduce the nature and level of hospital and medical stress. (See Kendall, 1983, for a description of work with catheterized patients and Wernick *et al.*, 1981, and Wernick, 1983, for work with burn patients.) In competitive sports, an SIT trainer can help athletes develop their coping skills in order to handle the stress of competition (Long, 1980; Mace & Carroll, 1986; Mace *et al.*, 1986, 1987), but as Smith (1980) observes, a trainer can also attempt to influence the behaviors of the athlete's coaches and parents, thus reducing a major source of competitive stress. Similarly, in work with victims of rape or terrorist attacks, the unfortunate "secondary victimization" of the distressed individuals from community agents (doctors, police, judges, teachers, administrators, health care providers, parents, and peers) can exacerbate the stress responses (see Ayalon, 1983; Veronen & Kilpatrick, 1983). It would be short-sighted to delimit SIT interventions to just the targeted victims or distressed clients and not to attempt to influence the stress-engendering behaviors and attitudes of significant others and community members. SIT has adopted the dual-track strategy of working directly with stressed clients, as well as with significant others and community agents who may inadvertently, and perhaps even unknowingly, exacerbate stress. SIT trainers search for and enlist "allies" to support the clients' ongoing coping efforts.

## How is SIT conducted?

One of the strengths of SIT is its flexibility. SIT has been carried out with individuals couples, families, and small and large groups. The length of the SIT intervention has varied, from as short as 20 minutes in preparing patients for surgery (Langer *et al.*, 1975) to 40 one-hour weekly and biweekly sessions administered to psychiatric patients with recurrent mental disorders and to individuals with chronic medical problems (Turk *et al.*, 1983). In most instances in the clinical domain, SIT consists of some 8–15 sessions, plus booster and follow-up sessions conducted over a 3- to 12-month period.

Obviously, the manners in which the three phases of SIT (conceptualization, skills acquisition and consolidation, application and follow-through) are conducted will vary, depending on the nature of the clients and the length of SIT training. The content of the conceptualization phase, the specific skills that will be emphasized and trained, and the nature of the application phase (inoculation trials) will each be specifically geared to the targeted population. There is, however, sufficient congruence across SIT application that a procedural flowchart of the SIT treatment procedure can be outlined, as shown in Table 7.3. More detailed clinical presentations of SIT are offered by Meichenbaum (1996, 2001).

## Illustrative applications of SIT

SIT has been employed in both a treatment and a preventative manner with a wide variety of medical and psychiatric populations and with a variety of diverse professional groups who experience high rates of job-related stress. Elsewhere (Meichenbaum, 1993; Wertkin, 1985), these diverse applications have been reviewed, and more recent reviews are also available (Maag & Kotlash, 1994; Saunders *et al.*, 1996). On a treatment basis, SIT and closely aligned cognitive-behavioral stress management procedures (Antoni *et al.*, 2001; Antoni, 2003; Cruess *et al.*, 2000), anxiety management approaches (Suinn, 1990), coping skills training (Folkman *et al.*, 1991), and cognitive-affective stress management training (Smith & Rohsenow, 1987) have been employed with a wide variety of clients. These clinical applications have been used with:

1. *Medical patients* who have various acute and chronic pain disorders, patients with breast cancer and those with essential hypertension, burn patients, ulcer patients, and patients with rheumatoid arthritis; on a *preventive basis*, SIT has been employed with medical and dental patients who are preparing for surgery or invasive medical examinations, with type A individuals, and with the caretakers of both child and adult patients who are medically ill.
2. *Psychiatric patients* with PTSD as a result of sexual assault; adults and adolescent patients with severe problems of anxiety (e.g., panic attacks) and those with anger-control problems and aggressive behaviors, such as in the case of abusive parents; aggressive individuals who are developmentally delayed; and chronically distressed outpatients with mental illnesses.

3. Individuals with *performance anxiety*, such as public-speaking and dating anxiety or debilitating anxiety in athletic competitions; and with individuals with *circumscribed fears* (animal phobias, fear of flying).

4. *Professional groups*, such as probation officers, nurses, teachers, military personnel, psychiatric staff members, and disaster and safety workers.

5. *Individuals* who have to deal with *stress of life transitions*, including coping with unemployment, or who are transitioning into new settings, such as high school or re-entering college, overseas placement, and joining the military.

In short, since its origin in 1976, SIT has been employed on both a treatment and a preventative basis with a wide variety of diverse clinical populations and with highly stressed occupational groups. Table 7.3 provides examples of some of these diverse applications.

**TABLE 7.3** A flowchart of SIT

### Phase 1: Conceptualization

- In a collaborative fashion, identify the determinants of the presenting problem or the individual's stress concerns by means of (1) interviews with the client and significant others; (2) the client's use of an imagery-based reconstruction and assessment of a prototypical stressful incident; (3) psychological and environmental assessments; and (4) behavioral observations. (As Folkman *et al.*, 1991, suggest, have the client address "who, what, where," and "when" questions: "Who is involved?" "What kind of situations cause stress?" "When is this kind of situation likely to occur?" "When did it occur last?" Also see interviews in Meichenbaum, 1996, 2001.)
- Permit the client to tell his or her "story" (solicit narrative accounts of stress and coping and collaboratively identify the client's coping strengths and resources). Help the client to transform his or her description from global terms into behaviorally specific terms.
- Have the client disaggregate global stressors into specific stressful situations. Then help him or her break stressful situations and reactions into specific behaviorally prescriptive problems. Have the client consider his or her present coping efforts and evaluate which are maladaptive and which are adaptive.
- Have the client appreciate the differences between changeable and unchangeable aspects of stress situations.
- Have the client establish short-term, intermediate, and long-term behaviorally specifiable goals.
- Have the client engage in self-monitoring of the commonalities of stressful situations and the role of stress-engendering appraisals, internal dialogue, feelings, and behaviors. Help the client appreciate the transactional nature of his or her stress. (Use the clock metaphor of a "vicious cycle" in Table 7.2.) Train the client to analyze problems (e.g., to conduct both situational and developmental analyses and to seek disconfirmatory data – "check things out").
- Ascertain the degree to which coping difficulties arise from coping-skills deficits or are the result of "performance failures" (namely, maladaptive beliefs, feelings of low self-efficacy, negative ideation, secondary gains).

*(continued)*

**TABLE 7.3** (Continued)

- Collaboratively formulate with the client and significant others a reconceptualization of the client's distress. Socratically educate the client and significant others about the nature and impact of stress and the resilience and courage individuals manifest in the face of stressful life events. Using the client's own "data," offer a reconceptualization that stress consists of different components (physiological, cognitive, affective, and behavioral) and that stress reactions go through different "phases," as described in Table 7.2. The specific reconceptualization offered will vary with the target population; the plausibility of the reconceptualization is more important than its scientific validity. In the course of this process, facilitate the discovery of a sense of meaning, nurture the client's hope, and highlight the client's strengths and feelings of resourcefulness.
- Debunk any client myths, as noted in Table 7.2.

## Phase 2: Skills acquisition and consolidation

A. *Skills training* (tailor to the needs of the specific population and to the length of training)
- Ascertain the client's preferred mode of coping. Explore with the client how these coping efforts can be employed in the present situation. Examine what intrapersonal or interpersonal factors are blocking such coping efforts.
- Train problem-focused instrumental coping skills that are directed at the modification, avoidance, and minimization of the impact of stressors (e.g., anxiety management, cognitive restructuring, self-instructional training, communication, assertion, problem-solving, anger control, applied cue-controlled relaxation training, parenting, study skills, using social supports). Select each skill package according to the needs of the specific client or group of clients. Help the client to break complex, stressful problems into more manageable sub-problems that can be solved one at a time.
- Help the client engage in problem-solving by identifying possibilities for change, considering and ranking alternative solutions and practicing coping behavioral activities in the clinic and *in vivo*.
- Train emotionally focused palliative coping skills, especially when the client has to deal with unchangeable and uncontrollable stressors (e.g., perspective-taking; selective attention-diversion procedures, as in the case of chronic pain patients; adaptive modes of affective expression such as humor, relaxation, reframing the situation, acceptance skills, and spiritual rituals).
- Train clients how to use social supports effectively (i.e., how to choose, obtain, and maintain support). As Folkman *et al.* (1991) observe, help clients identify what kind of support is needed (informational, emotional, tangible), from whom to seek such support, and how to maintain support resources.
- Aim to help the client develop an extensive repertoire of coping responses in order to facilitate flexible responding. Nurture gradual mastery.

B. *Skills rehearsal and consolidation*
- Promote the smooth integration and execution of coping responses by means of behavioral and imagery rehearsal.
- Use coping modeling (either live or videotape models). Engage in collaborative discussion, rehearsal, and feedback of coping skills.
- Use self-instructional training to help the client develop internal mediators to self-regulate coping responses.

**TABLE 7.3** (Continued)

* Solicit the client's verbal commitment to employ specific efforts.
* Discuss possible barriers and obstacles to using coping behaviors and ways to anticipate and address such barriers.
* Follow treatment guidelines to enhance the likelihood of transfer or generalization of coping skills (see Meichenbaum, 1996, 2001).

### Phase 3: Application and follow-through

A. *Encouraging application of coping skills in the form of stress inoculation trials*
* Prepare the client for application by using coping imagery, together with techniques in which early stress cues act as signals for coping.
* Expose the client in the session to graded stressors via imagery and behavioral exposure to stressful and arousing scenes.
* Use graded exposure and other response induction aids to foster *in vivo* responding.
* Employ relapse prevention procedures: Identify high-risk situations, anticipate possible stressful reactions, and rehearse coping responses.
* Use counterattitudinal procedures to increase the likelihood of treatment adherence (i.e., ask and challenge the client to indicate where, how, and why he or she will use coping efforts).
* Bolster self-efficacy by reviewing both the client's successful and unsuccessful coping efforts. Ensure that the client makes self-attributions ("takes credit") for success or mastery experiences (provide attribution retraining).

B. *Maintenance and generalization*
* Gradually phase out treatment and include booster and follow-up sessions.
* Involve significant others in training (e.g., parents, spouse, coaches, hospital staff, police, administrators), as well as peer and self-help groups.
* Have the client coach someone with a similar problem (i.e., put client in a "helper" or consultative role).
* Help the client to restructure environmental stressors and develop appropriate escape routes. Ensure that the client does not view the desire for escape or avoidance as a sign of failure but rather as a sign of taking personal control.
* Help the client to develop coping strategies for recovering from failure and setbacks, so that lapses do not become relapses.
* Work with clients to avoid revictimization.

## Patients with medical problems

The SIT interventions with medical patients have a heavy educational component in which patients and often their caretakers receive procedural and sensory information and are then afforded opportunities to practice coping skills. SIT highlights ways in which patients can use their own preferred idiosyncratic coping strategies. The coping training may include the use of coping-modeling films, both imaginal and behavioral rehearsal, and *in vivo* graded exposure. Such behavioral practice is accompanied by corrective feedback; personal attribution training, in which patients "take credit" for the changes they have been able to bring about; and relapse prevention strategies should lapses occur. The manner in which SIT is conducted needs to be individually tailored to the age of the patient and to the patient's preferred mode of coping. Finally, the research on the application of SIT to medical patients has underscored the need to ensure that the length of SIT treatment should be performance-based rather than time-based (an arbitrarily set number of sessions). Instead of all medical patients receiving treatment of a prescribed length, the length of treatment or the number of multiple practice and "inoculation" trials should be tailored to some behavioral criteria of mastery and accompanying expressed self-efficacy, especially for patients with intense and chronic medical problems. The following three examples illustrate the varied applications of SIT to medical problems.

1. Langer *et al.* (1975) provided 20 minutes' worth of coping skills training to medical patients prior to their surgeries. The conceptualization phase of SIT highlighted the manner in which stress can be affected by selective attentional and cognitive processes, how to focus on the benefits that can accrue from the surgery, and immediate coping efforts (relaxation, self-guided rethinking efforts, imaginal rehearsal). The SIT group, relative to both the informational and assessment control groups, evidenced significantly less preoperative anxiety and fewer postoperative requests for pain relievers and sedatives. The SIT-treated patients also stayed in the hospital for a shorter period of time. Siegal and Peterson (1980) have used a similar multifaceted coping skills package of relaxation training, calming self-talk, and guided imagery to help young dental patients reduce stress.

2. Jay and Elliott (1990) developed an SIT videotape film for parents of 3- to 12-year-old children with paediatric leukemia who have to undergo bone marrow aspirations and lumbar punctures. One hour prior to each child's medical procedure, the parents were shown a brief film of a model parent who employed coping self-statements, relaxation efforts, and coping imagery rehearsal. The parents were then given an opportunity to practice these coping skills. Relative to parents who received a child-focused intervention, the SIT-treated parents evidenced significantly less anxiety and enhanced coping skills. Videotaped SIT-modeling films have been used in a variety of clinical settings, including anger control, with rape victims preparing for forensic examination, and parenting (see Meichenbaum, 1996, 2001).

3. Finally, cognitive-behavioral stress management (CBSM), which overlaps with many of the features of SIT, has been used most impressively with female early-stage breast cancer patients. Like SIT, this 10-week group CBSM comprises (1) an educational component that debunks myths about breast cancer, enhances patients' awareness of stress and of ways to reduce it, and

nurtures hope; (2) a skills acquisition and practice phase in which patients learn ways to use intra- and interpersonal coping skills that range from emotional expression of concerns and feelings and acceptance skills to relaxation, problem-solving benefit finding, and ways to preserve and augment the patients' social support networks; and (3) an application phase in which patients are given opportunities and encouraged to practice the learned coping skills. Moreover, the patients are encouraged to take credit for the changes they are able to bring about in order to further promote a positive self-image. The CBSM not only resulted in improved behavioral adjustment and posttraumatic growth, but CBSM also continued to improve immune functioning (i.e., greater lymphocyte proliferative responses at a 3-month follow-up) relative to a control group (Cruess *et al.*, 2000).

## Psychiatric patients

SIT has been employed with a variety of psychiatric groups on both an inpatient and an outpatient basis. In most studies, SIT has been compared or combined with other multifaceted psychoeducational and pharmacological interventions; for example, Holcomb (1986) has examined the relative efficacy of eight 1-hour SIT sessions with and without psychotropic medications in the treatment of psychiatric inpatients. In terms of anxiety, depression, and overall subjective distress, Holcomb reported that SIT with and without medication was superior to pharmacological interventions alone; impressively, this relative improvement was evident at a 3-year follow-up, as indicated by fewer patient re-admissions for psychiatric problems.

SIT and related cognitive-behavioral interventions have been applied to psychiatric patients who have specific disorders such as panic attacks, PTSD, and anger-control problems and aggression. In many instances, these patients have overlapping comorbid disorders.

In the anxiety domain, the panic-control treatment procedures of Barlow (1988), Clark and Salkovskis (1989), and Rapee (1987) have extended the SIT treatment model to patients with anxiety disorders. During the initial conceptualization phase, the patients are offered an explanatory and conceptual model, based on their symptoms, that highlights the interactive role that hypervigilance about bodily cues, their "catastrophic" misinterpretations of their physiological arousal, and their hyperventilation play in eliciting and exacerbating their anxiety reactions. Such a reconceptualization of panic attacks readily leads to the second phase of treatment, which is the acquisition and practice of a variety of coping responses that include (1) relaxation skills in order to control physical tenseness and hyperventilation, (2) cognitive coping skills in order to control "catastrophic" misrepresentation, and (3) cognitive restructuring procedures in order to alter the patients' appraisal attributions, expectations, and avoidance behaviors.

Following the SIT model, the final application and follow-through phase provides the patients with "inoculation" trials by means of imaginal and behavioral rehearsal, both in the clinic and *in vivo*. The behavioral coping trials include opportunities to cope with self-induced hyperventilation and the symptoms of panic attacks, coping imagery to anxiety-producing scenes, and, finally, graduated exposure to panic-inducing situations. Relapse prevention and self-attribution treatment components are included in this last phase of treatment. Michelson and Marchione (1991) have documented the relative efficacy of this three-phase cognitive-behavioral intervention.

Another anxiety disorder that has been treated by means of SIT is PTSD. For instance, Veronen and Kilpatrick (1982) used SIT to successfully treat rape victims. The SIT intervention consisted of a psychoeducational component concerning the nature and impact of rape and the acquisition and practice of coping skills aimed at management of assault-related anxiety and postassault problems. The coping skills that were taught included cue-controlled relaxation, thought stopping, cognitive restructuring, guided self-dialogue, covert modeling, and role playing. Homework assignments consisted of patients practicing the various coping skills *in vivo*. Foa and her colleagues have also found that SIT can reduce PTSD symptoms that result from sexual assaults. These reductions were maintained at follow-up assessments conducted up to one year posttreatment (Foa *et al.*, 1991; Foa *et al.*, 1999). In two well-controlled studies, SIT demonstrated more improvement in PTSD symptoms than supportive counseling and wait-list conditions (Foa *et al.*, 1991; Foa *et al.*, 1999). In a study comparing SIT, prolonged exposure (PE), and PE/SIT, SIT demonstrated significant reduction in PTSD and related symptoms. There was a trend, however, for clients who received PE to obtain higher levels of overall functioning, as evident in a composite reduction of PTSD, anxiety, and depressive symptoms (Foa *et al.*, 1999).

In evaluating the relative efficacy of PE and SIT in these studies, it is important to keep in mind that, in the original SIT treatment protocol, clients were confronted with anxiety-engendering situations, either imaginally or by means of role playing and graded *in vivo* exposure. In the Foa *et al.* comparative studies, this exposure-rehearsal component that fosters inoculation was eliminated because of the possible overlap with the exposure comparison condition. Thus the SIT was delimited to only the initial two phases of psychoeducational and coping skills training. The critical exposure and accompanying self-attribution and relapse prevention components that constitute the final phase were omitted from the SIT comparison group.

The results of these studies (Foa *et al.*, 1991; Foa *et al.*, 1999) underscore the additional therapeutic benefits that accrue from including the third, experiential practice, component of SIT. Educating clients and teaching coping skills are necessary but there are insufficient components to lead to sustained improvement. Similar conclusions have been drawn by other clinical researchers who have used variations of cognitive therapy to treat clients with PTSD (Marks *et al.*, 1998; Resick & Schnicke, 1992; Tarrier *et al.*, 1999). The results of these studies have also highlighted the fact that various forms of cognitive-behavioral therapies, such as SIT, prolonged exposure, and cognitive restructuring, have broad effects in reducing associated negative emotional states such as anger, depression, and anxiety, as well as PTSD symptomatology. For example, Cahill *et al.* (2003) report that SIT, but not PE, produced a greater decrease in anger in female assault victims than did the combination treatment of PE/SIT. Thus those interventions that included SIT seem particularly well suited for treating clients with issues of anger control.

Cahill *et al.* (2003) caution that several clinical studies, both theirs and others', have also demonstrated that combining treatments (e.g., SIT with PE and cognitive restructuring) did *not* result in better outcomes and sometimes resulted in slightly worse outcomes than those obtained by individual treatments (Foa *et al.*, 1999; Marks *et al.*, 1998; Paunovic & Ost, 2001). Such attempts to combine various interventions within a time-limited treatment protocol may dilute the effectiveness of the respective interventions.

Anger is an often overlooked emotional disorder in the psychiatric community, although it overlaps with some 19 different psychiatric conditions. Anger is often experienced among various survivors of sexual assault, motor vehicle accidents, torture, and combat and among refugees. A number of clinical researchers, including Jerry Deffenbacher, Eva Feindler, Arthur Hains, and Ray Novaco and their colleagues, have applied SIT with adolescents and adults who have problems with anger control and aggressive behaviors (see Deffenbacher & McKay, 2000; Feindler & Ecton, 1986; Hains, 1992; Novaco, 1975). Novaco has also applied SIT to several occupational groups for whom anger control is an important part of their job (namely, law enforcement officers, probation officers, and Marine drill instructors; Novaco, 1977a, 1977b, 1980; Novaco *et al.*, 1983).

The potential usefulness of SIT and related cognitive-behavioral interventions with adolescents and adults who have anger-control problems and who manifest aggressive behaviors was highlighted by DiGuiseppe and Tafrate (2001). They conducted a meta-analytic review and concluded that the cognitive-behavioral treatments "seem to work equally well for all age groups and all types of populations and are equally effective for men and women. The average effect sizes across all outcome measures ranged from .67 to .99 with a mean of .70" (p. 263).

The results of this meta-analysis revealed that the cognitive-behavioral SIT was "moderately successful" (p. 263). Patients in the SIT group were better off than 76% of the control group of untreated patients and that 83% of the treated patients improved in comparison to their pretest scores. This level of improvement was maintained at a follow-up period that ranged from two to 64 weeks. These findings are similar to conclusions drawn by Beck and Fernandez (1998), who conducted a similar meta-analysis of 50 SIT and cognitive-behavioral interventions that involved 1,640 participants across the full age range. In both meta-analytic reviews, they found that those treatment programs that used standardized manuals and treatment fidelity checks were found to be most effective.

An example of SIT with individuals with anger-control problems was offered by Chemtob, Novaco, Hamada, & Gross (1997), who targeted the treatment of anger among a group of veterans who experienced both PTSD and elevated levels of anger. They added SIT to routine Veterans Administration clinical care and found that, relative to a control group that continued to receive only routine care, adding SIT was effective in significantly reducing state anger, increasing anger control and coping skills, decreasing general anxiety, and decreasing PTSD symptoms of re-experiencing. The SIT treatment of anger not only decreased the targeted level of anger but also decreased PTSD symptoms, highlighting the robustness of SIT. See Meichenbaum (2001) for a detailed description of how to apply SIT on both a treatment and preventative basis with individuals who have problems controlling their anger and their accompanying aggressive behaviors.

## Individuals with evaluative anxiety and those requiring transitional adjustment

From its origin, SIT has been employed with individuals who experience debilitating anxiety in evaluative situations. This may take the form of treating individuals with anxiety in such areas as testing, speech, math, computer use, dating, writing, and performance in an athletic competition (see Hembree, 1988, and Meichenbaum, 1993, for reviews of these studies). In most of these treatment studies, SIT was combined with population-specific skills training, such as public-speaking training, writing, and study skills. In each domain, SIT has been adapted to and "packaged" in ways that would make SIT most appealing. For instance, Smith (1980) has characterized the stress management features of SIT as a form of "mental toughness training" for athletes and their coaches. SIT was designed to help athletes "control their emotional responses that might interfere with performance and is also designed to help athletes focus their attention on the task at hand" (Smith, 1980, p. 157). The rationale of "mental toughness training" is more likely to be acceptable than the rationale of "reducing stress," as if stress is something to be avoided. Many athletes and coaches believe that athletes need to experience stress in order to achieve peak performance. Under the aegis of "mental toughness training," Smith (1980) has developed a cognitive-behavioral group-training program that is offered in six twice-weekly, one-hour sessions. The initial educational/conceptualization phase orients the participants to the nature of stress and emotions, the role mental processes play, and various ways to develop an "integrated coping response." The skills-acquisition phase focuses on cue-controlled relaxation, imagining stressful situations, and cognitive rehearsing of "antistress" coping self-statements. The goal of training is *not* to eliminate emotional arousal but rather to give athletes greater control over their emotional responses. The athletes are given an opportunity to rehearse their coping skills under conditions of trainer-induced high arousal and strong affect, which are stimulated by the trainer's offering of highly charged imagery scenes. In this inoculation fashion, the athletes are taught to focus their attention on intense feelings and then to practice refraining, accepting, and/or turning them off again in order to reduce and prevent high arousal levels from getting out of hand. The trainer also attends to the excessively high performance standards and distorted fear of the consequences of possible failure that distressed athletes, their coaches, and their parents may hold. In addition, the trainer, in collaboration with a coach and an athlete, can set up *in vivo* practice trials and can implement a training program to improve relevant sports skills. In short, SIT with athletes is packaged as an educational program in self-control, not as a form of psychotherapy.

Another anxiety-producing situation in which SIT has been employed successfully is that accompanying the transitional adjustment to unemployment. A randomized field experiment conducted by Caplan, Vinokur, Price, and van Ryan (1989) provides encouraging data. As part of a comprehensive intensive intervention, eight three-hour sessions were conducted with the unemployed over a two-week period. Following the educational phase on the impact of the stress of being laid off and the acquisition and practice of job-seeking and problem-solving skills, the participants were given inoculation trials concerning how to cope with possible rejection and setbacks. This comprehensive cognitive-behavioral intervention contributed to higher rates of re-employment, higher motivation, and greater job satisfaction in the SIT treatment group relative to a matched attention-control group.

Meichenbaum (1993) reviewed the literature on the potential usefulness of SIT in helping individuals adjust to entry into the military, senior students re-entering a university, and individuals taking up overseas assignments.

## Conclusions

The past 30 years have witnessed a broad application of SIT to a variety of stressed populations, in both a treatment and a preventative manner. In each instance, the clinical application of SIT has been individually tailored to the specific target population and circumstances. It is the flexibility of the SIT format that has contributed to its robust effectiveness. It should also be apparent that SIT is a complex, multifaceted cognitive-behavioral intervention that comprises key elements of nurturing a therapeutic working alliance with clients: psychoeducational features that include inductive Socratic discovery-oriented inquiry, collaborative goal setting that nurtures hope, and direct-action problem-solving and acceptance-based coping skills training that incorporates training generalization guidelines; relapse prevention; and self-attributional training procedures. In those instances in which clients have been victimized, SIT can be readily supplemented with symptom-specific interventions (e.g., cognitive-behavioral coping techniques to address physiological arousal, dissociation, emotional dysregulation, and physical pain) and "memory work" such as imaginal and *in vivo* exposure-based techniques. From an SIT perspective, the treatment goal is *not* merely to have clients relive and retell their abuse histories but rather to have them consider the nature of the "stories" they tell both themselves and others as a result of such trauma exposure. SIT is designed to help clients consider the conclusions that they draw about themselves, the world, and the future as a result of such trauma experiences. SIT is designed to help clients construct a more adaptive narrative and to change their views of themselves from "victims" to "survivors" to "thrivers." The SIT concludes with a consideration of how to help clients find meaning or to transform their emotional pain into healing processes and activities and to learn how to reclaim their lives. Finally, SIT focuses on ways to ensure that such victimized individuals are *not* revictimized.

In short, SIT is more than a mere collection and application of a variety of coping techniques. The coping-skills features of SIT are critical, but without the other contextual features of SIT, especially the "inoculation" trials and application opportunities, the skills-training components are unlikely to prove effective or sufficient. SIT is not a chapter heading for a collection of cognitive-behavioral coping techniques but rather a client-sensitive, highly collaborative intervention that is as much concerned about working with clients as it is about working with significant others and agencies who may inadvertently and unknowingly engender and help maintain even more stress. As noted, the SIT model embraces both the transactional model of stress and coping and the mandate for clinicians and trainers to be involved in assessing both the clients and their environments. Such an SIT treatment plan will go a long way toward helping individuals and communities cope more effectively in the stressful post-September 11 environment in which we live.

# References

Aldwin, C. M., & Levenson, M. R. (2004). Posttraumatic growth: a developmental perspective. *Psychological Inquiry*, 15, 19–22.

Antoni, M. H. (2003). *Stress Management Intervention for Women with Breast Cancer*. Washington, DC: American Psychological Association.

Antoni, M. H., Lehman, J. M., Kilburn, K. M., Boyers, A. E., Yont, S. E., & Culver, J. L. (2001). Cognitive-behavioral stress management intervention decreases the prevalence of depression and enhances the sense of benefit among women under treatment for early-stage breast cancer. *Health Psychology*, 20, 20–32.

Ayalon, O. (1983). Coping with terrorism: the Israeli case. In D. Meichenbaum & M. Jaremko (eds), *Stress Prevention and Management: A Cognitive Behavioral Approach*. New York: Plenum Press.

Barlow, D. (1988). *Anxiety and Its Disorders: The Nature and Treatment of Anxiety and Panic*. New York: Guilford Press.

Beck, R., & Fernandez, E. (1998). Cognitive-behavioral self-regulation of the frequency, duration and intensity of anger. *Journal of Psychopathology and Behavioral Assessment*, 20, 217–29.

Brewin, C. R., & Holmes, E. A. (2003). Psychological theories of posttraumatic stress disorder. *Clinical Psychological Review*, 23, 339–76.

Brody, H. (2000). *The Other Side of Eden.* New York: North Point Press.

Cahill, S. P., Rauch, S. A., Hembree, E. A., & Foa, E. B. (2003). Effect of cognitive-behavioral treatment for PTSD on anger. *Journal of Cognitive Psychotherapy*, 17, 113–31.

Calabrese, E. J., & Baldwin, L. A. (2002). Hormesis: a dose-response revolution. *Annual Review of Pharmacology and Toxicology*, 43, 175–97.

Caplan, R. D., Vinokur, A. D., Price, R. H., & van Ryan, M. (1989). Job seeking, reemployment, and mental health: a randomized field trial in coping with job loss. *Journal of Applied Psychology*, 74, 10–20.

Chemtob, C. M., Novaco, R. W., Hamada, R. S., & Gross, D. M. (1997). Cognitive-behavioral treatment for severe anger in posttraumatic disorder. *Journal of Consulting and Clinical Psychology*, 65, 184–9.

Clark, D. M., & Salkovskis, P. M. (1989). *Panic Disorder Treatment Manual.* Oxford: Pergamon Press.

Cruess, D. G., Antoni, M. H., McGregor, B. A. S., Kilbourn, K. M., Boyers, A. E., *et al.* (2000). Cognitive behavioral stress management reduces serum cortisol by enhancing benefit finding among women being treated for early-stage breast cancer. *Psychosomatic Medicine*, 62, 304–8.

Deffenbacher, J. L., & McKay, M. (2000). *Overcoming Situations and General Anger.* Oakland, CA: New Harbinger.

DiGuiseppe, R., & Tafrate, R. C. (2001). "Anger Treatment for Adults: A Meta-analytic Review." Unpublished manuscript, St John's University, Jamaica, New York.

Ehlers, A., & Clark, D. M. (2000). A cognitive model of posttraumatic stress disorder. *Behaviour Research and Therapy*, 38, 319–45.

Elliott, G. R., & Eisdorfer, C. (1982). *Stress and Human Health.* New York: Springer.

Feindler, E. L., & Ecton, R. B. (1986). *Adolescent Anger Control: Cognitive-Behavioral Techniques.* Elmsford, NY: Pergamon Press.

Foa, E. B., Rothbaum, B. O., Riggs, D. S., & Murdock, T. B. (1991). Treatment of posttraumatic stress disorder in rape victims: a comparison between cognitive-behavioral procedures and counseling. *Journal of Consulting and Clinical Psychology*, 59, 715–23.

Foa, E. B., Dancu, C., Hembree, E. A., Jaycox, L. H., Meadows, E. A., & Street, G. D. (1999). A comparison of exposure therapy, stress inoculation training and their combination for reducing posttraumatic stress disorder in female assault victims. *Journal of Consulting and Clinical Psychology*, 67, 194–200.

Folkman, S., Chesney, M., McKusik, L., Ironson, G., Johnson, D. G., & Coates, T. J. (1991). Translating coping theory into an intervention. In J. Eckenrode (ed.), *The Social Context of Coping.* New York: Plenum Press.

Hains, A. A. (1992). A stress inoculation training program for adolescents in a high school setting: a multiple baseline approach. *Journal of Adolescence*, 15, 163–75.

Harvey, J. H. (2000). *Embracing the Memory.* Needham Heights, MA: Allyn & Bacon.

Hembree, R. (1988). Correlates, causes, effects of test anxiety. *Review of Educational Research*, 58, 47–77.

Holcomb, W. R. (1986). Stress inoculation therapy with anxiety and stress disorders of acute psychiatric patients. *Journal of Clinical Psychology*, 42, 864–72.

Howard, G. S. (1991). Cultural tales: a narrative approach to thinking, cross-cultural psychology and psychotherapy. *American Psychologist*, 46, 187–97.

Janoff-Bulman, R. (1990). Understanding people in terms of their assumptive worlds. In D. J. Ozer, J. M. Healy, & A. J. Stewart (eds), *Perspectives in Personality: Self and Emotion.* Greenwich, CT: JAI Press.

Jay, S. M., & Elliott, C. H. (1990). A stress inoculation program for parents whose children are undergoing painful medical procedures. *Journal of Consulting and Clinical Psychology*, 58, 799–804.

Kendall, P. C. (1983). Stressful medical procedures: cognitive-behavioral strategies for stress management and prevention. In D. Meichenbaum & M. Jaremko (eds), *Stress Prevention and Management: A Cognitive Behavioral Approach*. New York: Plenum Press.

Langer, T., Janis, I., & Wolfer, J. (1975). Reduction of psychological stress in surgical patients. *Journal of Experimental Social Psychology*, 11, 155–65.

Lazarus, R. S., & Folkman, S. (1984). *Stress, Appraisal, and Coping*. New York: Springer-Verlag.

Long, B. C. (1980). Stress management for the athlete: a cognitive-behavioral model. In C. H. Nadeau, W. R. Halliwell, K. M. Newell, & G. C. Roberts (eds), *Psychology of Motor Behavior and Sport*. Champaign, IL: Human Kinetics.

Maag, J., & Kotlash, J. (1994). Review of stress inoculation training with children and adolescents: issues and recommendations. *Behavior Modification*, 18, 443–69.

McAdams, D. P., Reynolds, J., Lewis, M., Patten, A. V., & Bowman, P. J. (2001). When bad things turn good and good things turn bad: sequences of redemption and contamination in life narratives and their relation to psychological adaptation in midlife adults and in students. *Personality and Social Psychology Bulletin*, 27, 474–85.

Mace, R. D., & Carroll, D. (1986). Stress inoculation training to control anxiety in sports: three case studies in squash. *British Journal of Sports Medicine*, 20, 115–17.

Mace, R. D., Eastman, C., & Carroll, D. (1986). Stress inoculation training: a case study in gymnastics. *British Journal of Sports Medicine*, 20, 139–41.

Mace, R. D., Eastman, C., & Carroll, D. (1987). The effects of stress inoculation training in gymnastics on the pommel horse: a case study. *Behavioral Psychotherapy*, 15, 272–29.

McGuire, W. (1964). Inducing resistance to persuasion: some contemporary approaches. In L. Berkowitz (ed.), *Advances in Social Psychology* (Vol. 1). New York: Academic Press.

Marks, I., Lovell, K., Noshirvani, H., Livanou, M., & Thrasher, S. (1998). Treatment of post-traumatic stress disorder by exposure and/or cognitive restructuring: a controlled study. *Archives of General Psychiatry*, 55, 317–25.

Marlatt, G. A., & Gordon, J. R. (eds). (1988). *Relapse Prevention: Maintenance Strategies in the Treatment of Addictive Behaviors*. New York: Guilford Press.

Meichenbaum, D. (1975). Self-instructional methods. In F. H. Kanfer & A. P. Goldstein (eds), *Helping people change* (pp. 357–391). New York: Pergamon Press.

Meichenbaum, D. (1976). A self-instructional approach to stress management: a proposal for stress inoculation training. In C. Spielberger & I. Sarason (eds), *Stress and Anxiety in Modern Life*. New York: Winston.

Meichenbaum, D. (1977). *Cognitive Behavior Modification: An Integrative Approach*. New York: Plenum Press.

Meichenbaum, D. (1985). *Stress Inoculation Training*. Elmsford, NY: Pergamon Press.

Meichenbaum, D. (1993). Stress inoculation training: a 20-year update. In P. M. Lehrer & R. L. Woolfolk (eds), *Principles and Practice of Stress Management* (pp. 373–406). New York: Guilford Press.

Meichenbaum, D. (1996). *Treating Adults with Post-Traumatic Stress Disorder*. Waterloo, Ontario, Canada: Institute Press.

Meichenbaum, D. (2001). *Treating Individuals with Anger-Control Problems and Aggressive Behaviors*. Waterloo, Ontario, Canada: Institute Press.

Meichenbaum, D. (2005). Trauma and suicide: a constructive narrative perspective. In T. E. Ellis (ed.), *Cognition and Suicide: Theory, Research and Practice*. Washington, DC: American Psychological Association.

Meichenbaum, D., & Deffenbacher, J. L. (1988). Stress inoculation training. *Counseling Psychologist*, 16, 69–90.

Meichenbaum, D., & Fitzpatrick, D. (1993). A narrative constructivist perspective of stress and coping: stress inoculation applications. In L. Goldberger & S. Breznitz (eds), *Handbook of Stress* (2nd edn). New York: Free Press.

Meichenbaum, D., & Fong, G. (1993). How individuals control their own minds: a constructive narrative perspective. In D. M. Wegner & J. W. Pennebaker (eds), *Handbook of Mental Control*. New York: Prentice Hall.

Meichenbaum, D., & Jaremko, M. E. (eds) (1993). *Stress Reduction and Prevention*. New York: Plenum Press.

Meichenbaum, D., & Novaco, R. (1978). Stress inoculation: a preventative approach. In C. Spielberger & I. Sarason (eds), *Stress and Anxiety* (Vol. 5). Washington, DC: Hemisphere.

Meichenbaum, D., & Turk, D. C. (1976). The cognitive behavioral management of anxiety, anger and pain. In P. Davidson (ed.), *The Behavioral Management of Anxiety, Depression and Pain*. New York: Brunner/Mazel.

Meichenbaum, D., & Turk, D. C. (1987). *Facilitating Treatment Adherence: A Practitioner's Guidebook*. New York: Plenum Press.

Michelson, L. K., & Marchione, K. (1991). Behavioral, cognitive and pharmacological treatment of panic disorder with agoraphobia: critique and synthesis. *Journal of Consulting and Clinical Psychology*, 59, 100–114.

Neimeyer, R. A. (2001). *Meaning Reconstruction and the Experience of Loss*. Washington, DC: American Psychological Association.

Norcross, J. (2004). Empirically supported therapy relationships. *Clinical Psychologist*, 57, 19–24.

Novaco, R. (1975). *Anger Control: The Development and Evaluation of an Experimental Treatment*. Lexington, MA: Heath.

Novaco, R. (1977a). Stress inoculation: a cognitive therapy for anger and its application to a case of depression. *Journal of Consulting and Clinical Psychology*, 45, 600–8.

Novaco, R. (1977b). A stress inoculation approach to anger management in the training of law enforcement officers. *American Journal of Community Psychology*, 5, 327–46.

Novaco, R. (1980). Training of probation officers for anger problems. *Journal of Consulting Psychology*, 27, 385–390.

Novaco, R., Cook, T., & Sarason, I. (1983). Military recruit training: an arena for stress-coping skills. In D. Meichenbaum & M. Jaremko (eds), *Stress Prevention and Management: A Cognitive-Behavioral Approach*. New York: Plenum Press.

Paunovic, N., & Ost, L. G. (2001). Cognitive-behavioral therapy vs. exposure therapy in treatment of PTSD in refugees. *Behaviour Research and Therapy*, 39, 1183–97.

Rapee, R. (1987). The psychological treatment of panic attacks: theoretical conceptualization and review of evidence. *Clinical Psychology Review*, 7, 427–38.

Resick, P. A., & Schnicke, M. K. (1992). Cognitive processing therapy for sexual assault victims. *Journal of Consulting and Clinical Psychology*, 60, 748–56.

Saunders, T., Driskell, J. E., Johnston, J. H., & Salas, E. (1996). The effect of stress inoculation training on anxiety and performance. *Journal of Occupational Psychology*, 1, 170–86.

Segerstrom, S. C., & Miller, G. E. (2004). Psychological stress and the human immune system: a meta-analytic study of 30 years of inquiry. *Psychological Bulletin*, 130, 601–30.

Siegal, L. J., & Peterson, L. (1980). Stress reduction in young dental patients through coping skills and sensory information. *Journal of Consulting and Clinical Psychology*, 48, 785–7.

Smith, R. E. (1980). A cognitive-affective approach to stress management training for athletes. In C. H. Nadeau, W. R. Halliwell, K. M. Newell, & G. C. Roberts (eds), *Psychology of Motor Behavior and Sport*. Champaign, IL: Human Kinetics.

Smith, R. E., & Rohsenow, D. J. (1987). *Cognitive-Affective Stress Management Training: A Treatment and Resource Manual*. San Rafael, CA: Select Press.

Smucker, M. P., Grunet, B. K., & Weis, J. M. (2003). Posttraumatic stress disorder: a new algorithm treatment model. In R. L. Leahy (ed.), *Roadblocks in Cognitive-Behavioral Therapy* (pp. 175–94). New York: Guilford Press.

Suinn, R. M. (1990). *Anxiety Management Training*. New York: Plenum Press.

Tarrier, N., Pilgrim, H., Sommerfield, C., Faragher, B., Reynolds, M., Graham, E., *et al.* (1999). A randomized trial of cognitive therapy and imagined exposure in the treatment of chronic posttraumatic stress disorder. *Journal of Consulting and Clinical Psychology*, 29, 12–18.

Turk, D. C, Meichenbaum, D., & Genest, M. (1983). *Pain and Behavioral Medicine: A Cognitive-Behavioral Perspective*. New York: Guilford Press.

Veronen, L. J., & Kilpatrick, D. G. (1982, November). *Stress Inoculation Training for Victims of Rape: Efficacy and Differential Findings*. Symposium conducted at the annual convention of the Association for the Advancement of Behavior Therapy, Los Angeles.

Veronen, L. J., & Kilpatrick, D. G. (1983). Stress management for rape victims. In D. Meichenbaum & M. Jaremko (eds), *Stress Prevention and Management: A Cognitive Behavioral Approach*. New York: Plenum Press.

Wernick, R. L. (1983). Stress inoculation in the management of clinical pain: applications to burn patients. In D. Meichenbaum & M. Jaremko (eds), *Stress Reduction and Prevention: A Cognitive Behavioral Approach* (pp. 191–218). New York: Plenum Press.

Wernick, R. L., Jaremko, M., & Taylor, P. (1981). Pain management in severely burned adults: a test or stress inoculation. *Journal of Behavioral Medicine*, 4, 103–9.

Wertkin, R. A. (1985). Stress inoculation training: principles and applications. *Social Casework*, 12, 611–16.

Witkiewitz, K., & Marlatt, G. A. (2004). Relapse prevention for alcohol and drug problems: that was Zen, this is Tao. *American Psychologist*, 59, 224–35.

# 8

# ANGER MANAGEMENT

*Donald Meichenbaum*

Have you ever known someone who is hot-tempered and easily riled, who has a short fuse, overreacts to frustrating events, carries grudges, desires revenge and becomes aggressive too easily? Have you ever known someone who carries a chip on their shoulder, has their antennae up all the time, on the lookout for provocations, and takes slights personally, so that disagreements escalate quickly into confrontations?

What do these individuals do with their anger? Does their anger take the form of verbal and physical assaults (sarcasm, swearing, hitting) or does it turn into an indirect form of passive aggression (becoming silent, doing something to hurt others)?

## What is anger?

Anger is an emotion ranging from mild to intense fury, from feelings of irritation to ones of rage. Anger is a natural response to those situations where you feel threatened or believe you might be harmed, or where you believe that another person has wronged you on purpose. Often – but not always – anger is accompanied by the tendency to retaliate or undo the perceived wrongdoing. Anger is an accusatory response to some perceived misdeed.

Anger is associated with absolute judgments of "must," "ought," "should have," or "could have." Anger attacks may take various forms including irritability, emotional overreactions to minor annoyances, frustration, fury, and rage. Accompanying

– Reproduced by permission of Philip Allan (for Hodder Education). Meichenbaum, D. (2008). Anger management. *Psychology Review*, 14 (1), 2–5.

physical reactions include tightness of the chest, sweating, dizziness, shortness of breath, a racing heart, and feelings of being out of control.

## Consequences of anger

Anger becomes a problem when it is felt too frequently, felt too intensely, lasts too long (not letting the anger go), or is expressed inappropriately. Anger can take both a physical and a behavioral toll. It places extreme physical strain on the body. Anger, chronic cynicism, and hostility are implicated in contributing to high blood pressure (hypertension), heart disease, diminished immune system efficiency, and increased mortality. In short, anger can be a killer.

Hostile individuals who evidence high levels of social conflict and who have low levels of social support are particularly vulnerable to coronary heart disease (CHD). In fact, anger and hostility are recognized as key elements of what is called a type A personality. The negative health consequences of anger are compounded when they are accompanied by the use of substances like alcohol, drugs, and the presence of depression.

At the behavioral level, an inappropriate expression of anger (verbal abuse, intimidating and threatening behaviors) often results in negative social consequences from family members, friends, classmates and co-workers. If anger escalates into physical aggression, it can result in trouble with the police. However, not all forms of aggression involve anger.

## How widespread are anger episodes?

Studies by the psychologist Jim Averill found that in normal (non-clinical) populations, on average, individuals experienced one incident of anger per day (7.3 per week or 23.5 episodes of anger per month). In 88% of these anger episodes, the anger was directed at another person and in 75% of these instances, the targeted individual was familiar and liked by the angry individual. Only 13% of anger episodes involved strangers. Most interpersonal angry exchanges resulted from disputes between individuals who have an ongoing relationship. Over 85% of such angry exchanges were considered to be justified, but perceived to have been avoidable (for example, being treated with insufficient respect or people failing to fulfill commitments). Although overt physical aggression is rare (occurring in less than 10% of such episodes), angry individuals report frequent impulses toward verbal (80%) and physical aggression (40%) when they are angry. That is, many angry individuals are "on the brink" of saying or doing something to hurt others that they may feel sorry for afterwards. However, most angry people do not act out their feelings.

In fact, when one compares individuals who have a low level of anger with those who have a high level of anger, it turns out that they encounter a similar number of provocative situations, but the highly angry individuals respond to such perceived provocations with greater emotional response.

Anger is not only related to aggressive behavior, as in the case of family violence (where arguments and disagreements get out of hand), but it is also related to road rage, substance abuse, suicide, antisocial behaviors and, as noted, physical health problems. At the clinical level, anger is one of the most common symptoms occurring in some 19 different psychiatric disorders.

## Analysing anger

Anger consists of various components that include:

- appraising external and internal triggers;
- primary and secondary emotions;
- thinking patterns, forms of self-talk and images; accompanying beliefs and mental scripts;
- behavioral acts and their consequences.

Let us consider each of these components in turn and then look at the implications for ways to manage and control anger. A useful model is to think of these four elements as positions on a clock – see Figure 8.1.

At 12 o'clock you can put the concept of **triggers** – both **external triggers** (something someone does or does not do that you perceive as a provocation), or **internal triggers**, such as remembering a past harm, an "old anger" reappearing, a

**12 o'clock**
Internal/external
triggers

**9 o'clock**
Behaviour and
consequences (reactions of
others, physical emotions,
social consequences)

**3 o'clock**
Primary and
secondary
emotions

**6 o'clock**
Thinking patterns,
beliefs, self-talk images
and mental scripts

FIGURE 8.1   The vicious circle of anger

flashback, a feeling of apprehension about a possible future hurt or feelings of humiliation and disrespect. Research indicates that angry and aggressive individuals tend to carry with them a "hostility bias," where they are more likely to view the world through a prism of perceived provocations. Anger-prone individuals tend to respond negatively and misinterpret ambiguous social cues and they tend to disregard neutral and prosocial interpersonal cues.

At **3 o'clock** on the anger model are **primary** and **secondary emotions**. Angry individuals have a lower threshold for triggering emotional reactions and they show evidence of more extreme emotions, which last longer. They cannot seem to, or they will not, let those disturbing emotions go. In some instances, anger is a secondary emotion in response to the primary emotions of humiliation, embarrassment, rejection, insecurity, abandonment, disrespect, jealousy, fear, shame, and guilt. Moreover, high-anger prone individuals may hold a theory about their emotions (**meta-emotions**) that "These angry feelings just come," or "Once the anger blows, I can't do anything to stop it," or that "I am a walking time bomb ready to explode," or that "Anger is like a boiling kettle that just builds and builds until it blows."

Next at **6 o'clock**, we examine the role of the **thinking processes** of extremely angry and aggressive individuals. What do angry individuals have to tell themselves (and others) in order to not only get angry but to stay angry over a prolonged period of time? What is the self-talk, inner dialogue or conversation with oneself that perpetuates the anger cycle that can contribute to aggressive behaviours? See Table 8.1 for some examples.

This pattern of thinking and the learned accompanying scripts predispose angry individuals to "lose their cool" and become aggressive. Anger-prone individuals are more likely to view themselves quite favorably, and when their views are challenged or disputed by someone else's actions, they become angry and lash out, especially if they think the other person did it "on purpose."

The psychologist, Roy Baumeister, has characterized this highly favorable view that leads to anger and to a sense of entitlement as "threatened egotism," which acts like a mental script or blueprint (with implicit "if . . . then" rules) for anger and violence.

Finally, the **9 o'clock** features of this cycle are the **specific behaviors** and **resultant consequences**. In short, what does the individual do with all of his/her anger? Do they demonstrate their feelings by becoming sarcastic and verbally abusive or repress their anger and drink? What is the impact of such behavioral acts on others? When individuals act in an aggressive fashion, it often elicits counter-anger and counter-aggressive acts. Such responses from others confirm the anger-prone individual's beliefs and expectations. In this way, angry and aggressive individuals may inadvertently, unwittingly, and perhaps even unknowingly, produce the very reactions in others that confirm their view of the world. Life becomes a self-fulfilling prophecy. "You see, I am not making it up. They are picking on me." In summary, we can analyze anger as consisting of a vicious circle that feeds on itself.

**TABLE 8.1** Stoking up anger: what you have to tell yourself to increase your anger level

**Frustration tolerance**
"I can't stand it"
"They should have done it my way"

**Assign blame, attribute intentionality, be accusatory**
"He did it on purpose"
"She was out to get me"

**Lack of emotional responsibility**
"Anger just happens to me"
"Anger controls me"
"I can't stop it once it starts"

**Instrumental act**
"This is the only way to get them to listen"
"This is the way to show them I am no wimp"
"He dissed [disrespected] me and I am going to get even"
"Anger works!"

**Brooding behavior**
"Why did she do this to me?" (Continue to ask yourself "why" questions and mind-read the answers)
"I can't let go" (Ruminate)

**Over-generalized and black/white thinking**
"He is a ..." (insert inflammatory, emotionally-charged racial epithet)
"They are always doing it their way"
"It never goes my way'"

**Catastrophic thinking and 'MUSTerbation' thinking**
"It is a (horrible, awful, unbelievable, intolerable) hateful way to behave"
"They must do it my way"

## Ways of reducing anger

How can individuals prone to angry feelings and aggressive behavior learn to regulate their emotions? Perhaps you can use the clock metaphor to anticipate the therapeutic interventions that have been found to be helpful. Cognitive behavioral therapies can help angry individuals control their emotions and behaviors. I developed a stress inoculation intervention (SIT) that has been employed successfully with angry and aggressive individuals (see *Psychology Review*, Vol. 13, No. 2). This multifaceted SIT intervention includes:

- psycho education, where angry individuals learn about the negative and positive aspects of anger;
- the warning signs or "red flags" that anger builds;
- the impact of anger;

- the risk factors that exacerbate anger (alcohol, stress, anger-prone friends, availability of weapons);
- ways of regulating emotions and coping;
- ways of breaking the cycle of triggers, feelings, thoughts and behaviors.

Angry individuals learn ways to appraise events in a more benign less provocative fashion. If anger-prone individuals can learn to view potential provocations as problems to be solved, rather than as personal threats, then a more adaptive "script" can be called into play (12 o'clock interventions).

Angry individuals can also learn a variety of ways of regulating primary and secondary emotions and arousal by such means as relaxation (breathing retraining), acceptance, mindfulness, and time-out procedures. Such 3 o'clock-based interventions can, in turn, influence the angry individual's self-talk, so that they do not feel a victim of feelings, thoughts, and events.

Angry feelings usually do not just arrive unannounced. How anger-prone individuals appraise events, their ability to handle such emotions and what they say to themselves determines the ways in which they cope. A key element of the SIT intervention is to help angry individuals alter their thinking patterns and beliefs. There is a need to help individuals generate non-angry, non-aggressive behavioral alternatives and to practice these coping skills, both in treatment and in their everyday settings (9 o'clock interventions).

Angry and aggressive individuals need to learn how to become assertive without becoming aggressive. They need to fine-tune their communication and conflict resolution skills. There are adaptive ways of transforming angry feelings into effective interpersonal acts. Thus, there are several ways to break the cycle between angry feelings, anger-engendering thoughts and images, and aggressive behaviors. These are summarized in Table 8.2.

## In conclusion

Finally, it is important to recognize that there is nothing wrong with becoming angry. Anger is a useful and healthy emotion. People experience anger when there is a discrepancy between the way they think things should be and the way they are. Anger arises when you perceive injustice and lack of sensitivity. Without anger there would be no social changes, no Amnesty International, no Gay rights movement, no feminist movement, no efforts towards achieving civil rights and peace. It is not that individuals *become* angry. Rather, it is more a question of what they *do* with that anger.

Like other emotions such as anxiety, which acts as a warning sign, or depression, which is an occasion for others to provide support, anger can also be a bellwether emotion for action to be taken. Remember, high- and low-anger individuals have the same number of provocations. It is how they respond to such triggers that has major physical and social consequences.

**TABLE 8.2** Examples of anger management skills

| | |
|---|---|
| • Learn what triggers your anger. What do these various situations have in common? | • Learn the cues and warning signs: red flags that your anger is building or that you might be losing control. |
| • Develop an anger-control plan 'if…then rules which offer both immediate coping strategies and preventative strategies. | • Monitor your anger using a 1–10 scale, where 10 is when you lose control and experience negative consequences |
| • Keep a journal of your anger episodes. Analyse these episodes using the clock model (triggers, emotions, thoughts and behaviours) Ask yourself what you have done to make the anger cycle worse. Figure out what you can do to break that cycle. | • Change hostile attitudes. |
| • Question and challenge the self-talk which is making anger worse. | • Lower your arousal level and regulate emotions by using breathing and relaxation exercises. |
| • Blow off steam through physical exercise. | • Distract yourself with positive activities. |
| • Take 'time out' or cool down. Remove yourself from a provocative situation. | • View the provocation as a problem to be solved rather than as a personal threat. |
| • Talk to a friend about what is angering you. | • Imagine how a friend or relative who does not get angry would handle this situation. |
| • Act assertively (not aggressively) by standing up for your rights, but in a respectful way. Use 'I' statements; 'I feel X in situation Y when you do Z', instead of 'You' accusatory statements. | • Use your toolbox of coping strategies. |
| • Remind yourself that being angry will most often *not* help you achieve your goals and it may harm important relationships. | • Remind yourself that anger also hurts your physical health. |
| • Remind yourself that you pay a price for brooding and carrying a grudge. | • Remind yourself that there is nothing wrong with *being* angry. It is what you *do* with that anger that is critical. |

# References

Averill, J. R. (1982) *Anger and Aggression.* Springer.

Baumeister, R. F., Smart, C., and Boden, J. M. (1996) Relation of threatened egotism to violence and aggression. *Psychological Review,* vol. 103, pp. 5–33.

Meichenbaum, D. (2001) *Treatment of Individuals with Anger-Control Problems and Aggressive Behavior.* Institute Press.

See www.melissainstitute.org for information on how angry and aggressive behavior develops and means of prevention.

# 9

# A COGNITIVE-BEHAVIORAL APPROACH TO PAIN MANAGEMENT

*Dennis C. Turk and Donald Meichenbaum*

## Introduction

In recent years there has been a proliferation of multidisciplinary pain clinics, so that it is estimated that there are currently over 2000 such clinics in the United States alone. These pain clinics have employed a broad range of psychological as well as somatic treatments (Turk *et al.* 1983; Flor *et al.* 1992). Their multifaceted treatment approach is consistent with the increasing evidence that pain extends beyond the sole contribution of sensory phenomena to include cognitive, affective, and behavioral factors (Melzack & Wall 1983; Turk *et al.* 1993).

Despite the proliferation of pain clinics and treatment modalities, relatively few comprehensive programs have received systematic empirical evaluation (Flor *et al.* 1992). Turk *et al.* (1983) indicate that most research on the efficacy of pain management programs has focused on two approaches:

1.  the operant-conditioning approach developed by Fordyce and his colleagues (Fordyce *et al.* 1973)
2.  the cognitive-behavioral approach outlined by Turk *et al.* (1983; see also Holzman *et al.* 1986; Turk *et al.* 1986; Turk & Rudy 1993).

In this chapter we shall describe the central features of a cognitive-behavioral approach to pain management. For a detailed examination of the operant-conditioning approach, see Fordyce (1976).

## Rationale for the cognitive-behavioral approach

The cognitive-behavioral perspective on pain management evolved from research on a number of psychologically-based problems (e.g. anxiety, depression and phobias). Following the initial empirical research on cognitive-behavioral techniques in the early 1970s, there have been a large number of research and clinical applications (Meichenbaum 1977, 1985; Beck *et al.* 1979; Kendall & Hollon 1979). The common denominators across different cognitive-behavioral approaches include:

1. interest in the nature and modification of a patient's thoughts, feelings, and beliefs, as well as behaviors;
2. some commitment to behavior therapy procedures in promoting change (such as graded practice, homework assignments, relaxation, relapse prevention training).

In general, the cognitive-behavioral therapist is concerned with using environmental manipulations, as are behavior (operant-conditioning) therapists; but for the cognitive-behavioral therapist such manipulations represent informational feedback trials that provide an opportunity for the patient to question, reappraise, and acquire self-control over maladaptive thoughts, feelings, behaviors, and physiological responses. Thus, contrary to the suggestion of some authors (Ciceone & Grzesiak 1984; Rachlin 1985) there is no reason why the cognitive perspective and operant approaches should be viewed as incompatible or why they cannot or should not be integrated to create a cognitive-behavioral approach to treatment.

Although the cognitive-behavioral approach was developed originally for the treatment of psychologically-based disorders, the perspective has much in common with the multidimensional conceptualizations of pain that emphasize the contributions of cognitive and affective, as well as sensory phenomena (Melzack & Wall 1965). Both the cognitive-behavioral perspective and the Gate Control Model of pain emphasize the important contribution of psychological variables such as the perception of control, the meaning of pain to the patient and dysphoric affect. According to Melzack & Casey (1968):

> The surgical and pharmacological attacks on pain might well profit by redirecting thinking toward the neglected and almost forgotten contribution of motivational and cognitive processes. Pain can be treated not only by trying to cut down sensory input by anesthetic blocks, surgical interventions and the like but also by influencing the motivational-affective and cognitive factors as well.

Melzack (1980) has also suggested that "cognitive processes are at the forefront of the most exciting new psychological approaches to pain, fear and anxiety." The cognitive-behavioral approach focuses directly on cognitive processes as well as on affect, environmental and sensory phenomena. Each of the components of pain conceptualized in the Gate Control Model is incorporated within the cognitive-behavioral treatment program.

## Overview of the cognitive-behavioral perspective

It is important to differentiate the cognitive-behavioral perspective from cognitive-behavioral treatments. The cognitive-behavioral perspective is based on five central assumptions (Table 9.1) and can be superimposed upon any treatment approach employed with chronic-pain patients. In many cases the perspective is as important as the content of the therapeutic modalities employed, somatic as well as psychological (Turk & Holzman 1986; Turk & Rudy 1993).

The application of the cognitive-behavioral perspective to the treatment of chronic pain involves a complex clinical interaction and makes use of a wide range of tactics and techniques. Despite the specific techniques used, all cognitive-behavioral treatment approaches are characterized by being active, time-limited, and structured. Collaboration is central to the cognitive-behavioral approach. Therapists are not simply conveyers of information but serve as educators, coaches, and trainers. They work in concert with the patient (and sometimes family members) to achieve mutually agreed-upon goals.

A growing body of research has demonstrated the important roles that cognitive factors (appraisals, beliefs, expectancies) play in exacerbating pain and suffering, contributing to disability and in influencing response to treatment (Turk & Rudy 1992). Thus, cognitive-behavioral interventions are designed to help patients identify maladaptive patterns and acquire, develop, and practice more adaptive coping techniques. Patients are encouraged to become aware of, and monitor, the impact that negative pain-engendering thoughts and feelings play in the maintenance of maladaptive "pain behaviors." Additionally, patients are taught to recognize the connections linking cognition, affect, and behavior, together with their joint consequences. Finally, patients are encouraged to undertake "personal experiments" and to test the effects of their cognitions and beliefs by means of

**TABLE 9.1** Assumptions of the cognitive-behavioral perspective

- Individuals are active processors of information and not passive reactors.
- Thoughts (e.g. appraisals, expectancies, beliefs) can elicit and influence mood, affect physiological processes, have social consequences and can also serve as an impetus for behavior; conversely, mood, physiology, environmental factors and behavior can influence the nature and content of thought processes.
- Behavior is reciprocally determined by *both* the individual and environmental factors.
- Individuals can learn more adaptive ways of thinking, feeling, and behaving.
- Individuals should be active collaborative agents in changing their maladaptive thoughts, feelings, and behaviors.

selected homework assignments. The cognitive-behavioral therapist is concerned not only with the role that patients' cognitions play in contributing to their disorders, but, equally important, the therapist is concerned about the nature and adequacy of the patients' behavioral repertoire, since this affects resultant intrapersonal and interpersonal situations.

A cognitive-behavioral treatment program for pain patients involves a multi-faceted treatment program for individuals or groups and may be conducted on an inpatient or outpatient basis. A detailed presentation of the comprehensive treatment program is offered in Turk *et al.* (1983). In this chapter we will focus only on the psychological components of the cognitive-behavioral treatment; however, it is important to acknowledge that the psychological treatment modalities described need to be considered within a broader rehabilitation model that also includes physical components, vocational components, and to a greater or lesser extent involvement of significant others.

The cognitive-behavioral perspective outlined above should be considered not merely as a set of methods designed to address the psychological components of pain and disability, but as an organizing strategy for more comprehensive rehabilitation (Turk & Stieg 1987). For example, patients' difficulties arising during physical therapy may be associated not only with physical limitations, but with the fear associated with anticipation of increased pain or concern about injury. Therefore, from a cognitive-behavioral perspective, physical therapists need not only to address the patient's performance of physical-therapy exercises and the accompanying attention to body mechanics, but also to address the patient's expectancies and fears. These cognitive and affective processes, including self-management concerns, need to be considered, together with traditional instructions regarding the proper performance of exercise. The same attention to the individual's thoughts and expectancies should be adopted by all members of the interdisciplinary treatment team.

The cognitive-behavioral treatment consists of five overlapping phases that are listed in Table 9.2. Although the five treatment phases are listed separately, it is important to appreciate that they overlap. The distinction between phases is designed to highlight the different components of the multidimensional treatment. Moreover, although the treatment, as presented, follows a logical sequence, it should be implemented in a flexible, individually-tailored fashion. Patients proceed at varying paces and the therapist must be sensitive to these

**TABLE 9.2** Phases in cognitive-behavioral treatment

1. Initial assessment
2. Collaborative reconceptualization of the patient's views of pain
3. Skills acquisition and skills consolidation, including cognitive and behavioral rehearsal
4. Generalization, maintenance, and relapse prevention
5. Booster sessions and follow-up

individual differences. At times, the therapist may decide not to move on to the next phase of the treatment as would be expected, but instead will address some pressing problems or concerns of the patient that may be interfering with progress. In short, therapists must realize that flexibility and clinical skills have to be brought into play throughout the cognitive-behavioral treatment program.

The cognitive-behavioral treatment that we will describe is *not* designed to eliminate patients' pain per se, although the intensity and frequency of their pain may be reduced as a result of increased activity, physical reconditioning achieved during physical therapy, and by means of the acquisition of various cognitive and behavioral coping skills. The treatment is designed to help patients learn to live more effective and satisfying lives, despite the presence of varying levels of discomfort. Other goals include the reduction of excessive reliance on the healthcare system, reduced dependence on analgesic medications, increased functional capacity, and, whenever feasible, return to employment or usual household activities. Table 9.3 outlines the primary objectives of cognitive-behavioral treatment. The treatment program can readily supplement other forms of somatic, pharmacological and psychological treatment.

The overriding message of the cognitive-behavioral approach, one that begins with the initial contact and is woven throughout the fabric of treatment, is that patients are not helpless in dealing with their pain nor need they view pain as an all-encompassing determinant of their lives. Rather, a variety of resources are available for confronting pain, a pain that will come to be viewed by patients in a more differentiated manner. The treatment encourages patients to maintain a problem-solving orientation and to develop a sense of resourcefulness, instead of the sense of helplessness and withdrawal that revolves around bed, physicians, and pharmacists.

**TABLE 9.3** Primary objectives of cognitive-behavioral treatment programs

- To combat demoralization by assisting patients to change their view of their pain and suffering from overwhelming to manageable
- To teach patients that there are coping techniques and skills that can be used to help them to adapt and respond to pain and the resultant problems
- To assist patients to reconceptualize their view of themselves from being passive, reactive and helpless to being active, resourceful, and competent
- To help patients learn the associations between thoughts, feelings, and their behavior, and subsequently to identify and alter automatic, maladaptive patterns
- To teach patients specific coping skills and, moreover, when and how to utilize these more adaptive responses
- To bolster self-confidence and to encourage patients to attribute successful outcomes to their own efforts
- To help patients anticipate problems proactively and generate solutions, thereby facilitating maintenance and generalization

## Phase 1: Assessment

The assessment and reconceptualization phases are highly interdependent. The assessment phase serves several distinct functions as outlined in Table 9.4. Assessment information is obtained by interviewing patients and significant others, as well as by using standardized self-report measures and observational procedures (see Turk & Melzack 1992 for a detailed review of assessment methods). During the assessment phase, psychosocial and behavioral factors are evaluated and the integration of this information with biomedical information is used in treatment planning. There should be a close relationship between the data acquired during the assessment phase and the nature, focus and goals of the therapeutic regimen.

## Phase 2: Reconceptualization

A central feature of cognitive-behavioral treatment is to facilitate the emergence of a new conceptualization of pain during the course of treatment, thereby permitting the patient's symptoms to be viewed as circumscribed and addressable problems, rather than as a vague, undifferentiated, overwhelming experience. The reconceptualization process is designed to prepare the patient for future therapeutic interventions in a way designed to anticipate and minimize patient-resistance and treatment non-adherence (see Meichenbaum & Turk 1987 and Turk & Rudy 1991 for discussions of methods available to increase treatment adherence).

From both the assessment materials and information provided by the patient, the therapist attempts to alter the patient's conceptualization of his or her problem from one based on a sensory view of pain to a more multifaceted view with cognitive, affective, and socioenvironmental factors considered as contributors to the experience of pain. Through this process, patients are educated to think in terms

**TABLE 9.4** Functions of assessment

- To establish the extent of physical impairment
- To identify levels and areas of psychological distress
- To establish, collaboratively, behavioral goals covering such areas as activity level, use of the health-care system, patterns of medication use and response of significant others
- To provide baseline measures against which the progress and success of treatment can be compared
- To provide detailed information about the patient's perceptions of his or her medical condition, previous treatments, and expectations about current treatment
- To detail the patient's occupational history/goals vis-à-vis work
- To examine the important role of significant others in the maintenance and exacerbation of maladaptive behaviors and to determine how they can be positive resources in the change process
- To begin the reconceptualization process by assisting patients and significant others to become aware of the situational variability of the pain and the psychological, behavioral, and social factors that influence the nature and degree of pain

of a treatment that will be effective in enhancing and providing them with greater control over their lives, even if the pain cannot be completely eliminated (Turk *et al.* 1986).

## First contact with the patient

The reconceptualisation process begins with the patient's initial contact with the therapist. The therapist is concerned with establishing the source of the referral, general details of the pain complaint, the patient's general state of health, ongoing treatment (if any), the date of the last complete physical examination, and the patient's understanding of the reasons for which he or she has been referred to a nonmedical pain specialist. From the beginning, potential patients are directed toward viewing this opportunity as being unlike others they have experienced with health-care providers – they can be helped, but only if they are prepared to participate by making a serious commitment to take an active role in the intervention and in reshaping their lives. Patients are provided with information about the multiple effects of chronic pain on people's lives, general demands, and specific components of the treatment program.

As part of this initial contact, pain questionnaires are administered that are designed to elicit information regarding patients' thoughts and feelings about their capacity to exert control over pain and many other aspects of their lives (see the West Haven-Yale Multidimensional Pain Inventory (MPI), Kerns *et al.* 1985). In addition, by means of a structured interview, questions are asked that are designed to help patients view their severest pain episodes as having a definite beginning, middle, and ending; to see pain episodes as variable, but not being life-threatening; to interpret them as responses that can be controlled, and to view them as responsive to the passage of time, situational factors, and life circumstances. As part of this assessment, the therapist encourages the patient's spouse or significant other to identify the impact of the patient's pain on them, the effect of their behavior on the patient, as well as to provide the family members with an understanding of the cognitive-behavioral treatment approach. There is increasing evidence that significant others play an important role in the maintenance and exacerbation of pain, and, moreover, are themselves affected by living with a person with chronic pain (Kerns & Turk 1984; Flor *et al.* 1987a, 1987b).

At this point the therapist introduces the concept of "pain behaviors" and "operant pain" (following Fordyce) and discusses the important role that significant others may play in unwittingly, inadvertently, and perhaps unknowingly reinforcing the patient's overt expression of pain and suffering. Such behaviors as grimacing, lying down, avoiding certain activities, and moaning are offered as examples of "pain behaviors." The patient's significant other is encouraged to recall examples of the patient's specific pain behaviors. The spouse or significant other is also asked to complete a diary of the patient's pain behaviors and his or her responses. This homework assignment serves to highlight the role pain has come to have in their lives and the importance of significant others in the treatment. The question put to the spouse or significant other is: "How do you know when your spouse is experiencing severe pain?"

The patient may be asked to complete a self-report diary for 1–2 weeks. Patients are asked to record episodes each day when they view their pain as moderate to severe and also when they are feeling particularly upset or distressed. They are also asked to record the circumstances surrounding the episode, who was present, what they thought, how they felt, what they did, and whether or not what they did had any effect on the level of their pain. Diaries are designed so that the therapist will use them to assist patients to identify the links among thoughts, feelings, behaviors, pain intensity, and distress.

Finally, patients may be provided with pain intensity rating cards to record a two-week baseline of pain intensity. The pain-rating cards each contain a list of the hours of the day and a six-point scale of intensity with 0 = no pain to 5 = incapacitating, severe pain. Patients are instructed to rate the intensity of the pain they experience at various times during each waking day. Space is also provided on these cards for patients to indicate the time when medication is ingested and the specific incidents or thoughts and feelings that accompany intense pain (Turk *et al.* 1983).

The pain intensity rating cards are designed to demonstrate to the patients and spouse that, contrary to their expectations, the patient rarely experiences the most intense pain over extended periods and that the intensity of the pain tends to rise and fall. Patients often find this variability surprising in view of their earlier descriptions of their pain. The identification of the pain pattern functions to encourage a sense of control-through-predictability (i.e. pain peaks and troughs, once recognized, are amenable to self-management strategies). As therapists, we can ask questions, help patients juxtapose data and provide examples that facilitate a reconceptualization of the pain experience.

A note regarding homework assignments is in order. Since the conduct of homework assignments (such as keeping pain diaries, self-monitoring of pain levels, and so forth) are critical to cognitive-behavioral treatment, the therapist must ensure that the patient and significant other understand the rationale, goals, and actual procedures included with each homework assignment. A useful way to assess such understanding is to use a role-reversal procedure where the patient or significant other is required, in their own words, to explain the nature and rationale of the homework assignments to the therapist. The patient and significant other may be asked how they feel about the assignment, whether they believe they will be able to carry it out or whether they can foresee any problems or obstacles that would interfere with satisfactory completion of the assignments. If they can imagine problems developing, they are asked how they might deal with these should they occur. If no problems can be identified by the patients, the therapist may suggest some possibilities (e.g. they may forget to record a day, they may feel embarrassed to self-monitor). In order to reduce feelings of defensiveness on the part of patients, the therapist might preface specifying problems by suggesting that "although you do not foresee any problems, some patients have told us that a problem for them was ..." and "How would you suggest that you would deal with such a problem if it was to arise?" The therapist should anticipate and subsume any possible patient problems in conducting homework assignments within the therapeutic context.

Finally, it should be noted that the assessment should also focus on the patient's strengths and resources (e.g. coping abilities, competencies, social supports). These can be incorporated into subsequent treatment phases and contribute to the cognitive restructuring process.

## Preliminary formulation of treatment goals

At this point the patient, spouse and therapist *collaborate* in establishing treatment goals that will return the patient to optimal functioning in light of any physical restriction and that are consistent with the patient's wishes. From the cognitive-behavioral perspective, collaboration is essential because it helps patients to feel that they are responsible for what occurs in treatment and for the outcomes. It is often useful to use the information obtained from the structured interview, such as "How would your life be different if your pain could be relieved?", to generate specific goals. The goals for the patient must be specific and measurable. For example, a patient's goal "to feel better" is inadequate. The patient needs to specify what he or she will be doing that will indicate such improvement. We have found it useful to establish collaboratively short-term, intermediate and long-term goals in order that reinforcement by goal achievement can occur early in treatment, thus enhancing patients' self-confidence. The treatment goals agreed upon – guided rather than dictated by the therapist – typically include medication reduction, increased activity (recreational, exercise), specific tasks to accomplish at home and on the job, reduction in the inappropriate use of the health-care system, and other patient goals.

Towards the end of the reconceptualization phase it is appropriate to provide a brief description of what will occur in subsequent sessions such as education and practice of specific cognitive and behavioral coping skills. It is important that patients and significant others understand the kinds of demands and expectancies of the program and the likely impact their efforts will have on all phases of their lives. Clarification of the treatment demands at the earliest phases of the program helps to circumvent problems that often arise later during therapy.

## Graded exercise and activities

Many chronic-pain patients have developed a sedentary lifestyle that can exacerbate pain by reducing endurance, strength, and flexibility. Thus, the therapist, in collaboration with a physiotherapist and the patient's physician, should develop a graded exercise activity program appropriate to the patient's physical status, age, and gender. As is the case in operant-conditioning treatments, patients maintain activity-level charts of achievable, incremental goals from which progress can be gauged by the patient, as well as by the specific therapist and other family and treatment team members. Initial goals are set at a level that the patient should have little trouble achieving, with the requirements increasing at a gradual rate.

The exercise activity program has four major objectives. First, that of ameliorating physiological consequences that may exacerbate pain. Moreover, for chronic-pain patients and their families, pain is a major focus of attention. Each physical sensation, each environmental demand is viewed in terms of its significance for experiencing pain. Thus, the second objective of the exercise-activity program is to increase the likelihood that the pain patient and his or her family develop interests other than pain. In this way "pain" becomes more peripheral and competes for attention with other activities, rather than being the focal point of the patient's life. Thirdly, the graded exercise program provides for success experiences and thereby will help to reduce fear of activity. Finally, the graded exercise program reinforces the patient's perception of his or her own control and encourages self-attribution of successes.

## Medication reduction

Another important issue to discuss with the patient is the usage of analgesic medication. There is sufficient evidence to indicate that many patients are overmedicated and are often dependent on analgesics. It is advantageous to help patients reduce and eventually eliminate all unnecessary medication. Since reduction of some drugs is known to be accompanied by serious side-effects, consultation with the physician is imperative.

There are two schools of thought concerning the procedure to employ during drug withdrawal. Operant-oriented treatment programs like that of Fordyce and his colleagues (Fordyce 1976) require the patient to take medication at specific times rather than PRN (as required) and they mask the medication in a liquid medium (a "pain cocktail") with systematic reduction of the percentage of active ingredient by the treatment manager. The patient is informed of the process of reduction prior to the initiation of the program, but does not influence the schedule of the weaning process.

A second view regarding reduction of medication, one more congruent with the cognitive-behavioral perspective, also encourages the use of medication at specific intervals since self-control and responsibility are major factors in this approach. However, the therapist encourages the patient to systematically reduce his or her medication, helps the patient design procedures by which this can be accomplished, and shares major responsibility for medication control with the patient. The patient is required to record the quantity and time of medication intake. The importance of medication reduction is stressed and the patient's medication records are carefully monitored. If the patient does not follow the guidelines in reducing the dosage, then this becomes a focus of discussion. The attempt to control medication intake is looked upon as a personal responsibility and the reasons for failure are considered in depth.

## Translation process

At this time the translation or reconceptualization process begins in a more formal manner. A simplified conceptualization of pain based on the Gate Control Model of Melzack & Wall (1965) is presented and contrasted with the unidimensional sensory-physiological model held by many patients. The interaction of cognitions, affect and sensory aspects of a situation is presented in a clear, understandable fashion using the patient's self-monitored experiences as illustrations (Turk *et al.* 1983). For example, the impact of anxiety is briefly considered and related to the exacerbation of pain. Data from patient diaries are extremely useful to make this point more concrete. Patients can review recent stressful episodes and examine the course their pain followed at that time. One coronary patient, who had been aware of a connection between periods of tension and the intensity of his pain, attributed the pain to changes in the state of his heart. As the details of his situation were examined, an alternative explanation emerged, namely, that the nature of his pain was stress-related. Muscle tension in the chest and shoulders increased when he was feeling stressed, but the heart rate and pulse remained unchanged. The patient's misattribution prevented appropriate action from being taken to reduce the muscle contraction that aggravated the chest-wall pain. The reappraisal of the pain stimulus both improved his ability to control the pain through timely and target-appropriate interventions, which in turn improved his sense of self-efficacy (Bandura 1977; Dolce *et al.* 1986).

One item included in our pain questionnaire that we have found to be particularly suited to providing examples of how cognitive and affective factors, such as appraisal of the situation and coping resources, contribute to the pain experience asks the patient to close his or her eyes and to imagine the last time he or she had experienced intense pain ("5" on the pain-rating cards) and to record as many thoughts and feelings as possible that he or she had experienced before, during, and after the episode. One patient who suffered with migraine headaches provided the following response to the item:

> For hours and hours. God, will it ever end, how much longer do I have to live this way? I have outlived my usefulness … the hours are endless and I am alone. I wish someone could take a sharp knife and cut that artery … How long will it be until I am sent to a mental institution? Migraines are not fatal; doctors don't care. You live through one, only to be stricken with another in a few days. I am incapable of everything I used to do. How am I going to fill the rest of my life? Unemployed, can't do anything, and all alone!

This patient feels helpless, views her situation as hopeless and appraises her situation as one of continued deterioration. In such situations, patients are asked to consider the impact of such thoughts and feelings on the experience of pain and what they can do in such circumstances. In this manner, the therapist engages the patient in a Socratic dialogue in order to illustrate how such thinking may maintain and exacerbate pain and to consider alternative coping responses.

The example of Beecher's (1959) observation on the pain experienced by Second World War soldiers wounded at Anzio in Italy can be used as an example of how appraisal and meaning systems affect the perception of pain. Beecher noted that many soldiers did not report experiencing intense pain, despite having incurred life-endangering battle wounds. Beecher attributed these responses to the meaning of an experience and suggested that the individual's appraisal influences how much pain he or she perceives. The therapist uses examples from the patient's experience that illustrate similar processes.

Biofeedback equipment may be used to illustrate the relationship between stress and muscle tension. Patients can be attached to biofeedback equipment and asked to tense relevant muscles and to attend to the changes in the information fed back (visual or auditory). The therapist may then ask the patients to relax the muscles (may give some guidance on how to do this) and to observe the changes in the tones or lights. The therapist can call to patients' attention their ability to change physiological functions, thus relating muscle tension to the exacerbation of pain. This can often have a dramatic effect in helping patients to realize the relationship between thoughts, feelings, and muscle tension. Moreover, it can demonstrate to patients that they can, at least to some extent, control their own bodies. Consistent with the cognitive-behavioral perspective, biofeedback training has been found to increase pain patients' locus of control and self-efficacy, even if physiological changes have not occurred (Turk & Rudy 1992).

To facilitate this reappraisal process, the therapist introduces the notion that the patient's experience of pain can be viewed as consisting of several manageable phases, rather than one overwhelming undifferentiated assault. In this way the patient comes to view his or her pain as composed of several components that go through different phases which are, in part, influenced by his or her reactions. The patient is not the "helpless victim" of pain. The therapist and patient have collected data to support this more differentiated view of pain, thus providing the basis for the intervention program that will follow.

Examples are offered to show how pain can be subdivided into several steps, each of which is manageable by the patient. For example, when the patient rates his or her pain as 0 or 1 on a six-point scale (i.e. no pain or fairly low-level intensity) this is an opportunity for the patient to engage in productive coping activities. This period of low-intensity pain can function as a time when the patient can plan how he or she will deal with more intense levels of pain by means of employing cognitive and behavioral coping strategies that the patient will learn by the end of the treatment program. Similarly, the patient can develop coping skills to employ at the higher levels of pain intensity. The patient is encouraged to view pain as a problem to be prepared for and solved. A useful analogy is the way athletic teams develop game plans. Preplanning lowers the risk of the patient becoming overwhelmed at times of more severe pain, while implicitly fostering an expectation that episodes of severe pain will pass. Patients are also encouraged to self-reinforce their efforts throughout by taking credit for their coping efforts.

Negative thoughts, pain-engendering appraisals and attributions are reviewed in treatment in order that the patient will not be surprised when and if they do arise. Rather, the patient is encouraged to use the negatively-valenced cognitions and feelings as reminders or as cues to initiate more adaptive coping strategies. The pain diaries described earlier can provide information that becomes the focus of discussion. For example, patients who recorded thoughts that they felt "incompetent" and "helpless" in controlling their pain during a specific episode can be encouraged to become aware of when they engage in such thinking and to appreciate how such thoughts may exacerbate their pain and become a self-fulfilling prophecy. Alternative thoughts such as a realistic appraisal of the situation and of their coping resources are encouraged and patients reinforced for using one or more of the coping strategies covered during the skills training. The patient is encouraged to divide the situation into stages as described earlier and to acknowledge that the most severe pain is usually relatively transitory. Such "cognitive restructuring" is incorporated throughout the treatment regimen. The therapist also incorporates examples of when the patient has been resourceful in his or her life and considers how these skills can be applied in the pain situation.

## Phase 3: Skills-acquisition and skills-consolidation

The skills-acquisition and skills-consolidation phase begins once the basic initial goals of the treatment program have been agreed upon. During this third phase the therapist provides practice in the use of a variety of cognitive- and behavioral-coping skills that are geared toward the alteration of the patient's response to environmental contributors to pain, to bolstering coping skills (e.g. attention diversion, relaxation skills for dealing with specific symptoms), to changing maladaptive interpretations and to changing factors that might contribute to stress (e.g. maladaptive communication patterns).

The order in which the various cognitive and behavioral strategies are covered can be varied depending upon the patient's needs. In addition to helping the patient develop specific coping skills, this phase is also designed to help patients use skills they already possess and to enhance the patient's belief in his or her ability to exercise control, further enhancing a sense of self-efficacy. The point to be underscored is that the cognitive-behavioral approach does not deal exclusively with the pain symptoms per se, but with those self-statements and environmental factors that may instigate or maintain less than optimal functioning and subsequent pain exacerbations. Alterations in lifestyle, problem-solving, communication-skills training, relaxation skills, and homework assignments are woven into the fabric of the treatment.

## Problem-solving

A useful way to think about pain is as a set of sequential problems, rather than simply as the presence of pain being a single overwhelming problem. That is, many patients view pain as their overriding problem and their only problem. An alternative that is encouraged by cognitive-behavioral therapists is that chronic pain presents the sufferer with an array of small and large problems – familial, occupational, social, recreational, and financial, as well as physical. The therapist assists patients in identifying their problems in these areas and suggests that a method for dealing with these problems is to generate a set of alternatives and to weigh the relative advantages and disadvantages of each of these alternatives. The therapist also suggests that patients can select what they believe is the best solution and try it out to see if it resolves or reduces the problem. It is also suggested that patients can recycle through the problem-solving process.

There are several critical features of problem-solving skills training. The important first step in problem-solving is to have patients "operationalize" their problems in behaviorally prescriptive language (e.g. when X occurs in situation Y, I feel Z). The second step is to help patients identify what particular situations are associated with pain. The use of self-monitoring in patient diaries can help to identify such problematic situations. Patients need to think of the difficulties that they encounter as "problems to be solved." Next they must try out the alternative to achieve the desired outcome. Patients need to learn that there is usually not a single solution or alternative to solve problems and they need to weigh alternatives. In this way lack of success with any one attempt will not be taken as a complete failure, but rather such setbacks and lapses are viewed as learning trials and occasions to consider alternatives.

It is all too easy to conduct problem-solving during treatment but much harder to do so in the patient's natural environment. Patients may be given the homework task of formally identifying problems, generating alternative solutions, rating the solutions for likely effectiveness, trying them out and then reporting on the outcome. Throughout treatment, the therapist can use the language of problems and solutions to illustrate the value of using the problem-solving approach. The therapist uses terms and phrases like "notice," "catch," "interrupt," "plan," "game plan," "being in charge," "having choices," "performing experiments," "setting goals," and the like.

## Relaxation and controlled breathing

Relaxation and controlled-breathing exercises are especially useful in the skills-acquisition phase because they can be readily learned by almost all patients and they have a good deal of face validity. The relaxation and controlled breathing involve systematically tensing and relaxing various muscle groups, both general and specific to the particular area of pain reported by patients. Emphasis on controlled breathing is included, due to research demonstrating that the amplitude and frequency of respiration has an effect upon heart rate and the accompanying experience of anxiety (Turk et al. 1983). Instruction in the use of relaxation and controlled breathing is designed not only to teach an incompatible response, but also as a way of helping the patients develop a behavioral-coping skill that they can use in any situation in which adaptive coping is required. The practice of relaxation and controlled breathing strengthens the patients' belief that they can exert control during periods of stress and pain and that they are not helpless. Patients are encouraged to employ the relaxation skills in situations where they perceive themselves becoming tense, anxious or experiencing pain.

Relaxation is not achieved by only one method; in fact, there are a large number of relaxation techniques in the literature. At this point, there is no evidence that one relaxation approach is any more effective than any other. What is most important is to state these findings with these patients and to help them determine what relaxation technique, or set of techniques, is most effective for them. Thus, in a collaborative mode, the therapist will assist patients to learn coping strategies that they find acceptable. If the coping effort proves ineffective, this is not to be viewed as a failure of relaxation, nor a reflection of the incompetence of the patient, but rather an opportunity to seek another alternative. As in the case of problem-solving described above, it is suggested that there may not be any one best coping alternative, but rather different ones for different people, or for different situations.

## Attentional training

The role of attention is a major factor in perceptual activity and therefore of primary concern in examining and changing behavior. The act of attending has been described as having both selective and amplifying functions. Attention-diverting coping strategies (e.g. thinking about something pleasant) have been employed probably since man first experienced pain. Again it is important to underscore that the patient is viewed as a collaborator in the selection of the specific coping strategies he or she will employ. Several types of strategies are considered and the patient is encouraged to choose those that are most likely to evolve into personally-relevant resources. Patients are also assisted in generating strategies and techniques that they believe might be useful. Again, attempts are made to actively involve patients in their own treatment.

Prior to the description of the specific coping strategies, the therapist always prepares the patient for the intervention. In this instance the therapist describes to the patient how attention influences perception. The therapist notes that people can focus their attention on only one thing at a time and that people control, to some extent, what they attend to, although at times this may require active effort. Examples are used to make this point concrete (often coming from the patient's experience). For example, the therapist uses the analogy of the simultaneous availability of all channels on a TV, but only one channel can be fully attended to at any one time. Attention is like a TV channel-tuner: we can control what we attend to, what we avoid, and the channel to which we tune. With instruction and practice the patient can gain similar control over his or her attention. This discussion prepares the way for presentation of different cognitive-coping strategies.

Both nonimagery- and imagery-based strategies are employed. Although imagery-based strategies (refocusing attention on pleasant pain-incompatible scenes and so forth) have received much attention, the results have not consistently demonstrated that imagery strategies are uniformly effective for all patients (Rosensteil & Keefe 1983; Turner & Clancy 1986; Fernandez & Turk 1989). The important component seems to be the patient's imaginative ability and depth or degree of absorption in using specific images. Guided imagery training is given to patients in order to enhance their abilities to employ all sensory modalities (e.g. imagine such scenes as a lemon being cut on a plate, a tennis match or a pleasant scene that incorporates all five senses). The specifics of the images seem less important than the details of sensory modalities incorporated and the patient's involvement in these images.

Following this preparation, the therapist proceeds to describe different imagery categories (e.g. pleasant, fanciful, dissociative) and once again asks the patient to generate examples that are personally relevant. The therapist asks the patient to imagine circumstances along a continuum of pain and encourages the patient to see him- or herself employing the various images to cope with the pain more effectively. The purpose of the imagery rehearsal is to foster a sense of "learned resourcefulness" as compared to "learned helplessness" that characterizes many pain patients.

Some patients will have difficulty learning relaxation or making use of imagery techniques. In such circumstances it is often helpful to have patients use audiotapes or posters to help them focus their attention and to guide them with relaxation or imagery. The emphasis is not on one imagery method or technique, but rather on nurturing flexibility. The therapist models this by his or her own creativity in assisting patients to achieve their desired outcomes.

## Phase 4: Rehearsal and application training

Next is the rehearsal phase of the treatment program. After learning different skills, patients are asked to use them in imaginal situations in the therapist's office. For example, after learning different relaxation methods, patients can be asked to imagine themselves in various stressful situations and to see themselves employing the relaxation and coping skills in those situations. For example, patients imagine the last time their pain intensity was rated between 3 and 5 on the pain intensity rating card and to see themselves using the relaxation and other coping techniques at those times. The intent is to have the patients learn that relaxation can be employed as a general coping skill in various situations of stress and discomfort and to prepare themselves for aversive sensations as they arise.

In order to review and consolidate the training procedures, the patient may be asked to role-play a situation in which the therapist and the patient reverse roles. The patient is instructed that it will be his or her job to assume the role of the therapist and the therapist will assume the role of a new patient who has not received any cognitive-behavioral training. The role-reversal exercise is employed because research on attitude change indicates that when people have to improvise, as in a role-playing situation, they generate exactly the kinds of arguments, illustrations, and motivating appeals that are most convincing. In this way the patient tailors the content of his or her roles to accommodate idiosyncratic motives, predispositions, and preferences (Turk *et al.* 1983). Such role-playing also provides the therapist with a means of assessing any conflicting thoughts, feelings or doubts that the patient may harbor.

With success, the therapist can follow up with specific homework assignments that will consolidate the skills in the patient's natural environment. For example, patients are asked to practice relaxation techniques at home at least twice a day for 15 minutes, with one of the practice sessions occurring prior to the times of the most intense pain, if such times have been identified on the pain intensity rating cards. Patients are also asked to anticipate potential problems in performing the homework assignment that might arise (e.g. they forget, they fall asleep) and to generate ways that these obstacles might be addressed should they arise. In this way, attempts are made to anticipate potential difficulties before they arise and to convey the message to patients that they are capable of generating alternative solutions to problems.

As was the case with exercise, skills training follows a graded sequence. First, the therapist discusses the rationale for using a specific method. This is followed by assessing whether the skills are in the patients' repertoires, and teaching the patients needed skills and having them practice them in the therapeutic setting. As patients develop proficiency, they are encouraged and challenged to use them in their homes, first in the least difficult circumstance and then building up to more stressful or difficult situations (when their pain is greater, when they are engaged in an interpersonal conflict).

## Phase 5: Generalization and maintenance

Generalization and maintenance are fostered throughout treatment by means of the provision of guided exercise, imaginal and behavioral rehearsal, and homework assignments, each of which is designed to increase the patient's sense of self-efficacy. Following the skills acquisition and rehearsal phases, patients are encouraged to "try out" the various skills that have been covered during the treatment in a broad range of situations and to identify any difficulties that arise. During these sessions, the patient is encouraged to consider potentially problematic situations and is assisted in generating plans or scripts as to how he or she could handle these difficulties, should they arise. Plans are formulated for what the patient might do if he or she begins to lapse. The therapist attempts to anticipate problems and generate solutions, in a sense to "inoculate" the patient against difficulties that may occur (see Marlatt & Gordon 1980 for a discussion of such relapse prevention procedures). Finally, the patient is encouraged to evaluate progress, review homework assignments and, most importantly, to attribute progress and success to his or her own coping efforts.

It is not enough to have patients change; they must learn to "take credit" for such changes that they have been able to bring about. The therapist asks the patient a series of questions to consolidate such self-attributions. For example, "It worked? What did you do? How did you handle the situation this time differently from how you handled it last time? When else did you do this? How did that make you feel?"

## Phase 6: Treatment follow-up

During the final therapy session all aspects of the training are reviewed. Patients are provided with another set of pain intensity rating cards and a pain questionnaire (Kerns *et al.* 1985). At two weeks following termination, the patient is asked to return with these materials to review progress and the maintenance of skills. At 3–6 months and one year, follow-up appointments are made to consider any difficulties that have arisen. Patients are also encouraged to call for appointments between specific follow-up dates if they are having difficulty with any aspect of the training. Checking in with the therapist is not viewed as a sign of failure, but rather as an occasion to reevaluate coping options.

## Effectiveness of the cognitive-behavioral approach

Cognitive-behavioral approaches have been evaluated in a number of laboratory analogue and clinical pain studies. Laboratory studies have demonstrated the effectiveness of the cognitive-behavioral approach in the enhancement of tolerance to a variety of nociceptive procedures (Klepac *et al.* 1981). The clinical effectiveness of the approach has been demonstrated in well over 100 studies with a wide range of pain syndromes, including headaches (Newton & Barbaree 1987; Holroyd *et al.* 1991), arthritis (Bradley *et al.* 1987; O"Leary *et al.* 1988), temporomandibular pain disorders (Olson & Malow 1987), debridement of burns (Wernick *et al.* 1981), low-back pain (Linssen & Zitman 1984), atypical chest pain (Klimes *et al.* 1990), cumulative trauma injury (Spence 1989) and heterogeneous samples of chronic pain syndromes (Moore & Chaney 1985; Kerns *et al.* 1986; Thorn *et al.* 1986; Nicholas *et al.* 1992). Cognitive-behavioral approaches have been used with patients across the age-span from adolescents (Lascelles *et al.* 1989) to geriatric patients (Puder 1988). Additionally, cognitive-behavioral approaches have been employed in combination with other therapeutic modalities (Brena *et al.* 1981; Guck *et al.* 1985; Mayer *et al.* 1985). A number of these studies have reported follow-up data ranging from six months to two years, indicating that the improvements have been maintained.

In summary, the cognitive-behavioral approach offers promise for use with a variety of chronic-pain syndromes. The fact that the approach has been employed in an outpatient and in a group format appears to be a particular asset, both in terms of the cost-effectiveness and the potential for generalization and maintenance of the skills covered in the treatment program.

An important research question is whether or not certain individual differences or situational constraints limit the relative efficacy of the different components of the comprehensive, multifaceted cognitive-behavioral treatment package. We know almost nothing about which treatment combinations would be most effective for which type of patient. Moreover, there is little research to determine how best to combine such psychologically-based interventions with somatically-based interventions (medications, transcutaneous nerve stimulation and so forth). Research programs are now underway to:

- replicate the preliminary results with the inclusion of appropriate control groups (e.g. credible attention placebo and waiting-list groups);
- identify the relative effectiveness of the cognitive-behavioral treatment for different syndromes and patient populations;
- assess the efficacy of treatment over a long-term follow-up period;
- identify active ingredients of the treatment;
- match treatment components to patient psychosocial and behavioral characteristics.

Taken as an aggregate, the available evidence suggests that the cognitive-behavioral approach has a good deal of potential as a treatment modality by itself and in conjunction with other treatment approaches. The cognitive-behavioral perspective is a reasonable way for health-care providers to think about and to deal with their patients regardless of the therapeutic modalities utilized.

## Side-effects

Unlike more invasive medical and surgical treatments, the cognitive-behavioral approach has no known negative side-effects. However, prior to considering this approach, careful evaluation of the patient's physical condition must be conducted in order to eliminate any treatable physical causes of pain.

Finally, little is known about the limitations of the cognitive-behavioral approach. One study, conducted by Tan (1982), suggests that the cognitive-behavioral approach may have limited value for high-intensity pain with rapid onset (e.g. pain produced during knee arthrogram) and a follow-up study published by Sturgis *et al.* (1984) reported no long-term benefits of a cognitive-behavioral intervention for a heterogeneous group of pain patients. It is important to identify such limitations in order that decisions about their use in more general clinical contexts can be based on data. The central question that remains to be answered is which treatment modalities are most appropriate for patients with what particular characteristics (Turk 1990)?

Although many of the elements included in the present treatment have been used for many years, the cognitive-behavioral treatment approach attempts to integrate these diverse features into an organized clinically-sensitive and effective intervention.

## References

Bandura, A. (1977) Self-efficacy: toward a unifying theory of behavior change. *Psychological Review*, 84: 191–215.

Beck, A. T., Rush, A. J., Shaw, B. F., & Emery, G. (1979) *Cognitive Therapy of Depression*. Guilford Press, New York.

Beecher, H. K. (1959) *Measurement of Subjective Responses: Quantitative Effects of Drugs*. Oxford University Press, New York.

Bradley, L. A., Young, L. D., Anderson, K. O. *et al.* (1987) Effects of psychological therapy on pain behavior of rheumatoid arthritis patients. Treatment outcome and six-month follow-up. *Arthritis and Rheumatism*, 30: 105–114.

Brena, S. F., Chapman, S. L., Decker, R. (1981) Chronic pain as a learned experience: Emory University Pain Control Center. In L. N. Y. Ng (ed.) *New Approaches to Treatment of Chronic Pain: A Review of Multidisciplinary Pain Clinics and Pain Centers*. DHHS publication no. (DM) 81–1089. United States Government Printing Office, Washington, DC.

Ciceone, D. S., & Grzesiak, R. C. (1984) Cognitive dimensions of chronic pain. *Social Science and Medicine*, 19: 1339–46.

Dolce, J. J., Doleys, D. M., Raczynski, J. M., Loessie, J., Poole, L., & Smith, M. (1986) The role of self-efficacy expectancies in the prediction of pain tolerance. *Pain*, 27: 261–72.

Fernandez, E., & Turk, D. C. (1989) The utility of cognitive coping strategies for altering pain perception: a meta-analysis. *Pain*, 38: 123–35.

Flor, H., Fydrich, T., & Turk, D. C. (1992) Efficacy of multidisciplinary pain treatment centers: a meta-analytic review. *Pain*, 49: 221–30.

Flor, H., Kerns, R. D., & Turk, D. C. (1987a) The role of the spouse in the maintenance of chronic pain. *Journal of Psychosomatic Research*, 31: 251–60.

Flor, H., Turk, D. C., & Scholz, O. B. (1987b) Impact of chronic pain on the spouse: marital, emotional, and physical consequences. *Journal of Psychosomatic Research*, 31: 63–71.

Fordyce, W. E. (1976) *Behavioral Methods for Chronic Pain and Illness*. C.V. Mosby, St Louis.

Fordyce, W. E., Fowler, R., Lehmann, J., DeLateur, B., Sand, P., & Trieschmann, R. (1973) Operant conditioning in the treatment of chronic pain. *Archives of Physical Medicine and Rehabilitation*, 54: 399–408.

Guck, T. P., Skultery, F. M., Meilman, P. W., & Dowd, E. T. (1985) Multidisciplinary pain center follow-up study and evaluation with a no-treatment control group. *Pain*, 21: 295–306.

Hazard, R. G., Benedix, A., & Genwich, J. W. (1991) Disability exaggeration as a predictor of functional restoration outcome for patients with chronic low-back pain. *Spine*, 16: 1062–7.

Holroyd, K. A., Nash, J. M., Pingel, J. D., Cordingley, G. E., & Jerome, A. (1991) A comparison of pharmacological (Amitriptyline HCL) and nonpharmacological (cognitive-behavioral) therapies for chronic tension headaches. *Journal of Consulting and Clinical Psychology*, 59: 121–33.

Holzman, A. D., Turk, D. C., & Kerns, R. D. (1986) The cognitive-behavioral approach in treating chronic pain. In: A. D. Holzman, & D. C. Turk (eds), *Pain Management: A Handbook of Psychological Treatment Approaches*. Pergamon Press, Elmsford, New York.

Kendall, P. C., & Hollon, S. D. (1979) *Cognitive-Behavioral Interventions Theory, Research, and Procedures*. Academic Press, New York.

Kerns, R. D., & Turk, D. C. (1984) Depression, marital satisfaction, and perceived support among chronic pain patients and their spouses. *Journal of Marriage and the Family*, 46: 845–52.

Kerns, R. D., Turk, D. C., & Rudy, T. E. (1985) The West Haven-Yale Multidimensional Pain Inventory (WHYMPI). *Pain*, 23: 345–56.

Kerns, R. D., Turk, D. C., Holzman, A. D., & Rudy, T. E. (1986) Efficacy of a cognitive-behavioral group approach for the treatment of chronic pain. *Clinical Journal of Pain*, 2: 195–203.

Klepac, R. K., Klauge, G., Dowling, J., & McDonald, M. (1981) Direct and generalized effects of three components of stress inoculation for increased pain tolerance. *Behavior Therapy*, 12: 417–24.

Klimes, I., Mayou, R. A., Pearce, M. J., & Fagg, J. R. (1990) Psychological treatment for atypical non-cardiac chest pain: a controlled evaluation. *Psychological Medicine*, 20: 605–11.

Lascelles, M. A., Cunningham, S. J., McGrath, P., & Sullivan, M. J. L. (1989) Teaching coping strategies to adolescents with migraine. *Journal of Pain and Symptom Management*, 4: 135–44.

Linssen, A. C. G., & Zitman, F. G. (1984) Patient evaluation of a cognitive behavioral group program for patients with low back pain. *Social Science and Medicine*, 19: 1361–7.

Marlatt, G. A., & Gordon, J. R. (1980) Determinants of relapse: implications for the maintenance of behavioral change. In P. O. Davidson, & S. M. Davidson (eds), *Behavioral Medicine: Changing Health Lifestyles*. Brunner/Mazel, New York.

Mayer, T. G., Gatchel, R. J., Kishino, N. *et al.* (1985) Objective assessment of spine function following industrial injury. A prospective study with comparison group and one-year follow-up. *Spine*, 10: 482–93.

Meichenbaum, D. (1977) *Cognitive-Behavior Modification: An Integrative Approach*. Plenum Press, New York.

Meichenbaum, D. (1985) *Stress Inoculation Training*. Pergamon Press, New York.

Meichenbaum, D., & Jaremko, M. (1983) *Stress Reduction and Prevention*. Plenum Press, New York.

Meichenbaum, D., & Turk, D. C. (1987) *Facilitating Treatment Adherence: A Practitioner's Guidebook*. Plenum Press, New York.

Melzack, R. (1980) Pain theory: exceptions to the rule. *Behavioral and Brain Science*, 3: 313.

Melzack, R., & Casey, K. L. (1968) Sensory, motivational and central control determinants of pain; a new conceptual model. In D. Kenshalo (ed.), *The Skin Senses*. C. C. Thomas, Springfield, Illinois.

Melzack, R., Wall, & P. D. (1965) Pain mechanisms: a new theory. *Science*, 150: 971–9.

Melzack, R., Wall, & P. D. (1983) *The Challenge of Pain*. Basic Books, New York.

Moore, J. E., & Chaney, E. F. (1985) Outpatient group treatment of chronic pain: effects of spouse involvement. *Journal of Consulting and Clinical Psychology*, 53: 326–34.

Newton, C. R., & Barbaree, H. E. (1987) Cognitive changes accompanying headache treatment: the use of a thought-sampling procedure. *Cognitive Therapy and Research*, 11: 635–52.

Nicholas, M. K., Wilson, P. H., & Goyen, J. (1992) Comparison of cognitive-behavioral group treatment and an alternative non-psychological treatment for chronic low back pain. *Pain*, 48: 339–47.

O'Leary, A., Shoor, S., Lorig, K., & Holman, H. R. (1988) A cognitive-behavioral treatment for rheumatoid arthritis. *Health Psychology*, 7: 527–44.

Olson, R. E., & Malow, R. M. (1987) Effects of biofeedback and psychotherapy on patients with myofascial pain dysfunction who are nonresponsive to conventional treatments. *Rehabilitation Psychology*, 32: 195–205.

Puder, R. S. (1988) Age analysis of cognitive-behavioral group therapy for chronic pain outpatients. *Psychology and Aging*, 3: 204–7.

Rachlin, H. (1985) Pain and behavior. *Behavioral and Brain Sciences*, 8: 43–53.

Rosenstiel, A. K., & Keefe, F. J. (1983) The use of coping strategies in chronic low back pain: patients relationship to patient characteristics and adjustment. *Pain*, 17: 33–44.

Spence, S. H. (1989) Cognitive behavior therapy in the management of chronic occupational pain of the upper limbs. *Behavior Research and Therapy*, 27: 435–46.

Sturgis, E., Schaefer, C. A., & Sikora, T. L. (1984) Pain center follow up study of treated and untreated patients. *Archives of Physical Medicine and Rehabilitation*, 65: 301–3.

Tan, S. Y. (1982). Cognitive and cognitive-behavioral methods for pain control: a selective review. *Pain*, 12: 201–28.

Thorn, B. E., Williams, D. A., & Johnson, P. R. (1986) Individualized cognitive behavioral treatment of chronic pain. *Behavioral Psychotherapy*, 14: 210–25.

Turk, D. C. (1990) Customizing treatment for chronic patients; who, what and why. *Clinical Journal of Pain*, 6: 255–70.

Turk, D. C., & Holzman, A. D. (1986) Commonalities among psychological approaches in the treatment of chronic pain: specifying the meta-constructs. In A. D. Holzman, & D. C. Turk (eds), *Pain Management: A Handbook of Psychological Treatment Approaches*. Pergamon Press, New York.

Turk, D. C., & Melzack, R. (eds) (1992) *Handbook of Pain Assessment*. Guilford Press, New York.

Turk, D. C., & Rudy, T. E. (1991) Neglected factors in chronic pain treatment outcome studies – relapse, noncompliance, and adherence enhancement. *Pain*, 44: 24–43.

Turk, D. C., & Rudy, T. E. (1992) Cognitive factors and persistent pain: a glimpse into Pandora's box. *Cognitive Therapy and Research*, 16: 99–122.

Turk, D. C., & Rudy, T. E. (1993) An integrated approach to pain treatment: beyond the scalpel and syringe. In C. D. Tollison (ed.), *Handbook of Chronic Pain Management*, 2nd edn. Williams & Wilkins, Baltimore (in press).

Turk, D. C., & Stieg, R. L. (1987) Chronic pain: the necessity of interdisciplinary communication. *Clinical Journal of Pain*, 3: 163–7.

Turk, D. C., Holzman, A. D., & Kerns, R. D. (1986) Chronic pain. In K. A. Holroyd, & T. L. Creer (eds), *Self-Management of Chronic Disease*. Academic Press, New York.

Turk, D. C., Meichenbaum, D., & Genest, M. (1983) *Pain and Behavioral Medicine: A Cognitive-Behavioral Perspective*. Guilford Press, New York.

Turk, D. C., Rudym, T. E., & Boucek, C. (1993) Psychological factors in chronic pain. In C. A. Warfield (ed.), *Pain Management Techniques*. Martinus Nijhoff, Boston.

Turner, J. A., & Clancy, S. (1986) Strategies for coping with chronic low back pain: relationship to pain and disability. *Pain*, 24: 355–64.

Wernick, R., Jaremko, M. E., & Taylor, P. W. (1981) Pain management in severely burned patients: a test of stress-inoculation training. *Journal of Behavioral Medicine*, 4: 103–9.

# PART IV

# Trauma, Resilience and Recovery

Over the course of 45 years of clinical practice and training, I have had the unique experience and challenge of working with clinicians who treat victims of natural disorders (Hurricanes Katrina and Sandy) and victims of violence, such as returning soldiers from Iraq and Afghanistan, with native populations and individuals who have experienced sexual victimization, intimate partner violence, torture, and human trafficking, and with children who have experienced multiple forms of victimization (family and community violence, school bullying and shootings and fellow student and teacher suicides).

As noted in the following two chapters, no matter what the form of victimization experienced, most individuals in the aftermath of traumatic and victimizing experiences will be impacted, but some 75 percent go onto evidence resilience, or the ability to "bounce back." In contrast, some 25 percent of victimized individuals will "get stuck" and develop persistent PTSD, complex PTSD, and co-occurring disorders.

PTSD is essentially a disorder of non-recovery and resilience is the normative response. PTSD reflects a specific form of autobiographical memories. Individuals who experienced traumatic and victimizing events, in the recent or distant past, have to tell a "story" of what happened and its impact to others, as well as to themselves. It is proposed that it is the nature of the "stories" individuals tell that distinguishes the 75 percent resilient groups from the 25 percent clinical groups. A constructive narrative perspective of psychotherapy helps patients with PTSD better appreciate how they reconstruct the past, sculpt their memories, and can engage presently in meaning-making activities. Such positive engendering activities can help clients develop more coherent, redemptive "healing stories" and the accompanying coping behaviors.

The chapters in this part and the additional papers below provide the research basis for these observations. They highlight that each of us is indeed "homo narrans" – "a storyteller" – and consider the implications for psychotherapeutic interventions.

In my most recent book, *Roadmap to Resilience*, I provide specific ways to bolster resilience in six domains (physical, interpersonal, emotional, cognitive, behavioral, and spiritual) (see www.roadmaptoresilience.com).

The interested reader can also find up-to-date additional papers such as the following, which are available to view and download from the web address given on page xii:

- The Emerging Neurobiology of Resilience: Implications for Psychotherapeutic Interventions.
- A Constructive Narrative Perspective of Trauma and Resilience: The Role of Cognitive and Affective Processes.
- Approaches to Bolster Resilience in Victims of Human Trafficking: Core Tasks of Intervention.
- Ways to Bolster Resilience in LGBTQ (Lesbian, Gay, Bisexual, Transgender, Questioning) Youth.
- Resilience-Building as a Means to Prevent PTSD and Adjustment Problems in Military Personnel.
- Trauma, Spirituality and Recovery: Toward a Spiritually-Integrated Psychotherapy.
- Ways to Bolster Resilience in Older Adults.

# 10

# RESILIENCE AND POSTTRAUMATIC GROWTH

## A constructive narrative perspective

*Donald Meichenbaum*

### Prologue

I have a story to tell and so do the individuals and clients I see who have a history of having been "victimized." Whether the form of trauma exposure is due to intentional human design (e.g., some form of individual or group violence) or due to exposure to natural disasters (e.g., my having recently lived through four hurricanes in Florida over a short period of time), the need to tell "stories" to others, as well as to oneself, about what happened and the implications, is rather pervasive.

As a result, an individual's (or groups') sense of self and the world are established through the "stories" they tell others and themselves. As the adage goes, "Beware of the stories you tell yourself and others for you will be lived by them."

### The main proposal

The central premise of this chapter is that the nature of the self-narrative (and group narrative) plays a critical role in determining whether individuals and groups manifest chronic persistent distress and posttraumatic stress disorder (PTSD) or whether they will evidence resilience and posttraumatic growth (PTG). In short, a Constructive Narrative Perspective (CNP) of the concepts of resilience and PTG will be offered to explain the marked individual differences that occur in the aftermath of trauma exposure. The present thesis can be summarized in a simple, straightforward fashion.

– Meichenbaum, D. (2006). Resilience and posttraumatic growth: A constructive narrative perspective. In L. G. Calhoun & R. G. Tedeschi (eds), *Handbook of Posttraumatic Growth: Research and Practice*. Mahwah, NJ: Lawrence Erlbaum Associates (pp. 355–67). Reproduced by permission of Taylor and Francis Group, LLC, a division of Informa plc.

1.  While a number of trauma, pretrauma, and posttrauma factors have been found to influence reactions to trauma experience (see Dalgleish, 2004), it is proposed that the narratives that individuals and groups offer act as the "final common pathways" to influence the levels of adjustment and distress.

2.  The burgeoning literature on the impact of trauma, especially the role of cognitive and affective processes, has highlighted what individuals have to do and not do, think and not think, to develop persistent distress and PTSD. As summarized in the following text, the key elements of "negative" thinking that contribute to both individuals' and groups' narratives will be examined. Like an ethologist who studies the detailed features and the flow of animal behavior, a "cognitive ethologist" offers a description of the thinking processes of individuals following trauma exposure. One can look upon such a cognitive descriptive account as offering a formula or algorithm on how to increase the likelihood that an individual or a group will develop persistent PTSD and related forms of distress (or what the psychiatric community calls *comorbid disorders*).

3.  Individuals and groups may use a variety of means to engage in resilience-building activities and to foster PTG. These activities may range from using spiritual rituals to employing social supports, from using distraction procedures of keeping busy to retelling their stories in the form of artistic expression or commemorative activities. It is proposed that these varied activities "work" or contribute to healing because they reduce the likelihood of individuals and groups engaging in "negative" counterproductive storytelling and accompanying stress-reducing behaviors. It is proposed that a key feature of resilience is the ability to *engage in non-negative thinking*.

4.  Finally, it is proposed that to go beyond the resilient process of adapting well in the face of adversity to the point of experiencing "growth," more is entailed than the power of non-negative thinking. To experience PTG, individuals and groups have to engage in such activities as benefit finding, establishing a future orientation, and constructing meaning and the commensurate accompanying behaviors (Table 10.1).

## The challenge

The study of the impact of trauma experience on individuals and groups is a remarkable story of courage and resilience. Several major reviewers have documented the resilience or the "ability to go on with life" after handling adversity (Bloom, 1990; Linley & Joseph, 2002, 2004; McMillen, 1999; Tedeschi & Calhoun, 2004b; Tedeschi et al., 1988). These authors observe that such resilience reflects the ability to:

1.  Show positive adaptation in spite of significant challenging life experiences.
2.  "Bend, but not break" or rebound from adversities.
3.  Learn to live with ongoing fears and uncertainty.

**TABLE 10.1** A constructive narrative model of posttraumatic reactions

1. Human beings are storytellers and account makers, especially following trauma experience.
2. The type of "stories" individuals and groups offer themselves and others acts as the "final common pathway," determining the level of distress *versus* degree of resilience.
3. Research indicates the specific features of the "negative" thinking and accompanying behaviors that lead to chronic persistent distress and PTSD.
4. Various individual and group "healing" activities work in large part because of their ability to have individuals and groups engage in the "power of non-negative thinking."
5. To move from resilience to the point of experiencing PTG, individuals and groups need to engage in such activities as benefit finding, establishing a future orientation, and constructing meaning, and the commensurate accompanying behaviors.

To document the role of resilience, they highlight that while exposure to traumatic events (Criterion A events according to the Diagnostic Statistical Manual for the diagnosis of PTSD) is quite common (approximately 60% in men and 50% in women), PTSD is quite low in general (approximately 5% in men and 10% in women). Moreover, they observe that up to 75% of people who are confronted with irrevocable loss do *not* show intense distress. Such resilience in the face of unimaginable loss was evident in the aftermath of the terrorist attacks on September 11, as documented by Schuster and Stein (2001) and Sheehy (2003). Nolen-Hoeksema and Davis (2004) observe that following almost any imaginable trauma, approximately 50% of those most directly affected report at least one positive life change or benefit that they link directly to their traumatic experience. But, not all individuals and groups in the aftermath of trauma exposure evidence such "resilience." A sizeable minority (approximately 20% to 25%) will evidence long-term persistent chronic PTSD, even to the point of attempting suicide (see Meichenbaum, in press). Even after treatment, one-third of clients continue to suffer PTSD. The challenging questions are what distinguished those who evidence resilience *versus* those who manifest chronic persistent clinical levels of distress, and what can be done to nurture and foster resilience?

The absence of an answer to the former question of the distinguishing differential processes has *not* inhibited health care providers from offering extensive advice on how to nurture resilience. Consistent with the notion that resilience can indeed be developed, nurtured, and taught, the American Psychological Association (APA) has created a Help Center (www.APAHelpCenter.org or call 1-800-964-2000) to foster resilience in response to terrorism and other stressful events. They have created educational materials for various specialty groups that enumerate "Ten Ways to Build Resilience." These guidelines include:

1. Make connections. (They even include a list of places to look for help.)
2. Avoid seeing crises as insurmountable problems.
3. Accept that change is part of living.

4.   Move toward goals, but stay flexible.
5.   Take decisive action.
6.   Look for opportunities for self-discovery.
7.   Nurture a positive view of yourself.
8.   Keep things in perspective. Learn from your past.
9.   Maintain a hopeful outlook.
10.  Take care of yourself.

Like good "storytellers" who use analogies and metaphors to make their points, the authors of the APA educational brochure "The Road to Resilience" encourage their readers to "think of resilience as similar to taking a raft down a river." Such journeys, like life, require plans, flexibility, perseverance, and help from trusted companions.

Why should such analogies and "storytelling" be helpful? A CNP of resilience helps to explicate the reasons why such "storytelling" and the accompanying array of advice-giving (that surely is informed and guided by research finding) work.

## What is a constructive narrative perspective?

People are storytellers. They offer accounts that are designed to make sense out of the world and their place in it. They construct narratives that include descriptions of behavioral events and their and others' reactions to those events. As Mair (1990) observed, "We live through stories."

The observation that people are account makers and construct narratives is not new. From the philosophical musings of Immanuel Kant to those of Jean-Paul Sartre, from the psychological writings of Wilhelm Wundt to those of George Kelly, there is a long tradition of the importance of storytelling or the construction of personal meanings. Common to this tradition is the view that individuals do *not* merely respond to events, but they respond to their interpretations of events. This constructivist viewpoint has both a historical and a current tradition. The simplest rendering of the constructive narrative perspective is the Buddhist observation:

> We are what we think. All that we are arises with our thoughts. With our thoughts ["stories"] we make the world. (Dhammapada)

In modern form, Howard (1991) observed:

> We are lived by the stories we tell. Beware of the stories you tell yourself (and one might add tell others), for you will surely be lived by them.

Thomas (2003) has characterized such narratives as a form of "inner conversations," in the tradition of the social psychologist George Herbert Mead, who highlighted the manner in which individuals carry on inner conversations with themselves. In this tradition, consider what happens to people's stories when really bad things (traumatic events) are experienced. Several researchers have observed that when such traumatic events occur, the narratives, beliefs, appraisal processes, attributions, and ruminations are each significantly impacted (see Brewin & Holmes, 2003; Dalgleish, 2004; Ehlers & Clark, 2000; Harvey, 2002; Harvey et al., 1990; Janoff-Bulman, 1992). Meichenbaum (1997b) has observed that people's ordinary language often proves inadequate to capture their posttraumatic experiences. Instead, such victims of trauma often become "poets" of sorts, using metaphors to describe what they have experienced and the accompanying implications they draw about themselves, the world, and the future. Such metaphorical descriptions are *not* mere idle patterns of speech, but they can act as templates that color the ways events are appraised and the coping options that may be considered.

"I am a prisoner of the past."
"I am soiled goods."
"I am on sentry duty all the time."
"I stuff my feelings."

Consider the ongoing impact of telling themselves and others that they are "prisoners of the past" or that they are "soiled goods." The metaphors that are offered and the language individuals use to fashion their narratives have important implications for how they appraise events and how they cope with the sequelae of trauma exposure.

But it is *not* only the nature of the metaphors that are incorporated into one's narratives, but a variety of other features that contribute to negative counterproductive thinking. Table 10.2, which was gleaned from the literature on cognitive processes in chronic PTSD, highlights the features of the self-narrative that contribute to the persistence of the stress disorder and related clinical problems. These are the characteristics of thinking that lead survivors toward "being stuck" and experiencing higher levels of distress. Beyond the initial shock, disbelief, numbness, sadness, depression, fears, rage, guilt, and the panoply of intense emotions that follow trauma exposure, comes an appreciation that an individual's way of understanding the world and his or her place in it has been "shattered." As Janoff-Bulman (1992) aptly describes, trauma exposure violates one's implicit beliefs and challenges one's assumptions that the world is safe, controllable, and predictable, and that others are benevolent and can be trusted.

An examination of Table 10.2 highlights the features of a narrative that individuals and groups need to offer themselves and others to maintain persistent chronic distress following trauma exposure. The ingredients for the development of chronic PTSD include:

1.  Engaging in self-focused cognitions that have a "victim" theme and that undermine ("shatter") core beliefs.
2.  Supplementing the "victim" theme of one's narrative with a set of specific cognitive behaviors consisting of remaining hyper-vigilant, ruminating,

**TABLE 10.2** Characteristics of the narrative associated with persistent and higher levels of distress following trauma exposure

| Thinking pattern | Prototypic examples |
|---|---|
| Engage in contra-factual thinking[1] | "If only I had … this would not have happened." "Only if …" "I never thought this would happen to me." |
| Self-blaming and guilt-engendering thinking (blameworthy, ashamed, humiliated, full of regrets)[2] | "I should have …" "I failed to protect her." "I berate myself before others do." |
| Focus on blaming others[3] | "I have been betrayed." "I won't rest until there is justice." |
| Espouse culturally based blame attributions[4] | "People will wonder what kind of family we are because we allowed this to happen." "Because I was raped, people will think that (Black, White) women are loose." "They will think I am too weak to cope." |
| Engage in self-focused thinking[5] (Viewing self as a "victim," mentally defeated and permanently changed) | "I feel trapped." "I have no control over anything." "I am brain dead." "Dead man walking." "My body (reputation) is ruined forever." |
| Altered beliefs[6] (World is unsafe, future unpredictable, people are untrustworthy) | "No place is safe." "I can't trust my instincts (judgment) any longer." "You can't trust anyone." |
| Be hyper-vigilant[7] (Perceive ongoing threat and impending doom: distinctions between then and there and here and now are blurred) | "I live in fear." "I am on every day. Danger is everywhere." "I am on the lookout all the time." "I am a walking target." "I can't let the kids out of my sight." |
| Think negatively about the past, present, and future[8] (Fail to retrieve specific "positive" memories) Ruminate and brood about the past and focus on what has been lost[9] (Continually pine for the past) | "It will never be over." "My life is destroyed." "Time is my enemy." "I just wish life would go back to the way it was." "I can't rest until I get even." "I'll never get over it." |
| Ruminate about "near miss" experiences[10] | "It could have been us." "You know how close we were to being hurt?" "It percolates, over and over. There are reminders everywhere." "My thoughts are like an overcrowded train that jumps from track to track." |

**TABLE 10.2** (Continued)

| Thinking pattern | Prototypic examples |
| --- | --- |
| Dwell on negative implications of reactions[11] | "If I react like that, it must mean that I am going mad." "This is not normal. I can't control my emotions and this means …" |
| Engage in deliberate avoidant and safety behaviors, even if unwarranted[12] (Cognitive and behavioral avoidance that leads to being "stuck" and disengaging and giving up) | "I can't allow myself to think about it." "I delay seeking help." "I am not worthy of help." "I can't share this with anyone. No one would understand…" "I can't allow myself to have a good time." "If I deprive myself, then…" "I try and keep busy so I don't think about this." |
| Feel helpless, hopeless, demoralized, and feel victimized by one's thoughts, feelings, circumstances[13] | "These thoughts just keep coming." "I get gripped by my feelings of depression and fear." "I don't think I can stand the pain anymore." |
| Engage in upward social comparison[14] | "How come she is doing so well and she went through less?" "Others will see that I am a victim." "Why do I have to have problems other people don't have?" |
| Continually and extensively search for meaning, but fail to find satisfactory resolution[15] | "What did I do to deserve this?" "Why me?" "Why now?" "I lost faith in God." |

1 Davis & Lehman, 1995; Greenberg, 1995
2 Kubany & Manke, 1995; Lee et al., 2001
3 Janoff-Bulman, & Berger, 2002
4 Neville et al., 2004
5 Ehlers & Clark, 2000
6 Janoff-Bulman, 1999
7 Ehlers et al., 2002; Foa et al., 1989
8 Nolen-Hoeksema & Davis, 2004; Treyner et al., 2003
9 Holman & Silver, 1998: Nolen-Hoeksema & Davis, 2004; Wortman & Silver, 1987
10 Meichenbaum, 1997b
11 Ehlers et al., 2002
12 Ehlers & Clark, 2000; Ehlers & Steil, 1995
13 Meichenbaum, in press
14 McAdams et al., 2001
15 Silver et al., 1983; Tait & Silver, 1989

brooding, engaging in both contra-factual thinking and upward social comparisons, self-blame and blaming others, with the resultant guilt-engendering feelings and thoughts.
3. Viewing the implications of one's reactions to trauma as negative, not only for now but also in the future, while continuing to persistently pine for the past.
4. Searching for "meaning," as evident in continually asking "why" questions, for which there are no satisfactory answers, resulting in the absence of any resolution or closure.
5. Engaging in avoidant and safety behaviors, delaying help-seeking behaviors and failing to share one's trauma experiences with others ("keeping it a secret").

Ehlers and Clark (2000) have highlighted that the failure to share the "trauma story" with supportive others results in the individual's or group's story being fragmented, disjointed, disconnected from the past, and being poorly elaborated and disorganized. Such traumatic memories are subject to "perceptual priming" with sensory and motor aspects being highlighted in which the worst moments of the trauma stand out. Unshared traumatic stories are usually poorly integrated into existing autobiographical memories. The use of avoidant and safety behaviors to handle the impact of such storytelling may put individuals at risk for further revictimization.

## A constructive narrative perspective of resilience

The CNP advocates that the way individuals tell themselves and others stories will determine the nature of their future vulnerability, their coping efforts, and the levels of adjustment and resilience that follow exposure to trauma experience. Two important caveats need to be highlighted about these propositions. First, this is a dynamic interactive process. How successful an individual's coping efforts prove to be will influence the nature of his or her storytelling that will, in turn, influence resilience-enhancing efforts.

A good example of this comes from the treatment literature on exposure-based interventions with rape victims. Foa, Molner, and Cashman (1995) analyzed the narratives of rape victims at the beginning and at the end of successful therapy. The exposure-based treatment involved providing the client with a safe environment to tell and retell her victimization story to "emotionally process" the trauma and reduce the negative affect attached to the memories and residual triggers. In this way, the clients learned to "segment" the trauma story into a beginning, middle, and end, and now also a future. The opportunity to tell and retell such accounts helps clients better appreciate what they did to survive and provides them with data that offering such accounts of the "worst moments" of the victimization experiences does *not* result in their "falling apart." Such guided storytelling provides disconfirmatory information and helps clients take back control and experience a sense of mastery.

As the clients began to improve and assimilate and integrate the victimization experiences into the flow of their autobiographical memories, Foa *et al.* (1995) observed that the nature of the narratives ("stories") they told also changed. The improved clients' narratives evidenced a decrease in unfinished thoughts and repetitions and a greater sense of personal agency. Moreover, such narrative changes correlated with symptom improvement in the form of trauma-related anxiety. Van Minnen, Wessel, Dijkstra, and Roelefs (2002) replicated these findings of narrative changes that accompany symptom reduction. Thus, the changes in adjustment (symptom reduction and reduction of avoidance [safety] behaviors) influenced the changes in the clients' narratives, which in turn enabled further coping efforts. This, in turn, influenced the nature of the narratives of not only the clients, but also how supportive others can provide a way to craft narratives about the changes that have occurred. As Adler (1997, p. 30) observed: "When we are able to formulate the right story, and it is heard by the right listener, we are apt to deal more effectively with the experience."

Gail Sheehy (2003, p. 32), in her moving account of one town's passage from trauma to hope, following the World Trade Center terrorist attacks observed:

> The best way to build bridges from the land of the dead to the land of the living is to tell and retell the stories of those who are gone; that guarantees a measure of immortality. The key is to shift the emphasis from the way the victim died to the way he or she lived.
>
> *(Sheehy, 2003, p. 392)*

It is proposed that it is *not* only the opportunity to tell one's story, but how one changes the nature of the storytelling over time, that influences the adjustment process.

The *second caveat* when considering the CNP of resilience is the need to recognize the *gradual transformation of the individual's and group's narratives.* Individuals who manifest resilience may continue to evidence *co-concurrent* negative and positive features in their narratives, reflecting both bouts of pining for the past and transforming their mixed emotions into behavioral enactments and "missions" for the future.

With these two caveats concerning a dynamic interactive process and a gradual transformation in mind, we can reconsider why the "10 Ways to Build Resilience" offered by the knowledgeable authors of the APA brochures may work. The suggestions offered fall into the "do" and "not do" categories. Readers are explicitly guided to change their narratives (e.g., avoid seeing the crisis as insurmountable; keep things in perspective; look for opportunities for self-discovery; maintain a hopeful outlook; accept that change is part of living) or to engage in activities that will provide the conditions for changes to one's narrative and accompanying coping efforts (e.g., move toward goals; take decisive action; make corrections; take care of yourself). Each of these suggestions is designed to reduce the likelihood of negative thinking. The "power of such non-negative thinking" should be distinguished from the limited efficacy and misguided advocacy of "the power of positive thinking," as discussed by Held (2002); Meichenbaum (1997a); Meichenbaum and Fitzpatrick (1993); Taylor (1989); and Wortman (2004). The negative self-punitive elements of one's narratives and the negative elements of social interactions are more strongly related to mental health than are positive elements.

## A constructive narrative perspective of posttraumatic growth

The experience of PTG is more than the ability to engage in non-negative thinking and the coping activities that help to nurture and maintain a constructive narrative. Posttraumatic growth is the experience of *positive change* that occurs as a result of a struggle with highly challenging life crises. As enumerated in Table 10.3, the kind of thinking and accompanying behaviors that lead toward "growth" include:

1.  Seeking, finding, reminding, and constructing benefits for oneself and others.
2.  Establishing and maintaining a future orientation with altered priorities.
3.  Constructing meaning, a coherent narrative, and engaging in special activities or "missions" that transform loss into something good that will come out of it.

To illustrate resilience and "growth," I will conclude my story with a personal anecdote. Consider the case of Lynn and Michael Aptman whose daughter Melissa was murdered in 1995 during a carjacking. She was about to graduate from Washington University in St. Louis. How does one survive such a devastating tragedy? As Dr. Aptman, a neurologist (2002, p. 286), observed:

> I have tried not to be too harsh on myself ... I have survived by taking life one day at a time ... I cherish Melissa's memory even more now ... I have great joy in being father to my two surviving children ... As a result of Melissa's death I am more sensitive in working with difficult cases in the ICU ... Sad as it may sound, I have become a better person as a result of the death of my child ... I believe that through prayer and good deeds one can bind up the soul of a loved one as a source of eternal blessing ... I find that meditation helps cleanse my soul and allows me to feel closer to Melissa ... Every day since Melissa's death I have been the fortunate recipient of acts of kindness ... I believe we are defined by how we respond to that kind of pain.

The Aptmans responded to their pain by establishing an institute in Melissa's name to prevent violence and to treat victims of violence (see www.melissainstitute.org). I am privileged and honored to be the Research Director of the Melissa Institute and help a family transform their pain to something good. As it says on Melissa's gravestone, "Her memory lives in each of our hearts ... Together we must make a difference."

**TABLE 10.3** Kinds of thinking and behaviors that lead survivors toward "growth"

| Thinking pattern | Prototypic examples |
|---|---|
| Benefit seeking, finding, and reminding – SELF[1] | "I am wiser (stronger) as a result of this experience." "I am better prepared for whatever comes along." "I am less afraid of change." "I never knew I could get along on my own." "I am better now at helping others." |
| Benefit seeking, finding, and reminding – OTHERS[2] | "This brought us all together." "I learned I am my brother's keeper." "I learned not to immerse myself in other people's pain." |
| Engage in downward comparison[3] | "I think about others and how it could have been worse." "I recognize that I need to accept help." "My view of what is important in life has changed." |
| Establish a future orientation[4] | "My view of what is important in life has changed." "I see new possibilities and goals to work on." "I am now able to focus on the fact that it happened and not on how it happened." |
| Constructing meaning[3] | "We survived and we have a chance to live and we're choosing life." "I am no longer willing to be defined by my victimization." "I survived for a purpose. I accept that responsibility. I owe it to those who perished to tell their stories (honor their memory, share with others, prevent this from happening again)." "I moved from being a victim to becoming a survivor and even a thriver." "I can make a gift of my pain and loss to others." "I now know God." |

1 Affleck & Tennen, 1996; Linley & Joseph, 2002, 2004
2 McMillen, 2004; McMillen et al., 1995
3 Nolen-Hoeksema & Larson, 1999; Monk et al., 1997
4 Pals & McAdams, 2004; Tedeschi & Calhoun, 2004b
5 Frazier et al., 2001; Neimeyer, 2001; Pargament et al., 2000; Silver et al., 1983; Tait & Silver, 1989; Wortman et al., 1997

# Epilogue

The present analysis of the role that cognitive and affective factors play in the persistence of stress disorders and in the processes of resilience and PTG does *not* preclude the role of other sources of influence. For example, available evidence suggests that exposure to trauma often brings about permanent neurobiological changes that can cause persistent hyper-arousal, resulting in PTSD symptoms, such as difficulty concentrating and sleep problems. Similarly, research has also begun to implicate the neurochemical profile that characterizes resilience (i.e., the neurotransmitters, neuropeptides, and hormones that are known to be altered by exposure to traumatic stressors) (Southwick et al., 2003).

Perhaps, some day we will be able to identify a neurobiological resilience factor that may be tied to genetic vulnerability (see True *et al.*, 1993). For now, however, the present analysis argues that another important area to search for vulnerability factors is in the area of cognitive processes. The ways in which individuals who have experienced trauma tell "stories" or construct narratives to themselves and to others plays a critical role and is clearly worthy of further investigation.

## References

Adler, H. M. (1997). The history of the present illness in treatment: who is listening and why does it matter. *Journal of the American Board of Family Practice*, 10, 28–35.

Affleck, G., & Tennen, H. (1996). Constructing benefits from adversity: adaptational significance and dispositional underpinnings. *Journal of Personality*, 64, 899–922.

Aptman, M. (2992). Personal history: one in a million? *Neurology*, 59, 784–6.

Bloom, S. (1990). By the crowd they have been broken, by the crowd they shall be healed: the social transformation of traumas. In R. G. Tedeschi, C. L. Park, & L. G. Calhoun (eds), *Posttraumatic Growth: Positive Changes in the Aftermath of Crisis* (pp. 179–213). Mahwah, NJ: Lawrence Erlbaum Associates.

Brewin, C. R., & Holmes, E. A. (2003). Psychological theories of posttraumatic stress disorder. *Clinical Psychology Review*, 3, 339–76.

Dalgleish, T. (2004). Cognitive approaches to posttraumatic stress disorder: the evolution of multirepresentational theorizing. *Psychological Bulletin*, 130, 228–60.

Dalgleish, T. (1999). Counterfactual thinking and coping with traumatic life events. In N. J. Roese & J. M. Olson (eds), *What Might Have Been: The Social Psychology of Contrafactual Thinking* (pp. 353–74). Mahwah, NJ: Lawrence Erlbaum Associates.

Davis, C. G. & Lehman, D. R. (1995). Counterfactual thinking and coping with traumatic life events. In N. J. Roese & J. M. Olsen (eds), *What Have Been: The Social Psychology of Counterfactual Thinking* (pp. 353–74). Mahwah, NJ: Lawrence Erlbaum Associates.

Ehlers, A., & Clark, D. M. (2000). A cognitive model of posttraumatic stress disorder. *Behaviour Research and Therapy*, 38, 319–45.

Ehlers, A., Hackman, A., Steil, R., Clohessy, S., Wenninger, K., & Winter, H. (2002). The nature of intrusive memories after trauma: the warning signal hypothesis. *Behaviour Research and Therapy*, 40, 995–1002.

Ehlers, A., & Steil, R. (1995). Maintenance of intrusive memories in posttraumatic stress disorder: a cognitive approach. *Behavioural and Cognitive Psychotherapy*, 23, 217–49.

Foa, E. B., Molnar, C., & Cashman, L. (1995). Change in rape narratives during exposure therapy for PTSD. *Journal of Traumatic Stress*, 8, 675–90.

Foa, E. B., Steketee, G., & Olasov-Rothbaum, B. (1989). Behavioral/cognitive conceptualization of posttraumatic stress disorder. *Behavior Therapy*, 20, 155–76.

Frazier, P., Conlon, A., & Glaser, T. (2001). Positive and negative life changes following sexual assault. *Journal of Consulting and Clinical Psychology*, 69, 1048–55.

Greenberg, M. A. (1995). Cognitive processing of traumas: the role of intrusive thoughts and reappraisals. *Journal of Applied Social Psychology*, 25, 1262–96.

Harvey, J. H. (2002). *Perspectives on Loss and Trauma: Assaults on the Self.* Thousand Oaks, CA: Sage.

Harvey, J. H., Weber, A. L., & Orbuch, T. L. (1990). *Interpersonal Accounts: A Social Psychological Perspective.* Oxford: Basel Blackwell.

Held, B. S. (2002). The tyranny of the positive attitude in the U.S.: observation and speculation. *Journal of Clinical Psychology*, 58, 965–92.

Holman, E. A., & Silver, R. C. (1998). Getting "stuck" in the past: temporal orientation and coping with trauma. *Journal of Personality and Social Psychology*, 74, 1146–63.

Howard, G. S. (1991). Cultural tales: a narrative approach to thinking, cross-cultural psychology, and psychotherapy. *American Psychologist*, 46, 187–97.

Janoff, J. B., & Gunn, L. (1988). Coping with disease, crime and accidents: the role of self-blame attributions. In L. Y. Abramson (ed.), *Social Cognitions and Clinical Psychology: A Synthesis*. New York: Guilford.

Janoff-Bulman, R. (1992). *Shattered Assumptions: Toward a New Psychology of Trauma*. New York: Free Press.

Janoff-Bulman, R. (1999). Rebuilding shattered assumptions after traumatic events: coping processes and outcomes. In C. R. Snyder (Ed.), *Coping: The Psychology of What Works*. New York: Oxford University Press.

Janoff-Bulman, R., & Berger, A. (2002). The other side of trauma: toward a psychology of appreciation. In J. H. Harvey & E. D. Miller (eds), *Loss and Trauma: General and Close Relationship Perspectives* (pp. 29–44). Philadelphia: Brunner-Routledge.

Joseph, S., Williams, R., & Yule, W. (1997). *Understanding Posttraumatic Stress: A Psychosocial Perspective and Its Treatment*. Chichester: Wiley.

Kubany, E. C., & Manke, F. P. (1995). Cognitive therapy for trauma-related guilt: conceptual bases and treatment outlines. *Cognitive and Behavioral Practice*, 7, 27–62.

Lee, D. A., Scragg, P., & Turner, S. (2001). The role of shame and guilt in traumatic events: a clinical model of shame-based and guilt-based PTSD. *British Journal of Medical Psychology*, 74, 451–66.

Linley, P. A., & Joseph, S. (2002). Posttraumatic growth. *Counseling and Psychotherapy Journal*, 13, 14–17.

Linley, P. A., & Joseph. S. (2004). Positive change following trauma and adversity: a review. *Journal of Traumatic Stress*, 17, 11–21.

Mair, M. (1990). Telling psychological tales. *International Journal of Construct Psychology*, 3, 121–35.

Martin, L. L., & Tesser, A. (1996). Clarifying our thoughts. In R. S. Wyer (ed.), *Ruminative Thoughts: Advances in Social Cognition* (Vol. 9, pp. 189–209). Mahwah, NJ: Lawrence Erlbaum Associates.

McAdams, D. P., Reynolds, J., Lewis, M., Patten, A. H., & Bowan, P. J. (2001). When bad things turn good and good things turn bad. *Personality and Social Psychology Bulletin*, 27, 474–85.

McMillen, J. C. (1999). Better for it: how people benefit from adversity. *Social Work*, 44, 455–68.

McMillen, J. C. (2004). Posttraumatic growth: what is it all about? *Psychological Inquiry*, 15, 48–52.

McMillen, J. C., Smith, E. M., & Fisher, R. H. (1997). Perceived benefit and mental health after three types of disaster. *Journal of Consulting and Clinical Psychology*, 63, 1037–43.

McMillen, J. C., Zuravin, S., & Rideout, G. (1995). Perceived benefit from child abuse. *Journal of Consulting and Clinical Psychology*, 63, 1037–43.

Meichenbaum, D. (1997a). *Cognitive Behavior Modification: An Integrative Approach*. New York: Plenum Press.

Meichenbaum, D. (1997b). *Treating Individuals with Posttraumatic Stress Disorder*. Clearwater, FL: Institute Press.

Meichenbaum, D. (2000). Treating patients with PTSD: A constructive narrative approach. *NC-PTSD Clinical Quarterly*, 9, 55–9.

Meichenbaum D. (in press). Trauma and suicide. In T. Ellis (ed.), *Cognition and Suicide: Theory, Research and Practice.* Washington, DC: American Psychological Association.

Meichenbaum, D., & Fitzpatrick, D. (1993). A constructive narrative perspective in stress and coping. In L. Goldberger & S. Breznitz (eds), *Handbook of Stress: Theoretical and Clinical Aspects.* New York: Free Press.

Monk, G., Winslade, J., Crocket, E., & Epton, D. (eds) (1997). *Narrative Therapy in Practice.* San Francisco: Jossey-Bass.

Neimeyer, R. A. (2001). *Meaning Reconstruction and the Experience of Loss.* Washington, DC: American Psychological Association.

Neville, H. A., Heppner, M. J., Oh, E., Spanierman, L. B., & Clark, M. (2004). General and culturally specific factors influencing Black and White rape survivors' self-esteem. *Psychology of Women Quarterly*, 28, 83–94.

Nolen-Hoeksema, S., & Davis, C. G. (2004). Theoretical and methodological issues in the assessment and interpretation of posttraumatic growth. *Psychological Inquiry*, 15, 60–64.

Nolen-Hoeksema, S., & Larson, J. (1999). *Coping with Loss.* Mahwah, NJ: Lawrence Erlbaum Associates.

Pals, J. L., & McAdams, D. P. (2004). The transformed self: a narrative understanding of posttraumatic growth. *Psychological Inquiry*, 15, 65–9.

Pargament, K. I., Koenig, H. G., & Perez, L. M. (2000). The many methods of religious coping: developmental and initial validation of the RCOPE. *Journal of Clinical Psychology*, 56, 519–43.

Park, C. L. (1998). Stress-related growth and thriving through coping: the roles of personality and cognitive processes. *Journal of Social Issues*, 54, 267–77.

Schuster, M., & Stein, S. (2001). A national survey of stress reactions after the September 11, 2001 terrorist attack. *New England Journal of Medicine*, 345, 1507–12.

Sheehy, G. (2003). *Middletown, America: One Town's Passage from Trauma to Hope.* New York: Random House

Silver, R. C., Boon, S., & Stones, M. H. (1983). Searching for meaning in misfortune. *Journal of Social Issues*, 39, 81–102.

Southwick, S. M., Morgan, C. A., Vythilingam, M., Krystal, J. H., & Charney, D. S. (2003). Emerging neurobiological factors in stress resilience. *PTSD Research Quarterly*, 14, 1–3.

Tait, R., & Silver, R. C. (1989). Coming to terms with major negative life events. In J. S. Uleman & J. A. Bargh (eds). *Unintended Thought* (pp. 351–82). New York: Guilford.

Taylor, S. E. (1989). *Positive Distortions: Creative Self-Deception and the Healthy Mind.* New York: Basic Books.

Taylor, S. E., Kemeny, M. E., Reed, G. M., Bower, J. E., & Gruenewald, T. L. (2000). Psychological resources, positive illusions and health. *American Psychologist*, 58, 99–109.

Tedeschi, R. G. (1999). Violence transformed: Posttraumatic growth in survivors and their societies. *Aggression and Violent Behavior*, 4, 319–41.

Tedeschi, R. G., & Calhoun, L. G. (1996). The posttraumatic growth inventory: measuring the positive direction of trauma. *Journal of Traumatic Stress*, 9, 455–71.

Tedeschi, R. G., & Calhoun, L. G. (2004a). *Helping the Bereaved Parent: A Clinician's Guide.* New York: Brunner-Routledge.

Tedeschi, R. G., & Calhoun, L. G. (2004b). Posttraumatic growth: conceptual foundations and empirical evidence. *Psychological Inquiry*, 15, 1–18.

Tedeschi, R. G., Park, C. L., & Calhoun, L. G. (eds) (1988). *Posttraumatic Growth: Positive Changes in the Aftermath of Crisis.* Mahwah, NJ: Lawrence Erlbaum Associates.

Thomas, P. M. (2003). Protection, dissociation and internal roles: modeling and treating effects of child abuse. *Review of General Psychology*, 7, 364–80.

Thompson, N. (ed.) (2002), *Loss and Grief: A Guide for Human Service Practitioners*. New York: Palgrave.

Treynor, W., Gonzalez, R., & Nolen-Hoeksema, S. (2003). Rumination reconsidered: a psychometric analysis. *Cognitive Therapy and Research*, 27, 247–59.

True, W. R., Rice, J., Eisen, S. A., Heath, A. C., Goldberg, L., Lyons, M. J., *et al.* (1993). A twin study of genetic and environmental contributions to liability for posttraumatic stress symptoms. *Archives of General Psychiatry*, 50, 257–64.

Van Minnen, A., Wessel, I., Dijkstra, T., & Roelefs, K. (2002). Changes on PTSD patients' narratives during prolonged exposure therapy: a replication and extension. *Journal of Traumatic Stress*, 15, 255–8.

Wortman, C. B. (2004). Posttraumatic growth: progress and problem. *Psychological Inquiry*, 15, 81–90.

Wortman, C. B., Battle, E. S., & Lemkau, J. P. (1997). Coming to terms with sudden traumatic death of a spouse or a child. In R. C. Davis & A. J. Lurigio (eds), *Victims of Crime* (pp. 108–33). Thousand Oaks. CA: Sage.

Wortman, C. B., & Silver, R. C. (1987). Coping with irrevocable loss. In G. R. Van den Bos & B. K. Bryant (eds), *Cataclysms, Crisis and Catastrophes*. Washington, DC: American Psychological Association.

Wortman, C. B., & Silver, R. C. (2001). The myths of coping with loss revisited. In M. S. Stroebe, R. O. Hannsson, W. Stroebe, & H. Schut (eds), *Handbook of Bereavement Research: Consequences, Coping and Care* (pp. 405–29). Washington, DC: American Psychological Association.

# 11

# BOLSTERING RESILIENCE

## Benefiting from lessons learned

*Donald Meichenbaum*

## Prologue

A central issue is how to provide both prevention and treatment interventions designed to bolster resilience and build on existing and potential strengths in diverse, victimized, and high-risk groups of children, youth, families, and communities. What can be done at the primary prevention level, which focuses on the universal implementation of intervention for all children (for example, youth violence prevention, gun safety, and family strengthening interventions may reduce the risk of all children's exposure to psychological trauma and victimization)? What can be done at the secondary prevention level, which targets children and youth already at risk (for example, children who are living in high-risk poverty environments or high-risk situations with exposure to repeated natural disasters or ongoing violence)? What can be done at the tertiary level, which provides interventions for selected populations of children and youth who present with persistent needs and challenging behaviors, and who require comprehensive wrap-around services (for example, incarcerated youth who have a history of neglect and victimization, or children and youth who present with the psychiatric sequelae of sexual and physical abuse)?

The answers to these challenging questions should be informed by research on the developmental nature of risk and resilience, and studies that translate this research literature's findings into demonstrably effective methods of prevention and treatment. What are the lessons learned that should guide the development and evaluation of interventions addressing childhood victimization?

– Meichenbaum, D. (2009). Bolstering resilience: benefiting from lessons learned. In D. Brom, R. Pat-Horenczyk, and J. D. Ford (eds), *Treating Traumatized Children: Risk, Resilience and Recovery*. London: Routledge (pp. 183–91). Reproduced by permission of Taylor and Francis Group, LLC, a division of Informa plc.

## Lessons to be learned about resilience

First, there is a need to reduce or remove exposure to multiple risk factors, and a need to address the cumulative complex impact of multiple victimization experiences.

It is estimated that 25 percent of American youth experience serious traumatic events by their sixteenth birthday (Costello *et al.* 2002). Children and youth frequently experience different types of victimization on multiple occasions, rather than being exposed to singular experiences. There is an overlap of different types of victimization experiences, such as living in high-risk crime-saturated poverty areas, witnessing violence at home, or experiencing neglect and abuse. Most instances of exposure to violence occur within a youth's immediate environment (home, school, neighborhood) and are most often perpetrated by a family member or acquaintance (Finkelhor *et al.* 2005; Garbarino *et al.* 1992).

Second, there is a need to systematically assess for the cumulative exposure to adverse childhood experiences (Edwards *et al.* 2005; Finkelhor *et al.* 2005). Moreover, interventions to nurture resilience need to target multiple systems, including child welfare, children's mental health, public health, schools, social services, and juvenile justice.

Research indicates that it is the total number of risk factors present that is more important than the specificity of risk factors that impact developmental outcomes. Risk factors often co-occur and pile up over time. For example, Sameroff *et al.* (1992) studied the influence of social and family risk factors on the stability of intelligence from preschool to adolescence. They found that the pattern of risk was less important than the total amount of risk present in the child's life.

Third, there is a need to address explicitly the academic needs of victimized children, and work on enhancing their "school connectedness" or feeling of membership in the school they attend, by the use of mentoring programs (Dubois and Karcher 2005). Exposure to chronic traumatic stressors in the developing years can cause changes that impact memory and cognition. More specifically, exposure to violence can reduce the youth's ability to focus attention, organize and process information, as well as contribute to decreased IQ and reading ability, lower academic performance, increased days of school absence and decreased rates of high school graduation. The rates of suspensions and expulsions from school are also associated with the students' exposure to community violence (Wong *et al.* 2007). Moreover, low-income and ethnic minority youth disproportionately experience higher rates of violence with the consequent academic sequelae for which they usually do not receive intervention (Delaney-Black *et al.* 2002; Grogger 1997; Hurt *et al.* 2001). Violence exposure is associated with higher rates of school suspensions and expulsions and lower rates of attendance.

Fourth, there is a need to provide traumatized children with skills training to compensate for self-regulatory deficits, and with "metacognitive prosthetic devices" to compensate for the neurobiological deficits that follow chronic traumatic experiences (Ford 2005). Exposure to recurrent or prolonged trauma, especially if the onset occurs during early childhood, can cause neurobiological changes such as alterations in the volume and activity levels of major brain structures, such as the corpus callosum and the limbic system; impairment of the left hemisphere cortical functioning; altered hypothalamic–pituitary axis functioning and increased hypersensitivity to cortisol levels; and increased sympathetic nervous system activity (De Bellis 2002).

Such bodily changes can result in exaggerated startle responses, PTSD, a compromised immune system, increased vulnerability to depression and a failure to develop self-regulatory functions, especially in the development of language, attentional and memory capabilities (Curtis and Cicchetti 2003; De Bellis 2002; De Bellis *et al.* 1999; Fletcher 1996; Streech-Fisher and Van der Kolk 2000).

Metacognitive supports may include the use of advanced organizers, memory prompts, self-instructional training, and other forms of cognitive-behavioral interventions (described on www.teachsafeschools.org). In addition, there is a need to reduce high-risk behaviors that can lead to revictimization, such as substance abuse, aggressive behaviors, sensation-seeking behaviors, and sexual acting-out behaviors (Alvord and Grados 2005; Grotberg 2003).

Fifth, helpers need to make special efforts to develop and monitor a collaborative therapeutic alliance with traumatized youth and address behaviors that interfere with therapy (Bertolino 2003; Miller *et al.* 2007). Trauma exposure can have a negative impact on the development of attachment behaviors. For example, abused teenage girls are more likely to hold in their feelings and have extreme emotional reactions. They have fewer adaptive coping strategies and have problems handling strong emotions, particularly anger. They have limited expectations that others can be of help. They show deficits in the ability to self-soothe and modulate negative emotions (Berman *et al.* 1996; Haggerty *et al.* 1996; Kendler *et al.* 2000). As Masten and Reed (2002, p. 95) observe:

> The best documented asset of resilience is a strong bond to a competent caring adult, which need not be a parent. For children who do not have such an adult involved in their lives, it is the first order of business. Children also need opportunities to experience success at all ages.

Sixth, there is a need to incorporate into resilience-bolstering interventions the attributes and circumstances that can contribute to people's abilities to cope effectively in the face of adversities and difficulties. Not all children and youth who are exposed to traumatic events develop behavioral and mental health problems. In fact, resilience appears to be the general rule of adaptation. This conclusion holds whether the children who are studied have experienced premature birth, physical illness or surgery, maltreatment (abuse or neglect), are the offspring of mentally ill, alcoholic, or criminally involved parents, are exposed to marital discord, domestic violence, poverty, or the trauma of war or natural disasters (DeAngelis 2007;

Masten 2001, 2004; Masten and Gewirtz 2006). As Bernard (1995) observes, between half and two-thirds of children living in such extreme circumstances grow up and "overcome the odds," going on to achieve successful and well-adjusted lives.

The Search Institute (www.Search-Institute.org) has enumerated some forty developmental assets that are the building blocks of positive youth development. Interventions should nurture these assets, some of which are listed here:

- A commitment to learning, a motivation to do well in school, feeling connected to school, participating in school activities, completing homework, reading for pleasure.
- Positive values and a prosocial attitude of being empathic, understanding, honest, and responsible, and practicing self-restraint with regard to addictive substances and sexual activity.
- Social competence, as reflected in the ability to resolve conflicts peacefully, resist negative peer pressure and make friends.
- Positive identity, which includes assets such as having high self-esteem, a sense of purpose in life, and plans for the future.

Resilience is not a trait that a child is born with or automatically keeps once it is achieved. Resilience is a complex interactive process that entails characteristics of the child, the family, extra-familial relationships, and school and community factors.

Seventh, when considering the features of so-called resilient children, it is important to keep in mind that children may be resilient in one domain of their lives, but not in other areas (e.g. academic, social, self-regulating behaviors). As Zimmerman and Arunkumar (1994) observe:

> Resilience is not a universal construct that applies to all life domains ... [children] may be resilient to specific risk conditions, but quite vulnerable to others ... [Resilience] is a multidimensional phenomenon that is context specific and involves developmental changes. (p. 4)

Resilience should be viewed as being 'fluid over time'. The relative importance of risk and protective factors changes at various stages of life. A child who may be resilient at one developmental stage may not necessarily be resilient at the next one. Developmental transition points at school and during puberty are particularly sensitive times for the impact of traumas. Protective efforts at bolstering resilience should be sensitive to these developmentally vulnerable periods.

Eighth, the factors that influence resilience differ for males and females and interventions need to be gender-sensitive. Protective factors differ across gender, race, and culture. For instance, girls tend to bolster their resilience by building strong, caring relationships, while boys are more likely to build resilience by learning active problem-solving (Bernard 1995). Further evidence that resilience may have gender differences comes from the longitudinal research by Werner and Smith (1992), who found that scholastic competence at age ten was more strongly associated with successful transition to adult responsibilities for men than for women. In contrast, factors such as high self-esteem, self-efficacy, and a sense of personal control were more predictive of successful adaptation among the women than the men. In the stress domain, males were more vulnerable to separation and loss of caregivers in the first decade of life, while girls were more vulnerable to family discord and loss in the second decade of life.

Another source of variability to be considered in resilience-based interventions is the cultural background. For instance, Kataoka *et al.* (2006) provide a description of how a culturally sensitive faith-based community intervention can be used to bolster the resilience of children who have been exposed to neighborhood violence. They combined an evidence-based intervention (Cognitive-Behavioral Intervention for Trauma in Schools – CBITS) with spirituality, as reflected in the use of the religious coping strategies of prayer, religious relaxation imagery, and local faith-based healers. As one mother commented, "My boy was very afraid and from that day he was terrorized. He wouldn't go outside. I remember at night he would pray and ask Jesus to give him comfort" (Kataoka *et al.* 2006, p. 90). Nonetheless, faith and spirituality operate as a stronger protective factor in some cultures more than in others.

Ninth, it is important for mental health care providers to build upon the specific positive behaviors and coping techniques that individuals already use to deal with suffering and disability, and capitalize on, and nurture, their innate self-healing capacities. Health care providers can aid survivors in enhancing their coping skills by pointing out techniques, already in place that they have utilized in the recovery process.

There are multiple pathways to resilience. Resilient children and youth possess multiple skills in varying degrees that help them cope with adversities. These response skills can be strengthened, as well as learned. Among other skills resilient individuals make wise choices and they take advantage of opportunities (e.g. continuing their education, learning new skills, joining the military, choosing healthy life partners, and breaking away from deviant peers) (Werner and Smith 2001).

To help survivors, health care providers can encourage and recommend altruistic behaviors, independent activities, and the use of spirituality. By helping others, survivors are in effect helping themselves. Encouraging independent activities, such as schoolwork, or work in general, enhances the recovery process. Using spirituality, survivors can reclaim values, and foster meaning and hope (Kataoka *et al.* 2006; Mollica 2006).

For example, at a recent clinical consultation, a youth who had a remarkable history of victimization was encouraged and challenged to use his talent and interest in poetry as a form of healing and a way to transform his life. There is a need to help victimized youth use their "islands of competence" to foster a sense of accomplishment.

Finally, most victimized children and youth do not receive services, and very few are treated with evidence-based interventions. For example, only 25 percent of children with emotional and behavioral problems in the United States receive specific mental health services.

The hopeful news is that there are now several evidence-based interventions that have been employed successfully with traumatized children. Schools are the best settings to identify at-risk children and provide mental health interventions (Alvord and Grados 2005; Battistich *et al.* 1996; Cohen *et al.* 2006; Cowen 2000; Doll and Lyon 1998; Eber *et al.* 1996; Ennett *et al.* 2003; Huang *et al.* 2005; Jennings *et al.* 2000; Rutter *et al.* 1979; Stein *et al.* 2003; Tobler and Stratton 1997; Weisz *et al.* 2005; Wong *et al.* 2007).

## Conclusion

The research literature on resilience in children has yielded important lessons and guidelines to follow when implementing prevention and treatment interventions. But it will take more than research to bolster the resilience of victimized children. It will take political leadership and public commitment.

## References

Alvord, M. K., and Grados, J. J. (2005). Enhancing resilience in children: a proactive approach. *Professional Psychology: Research and Practice*, 36, 238–45.

Battistich, V., Scheps, E., Watson, W., and Solomon, D. (1996). Preventative effects for the Child Development Project. *Journal of Applied Developmental Psychology*, 11, 12–35.

Berman, S. L., Kurtines, W. M., Silverman, W. K., and Serafini, L. T. (1996). The impact of exposure to crime and violence on urban youth. *American Journal of Orthopsychiatry*, 66, 329–36.

Bernard, B. (1995). *Fostering Resiliency in Kids: Protective Factors in the Family, School and Community*. San Francisco, CA: Far West Laboratory for Educational Research and Development.

Bertolino, B. (2003). *Change-Oriented Therapy with Adolescents and Young Adults*. New York: Norton.

Cohen, J. A., Mannarino, A. P., and Deblinger, E. (2006). *Treating Trauma and Traumatic Grief in Children and Adolescents*. New York: Guilford.

Costello, E. J., Erkanli, A., Fairbank, J. A., and Angold, A. (2002). The prevalence of potentially traumatic events in childhood and adolescence. *Journal of Traumatic Stress*, 15(2), 99–112.

Cowen, E. (2000). Psychological wellness: some hopes for the future. In D. Cicchetti, J. Rappaport, I. Sandler, and R. P. Weissberg (eds). *The Promotion of Wellness in Adolescents* (pp. 477–503). Washington, DC: Child Welfare League of America Press.

Curtis, W. J., and Cicchetti, D. (2003). Moving research on resilience into the 21st century: theoretical and methodological considerations in examining biological contributions to resilience. *Development and Psychopathology*, 15, 773–810.

De Bellis, M. D. (2002). Developmental traumatology. *Psychoneuroendocrinology*, 27, 155–70.

De Bellis, M. D., Baum, A. S. Birmaher, B., Keshavan, M. S., Eccard, C. H., Boring, A. M., *et al.* (1999). Developmental traumatology. Part 1: Biological stress systems. *Biological Psychiatry*, 45(10), 1259–70.

DeAngelis, T. (2007). A new diagnosis for childhood trauma? *Monitor on Psychology*, 38(3), 32–4.

Delaney-Black, V., Covington, C., Ondersma, S. J., Nordstrom-Klee, B., Templin, T., Ager, J., *et al.* (2002) Violence exposure, trauma, and IQ and/or reading deficits among urban children. *Archives of Pediatrics and Adolescent Medicine*, 156(3), 280–5.

Doll, B., and Lyon, M. A. (1998). Risk and resilience: implications for delivery of educational and mental health services in schools. *School Psychology Review*, 27, 348–63.

Dubois, D. L., and Karcher, M. J. (eds) (2005). *Handbook of Youth Mentoring*. Thousand Oaks, CA: Sage.

Eber, L., Osuch, R., and Reddott, C. (1996). School-based application of the wrap-around process: early results in service provision and student outcomes. *Journal of Child and Family Studies*, 5, 83–99.

Edwards, V. J., Anda, R. F., Dube, S. R., Dong, M., Chapman, D. P., and Felitti, V. J. (2005). The wide-ranging health outcomes of adverse childhood experiences. In K. A. Kendall-Tackett and S. M. Giaromoni (eds), *Child Victimization* (pp. 8–12). Kingston, NJ: Civic Research Institute.

Ennett, S. T., Ringwait, C. L., Thorne, J., Rohrbach, L. A., Vincus A., Simons-Rudolph A., *et al.* (2003). A comparison of current practice in school-based substance use prevention programs with meta-analysis findings. *Prevention Science*, 4(1), 1–14.

Finkelhor, D., Ormrod, R., Turner, H., and Hamby, S. L. (2005). The victimization of children and youth: a comprehensive national survey. *Child Maltreatment*, 10(1), 5–25.

Fletcher, K. E. (1996). Childhood posttraumatic stress disorder. In E. Mash and R. Barkley (eds), *Child Psychopathology* (pp. 242–76). New York: Guilford.

Ford, J. D. (2005). Treatment implications of altered neurobiology, affect regulation and information processing following child maltreatment. *Psychiatric Annals*, 35, 410–19.

Garbarino, J., Dubrow, N., Kostelny, K., and Pardo, C. (1992). *Children in Danger: Coping with the Consequences of Community Violence*. San Francisco. CA: Jossey-Bass.

Grogger, J. (1997). Local violence and educational attainment. *Journal of Human Resources*, 32, 659–82.

Grotberg, E. H. (ed.) (2003). *Resilience for Today: Gaining Strength from Adversity*. Westport, CT: Praeger.

Haggerty, J., Sherrod, L., Garmezy, N., and Rutter, M. (1996). *Stress, Risk and Resilience in Children and Adolescents*. New York: Cambridge University Press.

Huang, L., Stoul, B., Friedman, R., Mrazek, P., Friesen, B., Pires, S., *et al.* (2005). Transforming mental health care for children and their families. *American Psychologist*, 60(6), 615–27.

Hurt, H., Malmud, E., Brodsky, N. L., and Giannetta, J. (2001). Exposure to violence: Psychological and academic correlates in child witnesses. *Archives of Pediatrics and Adolescent Medicine*, 155, 351–6.

Jennings, J., Pearson, G., and Harris, M. (2000). Implementing and maintaining school-based mental health services in a large urban school district. *Journal of School Health*, 70, 201–5.

Kataoka, S. H., Fuentes, S., O'Donoghue, V. P., Castillo-Campos, P., Bonilla, A., Halsey, K., *et al.* (2006). A community participatory research partnership: the development of a faith-based intervention for children exposed to violence. *Ethnicity and Disease*, 16(1), 89–97.

Kendler, K. S., Bulik, C. M., Silberg, J., Hettema, J. M., Myers, J., and Prescott, C. A. (2000). Childhood sexual abuse and adult psychiatric and substance abuse disorders in women: an epidemiological and co-twin control analysis. *Archives of General Psychiatry*, 57(10), 953–9.

Masten, A. S. (2001). Ordinary magic: Resilience processes in development. *American Psychologist*, 56, 227–38.

Masten, A. S. (2004). Regulatory processes, risk and resilience in adolescent development. *Annals of the New York Academy of Sciences*, 1021, 310–19.

Masten, A. S., and Gewirtz, A. H. (2006). Resilience in development: the importance of early childhood. In R. E. Tremblay, R. E. Barr, and D.V. Peters (eds), *Encyclopedia on Early Childhood Development* (pp. 1–6). Retrived from Centre of Excellence for Early Childhood Development website (www.excellence-earlychildhood.ca/documents/masten-gewirtzangxp.pdf).

Masten, A. S., and Reed, M. G. (2002). Resilience in development. In S. R. Snyder and S. J. Lopez (eds), *The Handbook of Positive Psychology*. Oxford: Oxford University Press.

Miller, A. L., Rathus, J. H., and Linehan, M. M. (2007). *Dialetical Behavior Therapy with Suicidal Adolescents*. New York: Guilford.

Mollica, R. E. (2006). *Healing Invisible Wounds: Paths to Hope and Recovery in a Violent World*. New York: Harcourt.

Rutter, M. B., Maughan, P., Mortimore, J., Ouston, J., and Smith, A. (1979). *Fifteen Thousand Hours*. Cambridge. MA: Harvard University Press.

Sameroff, A. J., Seifer, R., Baldwin, A., and Baldwin, C. (1992). Stability of intelligence from preschool to adolescence: the influence of social and family risk factors. *Child Development*, 64, 80–97.

Stein, B. D., Jaycox, L. H., Kataoka, S. H., Wong, M., Tu, W., Elliott, M. N., *et al.* (2003). A mental health intervention for schoolchildren exposed to violence: a randomized controlled trial. *Journal of the American Medical Association*, 290(5), 603–11.

Streech-Fisher, A., and Van der Kolk, B. A. (2000). Down will come baby, cradle and all: diagnostic and therapeutic implications of chronic trauma on child development. *Australian and New Zealand Journal of Psychiatry*, 34, 903–18.

Tobler, N. S., and Stratton, H. H. (1997). Effectiveness of school-based drug prevention programs: a meta-analysis of the research. *Journal of Primary Prevention*, 18, 71–128.

Weisz, J. R., Sandler, I. N., Durlak, J. A., and Anton, B. S. (2005). Promoting and protecting a youth mental health through evidence-based prevention and treatment. *American Psychologist*, 60(6), 628–48.

Werner, E. E., and Smith, R. (1992). *Vulnerable But Invincible: A Longitudinal Study of Resilient Children and Youth*. New York: Adams, Bannistar & Cox.

Werner, E. E., and Smith, R. (2001). *Journeys from Childhood to Midlife: Risk, Resilience, and Recovery*. Ithaca, NY: Cornell University Press.

Wong, M., Rosemond, M. E., Stein, B. D., Langley, A. K., Kataoka, S. H., and Nadeem, E. (2007). School-based mental health intervention for adolescents exposed to violence. *Prevention Researcher*, 14(1), 17–20.

Zimmerman, M. A., and Arunkumar, R. (1994). *Resiliency Research: Implications for Schools and Policy*, Social Policy Report of the SRCD, 8, 1–17.

# PART V

# Core Tasks of Psychotherapy

## What "Expert" Therapists Do

Throughout my career, I have been fascinated by the nature of "expertise." What makes some psychotherapists more effective than other therapists in obtaining better treatment outcomes? In an attempt to answer this question, consider the following set of findings:

1.  "Expertise" has been defined as the increased quality of performance that is gained with experience, as reflected in a positive relationship between the level of experience and the level of professional skills (Tracey *et al.*, 2014).

2.  Improvement in expertise has been noted in such professional groups as astronomers, test pilots, chess masters, mathematicians, accountants and insurance analysts.

3.  Several professional groups for whom improved expertise was *not* demonstrated over the course of their careers include college administration officers, court judges, personnel selection officers and *psychotherapists* (Shanteau, 1992).

4.  What does change with experience is the psychotherapist's self-confidence. Clinicians often have unrealistic appraisals of their own capabilities. Dawes (1994) observed that "psychotherapists' self-estimates of their ability continue to grow with experience, even though their actual ability (treatment outcomes) do not improve." This process of increased self-confidence can undermine their motivation to seek critical feedback in order to develop their expertise. Expert psychotherapists who obtain better outcomes systematically seek feedback on their patient's progress on a session-by-session basis and take time before and after each treatment session to reflect on the best ways to "fit" their psychotherapeutic interventions to the client's current needs (Lambert, 2010; Miller *et al.*, 2008).

5.  The most effective psychotherapists have a greater level of facilitative skills and are able to establish, maintain and monitor a good working therapeutic alliance across a range of patients.

The two chapters in this part enumerate the core psychotherapeutic skills that "expert" therapists implement. Each of these core skills reflects well organized and readily retrievable declarative and strategic knowledge and are the result of "deliberate practice," and the monitoring of treatment outcomes (Ericcson *et al.*, 2013).

Of the various core skills that "expert" psychotherapists, who obtain the most effective treatment outcomes, employ is the ability to establish, maintain and monitor routinely the quality and nature of the therapeutic alliance (TA). As highlighted in the second chapter in this part, the quality of the TA is the most robust predictor of therapeutic outcomes. The amount of change attributable to TA is seven times that of the specific treatment model, or the specific treatment techniques. The specific treatment accounts for *no more* than 15 percent of the variance of treatment outcomes. In comparison, some 36 to 51 percent of treatment outcome variance is attributed to the person of the therapist, which is three to four times that of the specific treatment approach. Moreover, it is not the therapist demographic factors (gender, ethnicity, discipline, or experience) that is predictive of treatment outcomes (Sperry & Carlson, 2013; Wampold, 2006).

An effective TA may develop as early as the first session, but an effective TA must be firmly in place by the third session if treatment is to be effective. High TA leads to better treatment results and greater likelihood of maintaining change (Skovholt & Jennings, 2004).

As Sperry and Carlson (2013) observe:

> It is the therapist and not treatment that influences the amount of therapeutic change that occurs. Relationship skills or developing a therapeutic alliance is the cornerstone of therapeutic excellence.

How many of these core tasks do you engage in? How "expert" are you in your clinical practice?

## References

Dawes, R. M. (1994). *House of Cards: Psychology and Psychiatry Built on Myth*. New York: Free Press.

Ericsson, K. A., Charness, N., Feltovich, P. J., & Hoffman, R. R. (eds) (2013). *The Cambridge Handbook of Expertise and Expert Performance*. Cambridge: Cambridge University Press.

Lambert, M. J. (2010). *Prevention of Treatment Failure: The Use of Measuring, Monitoring and Feedback in Clinical Practice*. Washington, DC: American Psychological Association.

Miller, S. D., Hubble, M., & Duncan, B. (2008). Supershrinks: what is the secret of their success? *Psychotherapy in Australia*, 14: 14–22.

Shanteau, J. (1992). Competence in experts: the role of task characteristics. *Organizational Behavior and Human Decision Processes*, 53: 252–66.

Skovholt, J. M. & Jennings, L. (2004). *Master Therapists: Exploring Expertise in Therapy and Counseling*. Boston: Allyn & Bacon.

Sperry, L. & Carlson, J. (2013). *How Master Therapists Work*. New York: Routledge.

Tracey, T. J., Wampold, B. E., Lichtenberg, J. W., & Goodyear, R. K. (2014). Expertise in psychotherapy: an elusive goal? *American Psychologist*, 69: 218–29.

Wampold, B. E. (2006). The psychotherapist. In J. C. Norcros, L. E. Beutler, & R. F. Levant (eds), *Evidence-Based Practices in Mental Health: Debate and Dialogue on Fundamental Questions*. Washington, DC: American Psychological Association, pp. 200–8.

# 12

# CORE TASKS OF PSYCHOTHERAPY

## What expert therapists do

*Donald Meichenbaum*

This is the fourth time I am presenting at an Evolution of Psychotherapy Conference. Each time I feel honored and privileged to be included with such esteemed psychotherapists from whom I have learned so much and whom I admire. But, I am also challenged, as are the participants in this conference, to determine what distinguishes this group of "experts," and moreover to determine what they have in common. I have always been fascinated by the nature of expertise. In fact, my colleague Andrew Biemiller and I have recently written a book on educational expertise entitled *Nurturing Independent Learners*, in which we reviewed the literature on expertise (Meichenbaum & Biemiller, 1998). Psychologists have studied experts in such varied areas as sports, artists, writers, computer programmers, jugglers, chess players, waiters, and psychotherapists. What do these various expert groups have in common and what is the relevance to understanding expert psychotherapists?

The research indicates that experts differ from novices and from experienced non-experts in terms of their:

a)  knowledge (know what, how, and when to do things, or what have been characterized as declarative, procedural, and conditional knowledge);

b)  strategies or plans for achieving their goals and their ability to monitor their strategies and performance and alter them accordingly (what is called meta-cognitive skills);

c)  motivation to excel (commitment, interest, persistence, goal-directed deliberate practice).

– Meichenbaum, D. (1992). Core tasks of psychotherapy: what expert therapists do. In J. Zeig (ed.). *The Evolution of Psychotherapy*. New York: Brunner Mazel, pp. 73–83.

Now let us apply these constructs of knowledge, strategies, and motivation to the area of psychotherapy. Imagine that you, or a family member or a friend, are in need of a psychotherapist. Who in your area would you turn to for help? Whom would you consider a "therapist's therapist," or an "expert"? What does this therapist know and do that warrants your vote of confidence? How has this competent therapist incorporated the findings from the research literature on psychotherapy into his or her clinical repertoire?

Another way to address these questions is to raise the concerns that my tennis instructor highlights during my tennis lessons. She works on simplifying and identifying the "core tasks" of tennis into their component features, viz., ground strokes of forehand or backhand, consisting of top spin, slice, drop shots, volleys, net game, and serve. Moreover, she not only helps me master these basic strokes, she also highlights how I need to alter them depending on the strengths and weaknesses of my competitor, the stage and situation of the match, and the level of my endurance. In the same way, I intend to break the craft (and science) of psychotherapy into its "core tasks."

My list of component core tasks that are enumerated in Table 12.1 are derived from three sources. First, the process research on psychotherapy (Garfield, 1980; Lambert, 1992; Orlinsky et al., 1994), and secondly, the evidence for empirically supported treatments (American Psychological Association Reports on Dissemination of Empirically-based Therapies, 1995; Barlow et al., 1999; Chambless et al., 1996, 1998; Nathan and Gorman, 1998; and Wilson, 1996). The importance of incorporating findings from empirically-based treatments was underscored by Shadish et al. (1997) who have documented that these empirically-based treatment procedures can be applied to a wide range of clinical populations. They examined 56 treatment studies using meta-analytic procedures and categorized the studies on a continuum from least clinically representative to most clinically representative. They found similar effect sizes evident across all points of the treatment continuum. Thus, any enumeration of "core tasks" must be attuned to the findings of these empirically supported treatment procedures.

The final source for deriving the core tasks comes from 35 years of practicing psychotherapy, supervising and teaching novice and experienced therapists. Space does not permit me to review in detail the basis for each of the enumerated core tasks. I will, however, describe in general some of the core tasks and ways to achieve them. Throughout the remainder of this Evolution Conference, I will demonstrate how these core tasks can be implemented with such varied clinical populations as patients experiencing mixed anxiety-depression, PTSD, anger-control, and borderline personality disorder. Detailed treatment guidelines of the "how to" features of the core tasks have been made available at the conference bookstore, and a book on "How to Become a More Expert Therapist" is in preparation.

**TABLE 12.1** Core tasks of psychotherapy: what expert therapists do

1. Develop a *therapeutic alliance*.
2. *Educate* the patient about his/her problems and possible solutions.
3. Help the patient *reconceptualize* his or her problems in a more hopeful fashion: *nurture hope*.
4. Ensure that the patient has *coping skills*.
5. Encourage the patient to *perform "personal experiments"* in vivo: ensure that the patient takes "data" as evidence to *unfreeze their beliefs* about self and world.
6. Ensure that the patient *takes credit* for change: *nurture a sense of personal agency/sense of mastery*.
7. Conduct *relapse prevention*.

*Additional psychotherapeutic tasks for treating patients with a history of ongoing victimization*

8. Address the patient's *basic needs, safety* and help him/her develop *symptom regulation* including any *comorbidity features*.
9. Address *memory work* and *help the patient retell* his/her story, but *help the patient* to alter *his or her belief system and implications*.
10. Help the patient *find meaning* and *transform pain*.
11. Help the patient *reconnect with others* who are not "victims": address impact of trauma and disorder on *significant others*.
12. Address issues of *possible revictimization*.

## In search of "expert" therapists

The search for the features of "expert" therapists and the common mechanisms of behavior change was given a major impetus by Jerome Frank (1973). This search has taken varied modern forms as illustrated by the research efforts of Goldfried *et al.* (1991), Jennings and Skovholt (1999), Stiles *et al.* (1998), Tharp (1999), and Skovholt *et al.* (1997). A review of this literature is beyond the scope of this chapter. In the enumeration of therapist factors, however, it is important to keep in mind that patient characteristics and relationship factors (bi-directional influences between the therapist and the patient) account for most of the variance in treatment outcome. As Lambert (1992) observes, 30 years of psychotherapy research have demonstrated that the client factors, including their strengths and resources, their social supports, and the environment in which they live, are most important in predicting outcome.

This means that if therapists wish to be successful or if they want to see most improvement in their patients, the most important thing they can do is to *choose their patients carefully*. They should work with what are called YAVIS patients (e.g., young, attractive, verbal, intelligent, and successful). They should stay away from difficult patients who are chronically distressed with comorbid features of psychiatric and physical disorders (e.g., Axis II disorders), who have been or are being repeatedly victimized, and who have multiple problems and who are unmotivated, noncompliant and who live in an environment that undermines treatment. Such difficult patients, however, constitute an increasing majority of patients therapists see. In most instances, therapists *cannot* choose who they see in therapy, and often they seek the challenge of working with difficult patients.

Well, if therapists cannot choose whom they see in therapy, then what can they do? My answer to this question is the enumeration of the core tasks of psychotherapy. The first seven core tasks are common to all forms of psychotherapy, no matter what the therapeutic approach that is being employed; no matter what the theoretical orientation that is being adapted; and no matter the patient population.

The last five core tasks enumerated in Table 12.1 derived from working with psychiatric patients who have a history of victimization or who are suffering from PTSD and complex PTSD. Epidemiological studies indicate that up to 50% of psychiatric patients have a history of victimization, often overlooked by the mental health community. For example, consider that 34% to 53% of patients with severe mental illness report childhood sexual and physical abuse (Meichenbaum, 1995). Mueser *et al.* (1998) reported that among severely mentally ill patients (schizophrenia and bipolar disorders), 96% report exposure to at least one traumatic event and 43% meet the diagnostic criteria of PTSD, but only 2% had a diagnosis of PTSD in their clinical charts. The expert therapist needs to systematically assess and alter treatment accordingly when a history of or ongoing victimization is evident. The last five core tasks need to be implemented whenever PTSD is a consideration. Let us consider these core tasks of therapy.

## 1. Develop a therapeutic alliance

One of the robust findings in the psychotherapeutic research literature is that the quality of the alliance, as measured in different ways, from different perspectives, and in different treatment models, is a powerful predictor of treatment outcome (e.g., Horvath & Symonds, 1991). These studies indicate that the quality of the alliance is a function of the agreement between the therapist and the patient regarding the therapeutic tasks and agreement of goals of therapy, as originally suggested by Bordin (1979). In fact, Safran & Muran (2000) have argued that the quality of the therapeutic alliance is more important than the treatment techniques that are employed. Lambert (1992) has highlighted that the quality of the therapist's interaction, warmth, empathy, ability to establish and maintain a therapeutic alliance, are critical in predicting treatment outcome. Similarly Strupp (1995) observes, "Empathy is the single most important human and technical tool at the therapist's disposal."

The importance of the therapeutic alliance is also underscored by the findings that the pattern of patient participation within the first three therapy sessions is predictive of outcome (e.g., patient's affective bond, ability to work purposefully in therapy).

## 2. Educate the patient

Inherent in all forms of psychotherapy is an effort to educate patients about the nature of their disorders, about the variety of factors that contribute to their problems (i.e., collaboratively co-create a case conceptualization), and about the goals and tasks of psychotherapy. This educational process is *not* didactic, but Socratic and ongoing. There is also a need to educate patients about their "strengths" or what they have been able to accomplish *in spite* of their psychiatric disorders and distress. Moreover, an examination of how they have survived and thrived will help nurture the patients' sense of hope.

The ongoing assessment processes that the therapist employs with patients helps them to become more aware of what they are doing, thinking, and feeling, and how these processes interconnect. Elkin *et al.* (1999) have also highlighted the value of assessing the patient's beliefs about the causes of his or her problems and his or her notions about what will be helpful in treatment. The expert therapist can then incorporate and tailor treatment to the patient's understanding. The more compatible the treatment approach is to the patient's predilections the greater the likelihood for successful treatment outcome (see Beutler & Clarkin, 1990).

The therapist may use a variety of procedures to conduct such educational efforts. Among others, these include:

a)  convey information as part of social discourse, use written materials;
b)  have patients engage in self-monitoring and situational analyses;
c)  use videotape modeling films;
d)  use therapist and group feedback (if treatment is offered in couples, family or group basis).

Also note that therapists provide a rationale for the treatment which frames the intervention and helps motivate patients to change (e.g., use of motivational interviewing).

## 3. Nurture hope

A number of theorists have highlighted the role of hope in the change process (Frank, 1973; Kirsch, 1990; Snyder, 1994). In fact, one can look upon the history of psychotherapy, and to some degree the history of medicine, as a testament to the role that hope plays in the healing process. As Shapiro (1960) astutely observes, many forms of medical and psychological treatments that were considered helpful were indeed using ineffective ingredients and inert components. Their effectiveness instead can be attributed to the *placebo effect* or due to the hope they nurtured in their patients and therapists.

Research (reviewed by Snyder, 1994) has indicated that when individuals have hope or hold the perception that something desired may happen or the perception that their goals can be met, then they are more likely to:

a)   generate successful plans ("will and ways") to reach their goals;
b)   persist in the face of frustration;
c)   produce emotional states that nurture and enhance performance.

Expert therapists help their patients to believe that tomorrow and the future tomorrows can be different from the todays and the yesterdays. The positive effects of psychotherapy are basically mediated by increases in hope and nurtured by a sense of positive goal-related expectances in their lives.

Space does not permit a detailed discussion of the core tasks of how to teach skills and ensure for the generalization and maintenance of change (Core Task 4), nor a consideration of how to conduct the cognitive restructuring and problem-solving procedures that will ensure that patients perform personal *in vivo* experiments so they can collect data that are incompatible with their prior expectations and beliefs (Core Task 5). Inherent in both Core Tasks 4 and 5 is an evidential model of change, as discussed by Meichenbaum (1995).

Lambert (1992) has highlighted that patients who attribute change to their own efforts are more likely to maintain such change. The expert therapist ensures that patients "take credit" for improvement. In order to accomplish this core task the therapist may ask the patient such questions as:

> *You said, "It worked."*
> *What exactly did you do in situation X?*
> *Worked? How do you know it worked? What differences did you notice? Who else noticed these differences?*
> *How did you handle it this time compared to how you handled the situation in the past?*
> *Where else did you do this?*
> *Are you telling me, are you saying to yourself, that you could notice, catch, interrupt, use your game plan, had choices, etc....* [therapist chooses among these when reflecting]?
> *What does this mean about you as a person?*

Research reviewed by Meichenbaum (1995) indicates that such self-attributional processes also need to be nurtured, even when the improvement results from medication. Insofar as the patient can attribute behavior change to what the medication has allowed him or her to do (as compared to attributing the improvement just to the medication), the improvements are sustained.

In short, it is not just the fact that patients change, but the explanations they offer that are critical to the maintenance of change. Expert therapists do *not* leave such attributions to chance. They ensure that patients express personal agency and self-efficacy about the change process.

## 7. Relapse prevention

In most instances, psychiatric disorders are episodic in nature. For example, in the area of depressive disorders, despite aggressive pharmacological and psychotherapeutic approaches, approximately 15% of patients remain chronically depressed. Fifty percent of individuals who are depressed will experience another episode and the risk of recurrence increases with each episode. After the second episode, the risk is 70% of reoccurrence; 80% after the third episode; and 90% after the fourth episode (Teasdale, 1999).

In the area of addictions, where the initial interventions using relapse prevention were first employed (Marlatt and Gordon, 1985), the rate of relapse is very high. Sixty percent of those successfully treated revert to their prior behavior patterns within three months after therapy, increasing to 60% at six months, and 75% at 12 months (Meichenbaum & Turk, 1987).

Another form of concern about relapse arises in the case of anniversary effects for individuals who have experienced traumatic events. The occurrence of reminders can trigger recurrent distress (Meichenbaum, 1995).

Whether it is depression, substance abuse, or PTSD, the expert therapist must help patients to identify high-risk situations, notice prodromal warning signs and enhance the patient's skills for coping with these triggers and situations. An important task in therapy is to help patients manage lapses, as well as restructure the patient's perceptions of the relapse process (see Larimer et al., 1999).

The expert therapist recognizes that major depression and chronic PTSD, both of which often co-occur with other psychiatric disorders, are often lifelong disorders. Following from an initial episode, future relapse and recurrence are the norm. While research has indicated that cognitive-behavioral therapy often produces prophylactic effects or reduction of relapse of approximately 40%, there is still a need to provide ongoing support and to teach skills even for patients who have recovered from recurrent disorders such as depression. A core task is to help patients learn skills to reduce the risk of relapse and to reduce their vulnerability to future lapses. Teasdale (1999) observes that patients must learn to "nip in the bud" any incipient relapse by using their coping skills and come to view lapses, should they occur, as "learning opportunities," rather than as occasions to escalate the lapse incident into a complete relapse episode. By helping patients to learn to "notice, catch, interrupt, anticipate, and plan for" such lapses, they can learn to make conscious choices and decisions, rather than go on "automatic pilot" and "time-slide" into old, well-worn, habitual dysfunctional feelings, thoughts and behaviors that led to their initial distress.

The expert therapist recognizes that some patients will need recurrent help or what has been called intermittent brief therapies throughout the life cycle (Cummings, 1986).

Core Tasks 8 through 12 have been designed to be employed with patients who have a history of victimization or who are currently experiencing (re)victimization. The selection of these core tasks was derived from a comprehensive review of the PTSD literature by Meichenbaum (1995). Some of the major illustrative findings underscore the inclusion of these core tasks.

a) The unique features of PTSD (namely intrusive ideation, avoidance behavior and hyperarousal) require specific interventions. Avoidance behavior has been indicated as being highly correlated with poor treatment outcome and relapse.

b) 98% of patients with PTSD have at least one comorbid disorder. For example, PTSD and substance abuse are strongly linked for women, and thus require an integrated intervention approach that treats both disorders concurrently (see Najavits et al., 1998).

c) Traumatized individuals who have shared their accounts of victimization with others have a better outcome than those who have not engaged in retelling (Pennebaker, 1990).

d) It is not merely the self-disclosure of trauma, but rather how patients make sense of the impact of the victimization experience that is critical to adjustment (Silver et al., 1983).

e) There is a high incidence of revictimization. For example, up to 50% of rape victims report revictimization (Gold et al., 1999).

Expert therapists need to develop specific interventions that address issues of comorbidity, revictimization, and ways of finding meaning. Meichenbaum (1995) has described the specific ways these core therapeutic tasks can be implemented. A constructive narrative perspective provides a useful framework for helping patients tell their stories in a more hopeful fashion, as they move from being a "victim" to being a "survivor" who can thrive.

Like patients, expert therapists have a story to tell. As we listen to the esteemed therapists tell their stories over the course of the Evolution conference, consider how many of the core tasks of psychotherapy are evident. How do these expert therapists:

a) develop a therapeutic alliance;

b) educate and nurture hope in their patients;

c) teach skills and encourage their patients not only to perform personal experiments, but also to take credit for the changes they brought about;

d) anticipate and cope with possible lapses and possible revictimization;

e) assess for and address the impact of victimization and help patients retell their stories in a more helpful fashion that highlights what they did to survive;

f) help patients fashion meaning and transform their pain with the help of others into a tale of courage and resilience?

# References

American Psychological Association (1995). *Template for Developing Guidelines: Interventions for Mental Disorders and Psychological Aspects of Physical Disorders* (available from Division 12 of APA, 750 First Street NE, Washington, DC 20002–4242).

Barlow, D. H., Levitt, J. T., & Bufka, L. F. (1999). The dissemination of empirically supported treatments: a view to the future. *Behaviour Research and Therapy*, 32, 147–62.

Beutler, L. E., & Clarkin, J. F. (1990). *Systematic Treatment Section: Toward Targeted Therapeutic Intervention*. New York: Brunner/Mazel.

Bordin, E. S. (1979). The generalizability of the psychoanalytic concept of the working alliance. *Psychotherapy*, 16, 252–60.

Chambless, D. L., Baker, M. J., Baucom, D. H., *et al.* (1998). Update on empirically validated therapies II. *Clinical Psychologist*, 51, 3–15.

Chambless, D. L., Sanderson, W. C., Shoham, V., *et al.* (1996). An update on empirically validated therapies. *Clinical Psychologist*, 49, 5–18.

Cummings, N. A. (1986). The dismantling of our health system. *American Psychologist*, 41, 426–31.

Elkin, L., Yamaguchi, J. L., Arnkoff, D. B., Glass, C. R., Sotsky, S. M., & Krupnick, J. L. (1999). Patient-treatment fit and early engagement in therapy. *Psychotherapy Research*, 9, 437–51.

Frank, J. D. (1973). *Persuasion and Healing: A Comparative Study of Psychotherapy* (rev. edn). New York: Schocken Books.

Garfield, S. L. (1980). *Psychotherapy: An Eclectic Approach*. New York: Wiley.

Glass, C. R., Arnkoff, D. B., & Rodriguez, B. F. (1998). An overview of directions in psychotherapy integration research. *Journal of Psychotherapy Integration*, 8, 187–209.

Gold, S. R., Sinclair, B. B., & Balge, K. A. (1999). Risk of sexual victimization. *Aggression and Violent Behavior*, 4, 457–70.

Goldfried, M. R. (1991). Research issues in psychotherapy integration. *Journal of Psychotherapy Integration*, 1, 5–25.

Horvath, A. O., & Symonds, B. D. (1991). Relation between working alliance and outcome in psychotherapy: a meta-analysis. *Journal of Counseling Psychology*, 38, 139–49.

Irvin, J. E., Bowers, C. A., Rawson, N. S., & Oppenheim, A. N. (1999). Efficacy of relapse prevention: a meta-analytic review. *Journal of Consulting and Clinical Psychology*, 67, 563–70.

Jennings, L., & Skovholt, T. M. (1999). The cognitive, emotional and relational characteristics of master therapists. *Journal of Counseling Psychology*, 46, 3–11.

Kirsch, I. (1990). *Changing Expectations: A Key to Effective Psychotherapy*. Pacific Groves, CA: Brooks Cole.

Lambert, J. J. (1992). Psychotherapy outcome research: implications for integrative and eclectic therapists. In J. C. Norcross and M. R. Goldfried (eds), *Handbook of Psychotherapy Integration*. New York: Basic Books.

Larimer, M. E., Palmer, R. S., & Marlatt, G. A. (1999), Relapse prevention. *Alcohol Research and Health*, 23, 151–60.

Luborsky, L., McLellan, T. A., *et al.* (1985). Therapist success and its determinants. *Archives of General Psychiatry*, 42, 602–11.

Marlatt, G. A., & Gordon, J. R. (eds) (1985). *Relapse Prevention: Maintenance Strategies in the Treatment of Addictive Behavior*. New York: Guilford Press.

Meichenbaum, D. (1995). *Clinical Handbook on Assessing and Treating Adults with Stress Disorder*. Waterloo, ON: Institute Press. (Handbook is available directly from Don

Meichenbaum, University of Waterloo, Department of Psychology, Waterloo, Ontario, Canada N2L 3G1.)

Meichenbaum, D., & Biemiller, A. (1998). *Nurturing Independent Learners*. Brookline, MA: Brookline Books.

Meichenbaum, D., & Turk, D. (1987). *Facilitating Treatment Adherence*. New York: Plenum.

Mueser, K. T., Goodman, L. B., et al. (1998). Trauma and PTSD in severe mental illness. *Journal of Consulting and Clinical Psychology*, 66, 493–9.

Najavits, L. M., Weiss, R. D., Shaw, S. R., & Muenz, I. R. (1998). "Seeking safety": outcome of a new cognitive-behavioral psychotherapy for women with PTSD and substance dependence. *Journal of Traumatic Stress*, 11, 437–56.

Nathan, P. E., & Gorman, J. M. (1998). *A Guide to Treatments that Work*. New York: Oxford University Press.

Nezu, A. M., & Nezu, C. M. (1993). Identifying and selecting target problems for clinical interventions: a problem-solving model. *Psychological Assessment*, 5, 254–63.

Orlinsky, D. E., Grawe, K., & Parks, B. K. (1994). Process and outcome in psychotherapy. In A. E. Bergin & S. L. Garfield (eds), *Handbook of Psychotherapy and Behavior Change* (4th edn, pp. 270–376). New York: Wiley.

Pennebaker, J. W. (1990). *Opening Up: The Healing Power of Confiding in Others*. New York: Avon.

Safran, J. D., & Muran, J. C. (2000). *Negotiating the Therapeutic Alliance: A Relational Treatment Guide*. New York: Guilford.

Safran, J. D., Crocker, P., McMain, S., & Murray, P. (1990). Therapeutic alliance rupture as a therapy event for empirical investigation. *Psychotherapy*, 27, 154–65.

Sexton, T. L., & Whiston, S. C. (1994). The status of the counseling relationship: an empirical review, theoretical implication, and research direction. *Counseling Psychologist*, 22, 6–78.

Shadish, W. R., Matt, G. E., Navarro, A. M., et al. (1997). Evidence that therapy works in clinically representative conditions. *Journal of Consulting and Clinical Psychology*, 65, 355–65.

Shapiro, A. R. (1960). A contribution to the history of the placebo effect. *Behavior Science*, 5, 109–135.

Silver, R. L., Boon, C., & Stones, M. H. (1983). Searching for meaning in misfortune. *Journal of School Issues*, 39, 81–102.

Skovholt, T. M., Ronnestad, M. H., & Jennings, L. (1997). In search of expertise in counseling, psychotherapy and professional psychology. *Educational Psychology Review*, 9, 361–9.

Snyder, C. R. (1994). Hope and optimism. In *Encyclopedia of Human Behavior*, Vol. 2. New York: Academic Press.

Stiles, W. B., Honos-Webb, L., & Sarko, M. (1998). Responsiveness in psychotherapy. *Clinical Psychology: Science and Practice*, 5, 439–58.

Strupp, H. H. (1995). *Lasting Lessons from Psychotherapy Practice and Research*. Paper presented at the APA meeting in New York.

Task Force on Promotion and Dissemination of Psychological Procedures (1995). Training in a dissemination of empirically-validated psychological treatments. *Clinical Psychologist*, 48, 3–23.

Teasdale, J. D. (1999). Emotional processing, three modes of mind and the prevention of relapse in depression. *Behavior Research and Therapy*, 37, 53–77.

Tharp, R. G. (1999). Therapist as teacher: a developmental model of psychotherapy. *Human Development*, 42, 18–25.

Wilson, G. T. (1996). Manual-based treatments: the clinical application of research findings. *Behavior Research and Therapy*, 34, 295–314.

# 13

# THE THERAPEUTIC RELATIONSHIP AS A COMMON FACTOR

## Implications for trauma therapy

*Donald Meichenbaum*

Here is the challenge. I recently retired from my university to assume the position as Research Director of the Melissa Institute for Violence Prevention (see www.melissainstitute.org). In this capacity, I am invited to consult and train clinicians on ways to work with clients who have experienced traumatic events and victimizing experiences. The clients usually have received a diagnosis of Post Traumatic Stress Disorder (PTSD) and an array of comorbid disorders such as substance abuse and depressive disorders. For instance, I have been training clinicians who are working with returning service members, torture victims, Native populations who have been sexually abused, as well as clinicians who work in Residential Treatment Centers. If you were in my shoes, what advice would you offer these clinicians? What specific interventions would you recommend?

Consider the treatment options that can most succinctly be summarized in a list of acronyms. In fact, I have come to the conclusion that you cannot formulate a treatment for patients with PTSD and related disorders unless you have an acronym. In fact, I think that therapists must come up with the acronym first, and then develop the therapy. You can choose from the following list:[1] DTE, VRE, CPT, EMDR, SIT, AMT, MBSR, MAGT, ACT, CR, TF–CBT, IBT, CP, CMT, IPT, IRT, and others.

In addition, you can select from an additional array of treatment approaches that have been developed to address the presence of comorbid disorders such as SS, TARGET and STAIR–MPE.[2] This list of treatment options could be extended if we consider specific interventions that address patient dominant emotional

– Meichenbaum, D. (2014). The therapeutic relationship as a common factor: Implications for trauma therapy. In D. Murphy, S. Joseph, & B. Harris (eds), *Trauma, Recovery and the Relationship*. London: Palgrave Macmillan.

concerns such as complicated grief, guilt, shame, anger, moral injuries and spiritual based interventions.

Remember, as a consultant I am getting paid to help psychotherapists choose the "best" most-effective interventions. The catch-words are "evidence-based" and "evidence-informed" interventions.

Now, here is the rub. In my desire to be an "honest broker" and not a specific advocate of any one acronym therapy, I find myself on the "horns of a dilemma." On the one hand, there is the report of the Institute of Medicine (2008) of the efficacy of exposure-based therapies with patients who suffer from PTSD and the Veteran's Administration endorsing and training their clinical personnel on Direct Therapy Exposure and Cognitive Processing Therapy.

On the other side of the debate, there are a number of meta-analytic reviews that question the relative differential efficacy of so-called evidence-based therapies *versus* bona fide comparison groups that are "intended to succeed." Reviews by Benish *et al.* (2008), Imel *et al.* (2008), Keijsers *et al.* (2000), Norcross (2002) and Wampold *et al.* (1997, 2010) have seriously challenged the proposition that any one acronym form of treatment is the "winner of the race" and should be embraced and advocated by me in my consultative capacity. Moreover, Webb *et al.* (2010) have reported that the therapist's adherence to evidence-based treatment manuals is not related to treatment outcome. In fact, "loose compliance" that is tailored to the patient's individual needs may be the best treatment approach.

Such meta-analytic reviews have not gone without their critics, as highlighted by Ehlers *et al.* (2010). But, keep in mind that the clinicians that I am called upon to train still want to know specifically what to do with their challenging patients.

For the moment, let us assume that each of the acronym therapeutic approaches, does indeed, lead to favorable outcomes with patients diagnosed with PTSD and comorbid disorders. What are the common mechanisms that contribute to such patient improvements?

Another way to frame this question is to share an example of my supervisory role of clinical graduate students at the University of Waterloo in Ontario, Canada. In our clinic, we had several interview rooms side-by-side, each with one-way viewing mirrors. I would sit on a high-backed chair which had wheels and I could roll up and down the viewing corridor watching several students at one time. Okay, so imagine in each clinical interview room you could watch Edna Foa conducting Direct Therapy Exposure, Barbara Rothbaum using amplified Virtual Reality Exposure, Pat Resick conducting Cognitive Processing Therapy, Francine Shapiro conducting EMDR, Marsha Linehan teaching skills in Dialectical Behavior Therapy, and so forth. What makes these psychotherapists effective? What do "expert" therapists do, and not do, that leads to positive treatment outcomes?

In answering this question, keep in mind that there is little or no evidence of the "specificity" of treatment effects. Interventions that are designed to alter specific behavioral skill areas do not usually evidence changes in that domain. Moreover, when dismantling treatment studies are conducted, with the key treatment ingredients omitted or altered, favorable treatment results are still evident (see Rosen & Frueh, 2010).

Hopefully, you are beginning to appreciate the source of my challenge. What would you do? My solution has been to identify and enumerate the "Core Tasks" that underline treatment improvement. My list is gleaned from both the research literature and my 40 years of clinical work.

## Core tasks of psychotherapy

What are the core tasks that characterize the performance of psychotherapists who achieve positive treatment outcomes? This question has been addressed from Carl Rogers' (1957) initial examination of the necessary and sufficient prerequisite conditions of psychotherapy to Jerome Frank's (Frank & Frank, 1991) analysis of common persuasive features of behavior change to a search for the "heart and soul" of change by Miller *et al.* (2010).

In each instance, a set of common psychotherapeutic tasks have emerged. These tasks are dependent upon the quality and nature of the therapeutic relationship as being central to patient behavioural change. As highlighted by Ackerman & Hilsenroth (2003), Martin *et al.* (2000), Messer & Wampold (2002), Norcross (2002), Safran & Muran (2000) and Wampold (2001), the quality and nature of the therapeutic alliance accounts for a significantly larger proportion of treatment outcome variance than do therapist effects and the specific treatment interventions, or the specific form of acronym therapy that is being implemented. Approximately, one-third of treatment outcome is accounted for by the therapeutic relationship, significantly more than the specific type of therapy (Duncan *et al.*, 2009). The therapeutic alliance relationship is the "cornerstone" of effective therapy (Norcross, 2009). As Irvin Yalom (2002, p. 34) stated, "the paramount task of psychotherapy is to build a relationship together that will become the agent of change." Walsh (2011, p. 585) observed that "Ideally, therapeutic relationships then serve as bridges that enable patients to enhance life relationships with family, friends and community."

The correlation between the quality of the therapeutic alliance and treatment outcome is approximately 0.26, which corresponds to a moderate effect size. The pattern of patient participation and the degree of patient therapeutic engagement in the first three therapy sessions is predictive of treatment outcome. Patients with weaker therapeutic alliance scores are more likely to drop out of psychotherapy (Sharf *et al.*, 2010).

The relationship between the quality and nature of the therapeutic alliance and the treatment outcomes is further strengthened when psychotherapists assess and employ ongoing real-time patient feedback. Lambert and his colleagues (Lambert, 2010; Lambert *et al.*, 2005; Shimokawa *et al.*, 2010) and Miller *et al.* (2007) have demonstrated that measuring, monitoring, and alerting psychotherapists to potential patient treatment failure on a session-by-session basis by soliciting patient feedback of treatment response maximizes treatment outcomes. Such feedback permits the psychotherapist to individually alter and tailor the intervention to the patient's needs, and thereby strengthens the therapeutic alliance.

The role of the therapeutic alliance in impacting treatment outcome has now been demonstrated with diverse clinical populations. For example, a meta-analysis of 24 studies of couple and family therapy using a variety of self-report alliance measures (Working Alliance Inventory, Couple Therapy Scale and Family Therapy Alliance Scale) found that the interplay of each family member's alliance with the therapist was related to treatment retention and outcomes. Patients who reported feeling "safe" within therapy, with the avoidance of excessive cross-blaming, hostility, and sarcasm in sessions, reported stronger therapeutic alliances and better treatment outcomes. Insofar as a shared sense of purpose and the establishment of overarching familial systemic goals were achieved, rather than individual goals, therapeutic alliance development and treatment outcome were enhanced (Escudero *et al.*, 2011; Friedlander *et al.*, 2011). McLeod (2011) conducted a similar meta-analysis of the relationship of therapeutic alliance and treatment outcome in youth psychotherapy and reported similar findings.

A different research approach to studying the role of therapeutic relationship in influencing treatment outcome has been to ask patients what they have found helpful and unhelpful on the part of their therapists. Hamilton & Coates (1993) interviewed abused women who offered the following observations of their psychotherapists.

Helpful psychotherapists
- "Listened respectfully and took me seriously."
- "Believed my story."
- "Helped me see if I was still in danger and explored with me how I could deal with this situation."
- "Helped me see my strengths."
- "Helped me understand the impact of traumatic events on myself and on others."
- "Helped me plan for change."

In contrast, unhelpful psychotherapists
- "Did not listen and did not have an accepting attitude."
- "Questioned and doubted my story."
- "Dismissed or minimized the seriousness of my situation."
- "Gave advice that I did not wish to receive."
- "Blamed or criticized me."

A similar profile of patient reactions was reported by Elliott (2008).

Whether one considers the findings of meta-analytic studies or the results of interview studies with patients, the degree to which the patient feels respected, heard, accepted, empathically understood, validated, and hopeful enhances the likelihood of positive treatment outcomes. The felt sense of collaboration between the therapist and patient, including an emotional bond and negotiation of therapy tasks and goals has consistently predicted favorable treatment outcomes (Horvath *et al.*, 2011).

The therapeutic alliance has come to be defined as the extent to which the patient and the psychotherapist jointly agree on the goals of treatment and the means or tasks by which to achieve these goals ("pathways thinking") and the quality of the affective bond that develops between them (Bordin, 1979; Horvath & Bedi, 2002; Norcross, 2002). McFarlane (1994) observes that trust is also an essential feature of the therapeutic relationship with traumatized patients. The patient must feel secure and confident that the therapist is genuine, empathetic and warm, and, moreover, that the therapist can cope with bearing witness to the patient's reported trauma and understand its significance. These various authors are highlighting that the therapeutic alliance is the "primary vehicle," "prerequisite," "process," "glue," that permits patients to develop the courage to avoid avoidance, reexpose themselves to traumatic events, reminders, cues, and reengage life.

## Additional core tasks of psychotherapy

If we now revisit the various trauma psychotherapists (Foa, Rothbaum, Shapiro, Linchan, and the other acronym therapists), what do they have in common? Clearly, one thing is their ability to establish, maintain, monitor the therapist alliance and address any potential "ruptures" accordingly. But they do much more within the relationship with their patient. They each:

- Assess for the patient's safety (conduct risk assessment) and ensure that basic patient needs are being met.
- Educate the patient about the nature and impact of trauma, PTSD, and accompanying adjustment difficulties and discuss the nature of treatment.
- Address issues of confidentiality billing, logistics, and the like, but always conveying a "caring" attitude.
- Conduct assessments of the patient's presenting problems, as well as their strengths. What have the patients done to "survive" and "cope"? They tap the "rest of the patient's story."
- Solicit the patient's implicit theory about his/her presenting problems and his/her implicit theory of change. The therapist provides a cogent rationale for the treatment approach and assesses the patient's understanding, and makes the therapy process visible and transparent for the patient.
- Alter treatment in a patient-sensitive fashion, being responsive to cultural, developmental, and gender differences.
- Nurture "hope" by engaging in collaborative goal setting, highlighting evidence of patient, family, cultural, and community resilience.
- Teach intra- and interpersonal coping skills and build into such training efforts the ingredients needed to increase the likelihood of generalization and maintenance of treatment effects.

- The effective therapist does not merely "train and hope" for generalization, but explicitly builds in such features as relapse prevention, attribution retraining, aftercare, putting patients in a consultative mode (or in the "driver's seat"), so they become their own therapist.
- Provide interventions that result in symptom relief and address the impact of comorbid disorders.
- Encourage, challenge and cajole patients who have been avoidant to reexperience, reexpose themselves to trauma reminders, cues, situations, and memories. Enlist the support of significant others in these reexposure activities.
- Teach patients a variety of direct-action problem-solving and emotionally palliative coping skills (for example, mindfulness activities), to the point of mastery, addressing issues of treatment non-adherence throughout.
- Help patients reduce the likelihood of revictimization.

Finally:

- Engage patients in developing "healing stories".

In short, whatever the proposed acronym-based intervention (direct exposure, cognitive reprocessing, self-regulatory emotional controls, and the like), it is critical to remember that such specific interventions are embedded in a contextualized process. How much of the patient change that is achieved in trauma therapy should be attributed to each of these component steps and how much to "manualized" treatment procedures?

Table 13.1 is the Psychotherapist Checklist I use in my consulting role. This checklist highlights how to make the so-called non-specifics of psychotherapy specific, trainable, and measurable. It enumerates ways to enhance therapeutic alliance and treatment outcomes. The importance of these psychotherapeutic skills are highlighted by a better appreciation of the goals of trauma therapy from a Constructive Narrative Perspective.

## Constructive Narrative Perspective

Most individuals (70–80%) who have experienced traumatic and victimizing experiences evidence resilience, and in some instances, post-traumatic growth (Bonanno, 2004; Meichenbaum, 2006, 2007, 2009, 2011, 2012). The 20–30% of the traumatized population who evidence adjustment difficulties and who are candidates for some form of trauma therapy evidence a cognitive emotional, behavioral and spiritual style that contributes to persistent PTSD. Patients who receive the diagnosis of PTSD are likely to engage in:

- self-focused, mental defeating ruminative style of thinking;
- avoidant thinking processes of deliberate suppressing thoughts, using distracting behaviors that inadvertently reinforce avoidant behaviors and PTSD symptoms;

**TABLE 13.1** Checklist of therapy behaviors to facilitate the therapeutic alliance

- Convey respect, warmth, compassion, support, empathy, a caring attitude, and interest in helping. Be non-judgemental. Listen actively and attentively and let your patient know you are listening so he/she feels understood.
- Convey a relaxed confidence that help can be provided and a sense of realistic optimism, but not false hope. Communicate a positive expectancy of the possibility of change. Use phrases such as "As yet," "So far," and "RE" verbs such as RE-frame, RE-author, RE-engage. Emphasize that your patient can be helped, but it will require effort on both of your parts.
- Validate and normalize the patient's feelings. ("Given what you have been through, I would be deeply concerned, if *at times* you were not feeling overwhelmed and depressed.")
- Use guided discovery and Socratic Questioning. Use "How" and "What" questions. Stimulate the patient's curiosity, so he/she can become his/her own "therapist," "emotional detective."
- Enter the narrative text of the patient, using his/her metaphors. Assess the "rest of the patient's story" and collaboratively discover what the patient did and was able to achieve *in spite of* traumatic/victimizing experiences.
- Explore the patient's lay explanations of his/her problems and his/her expectations concerning treatment. Collaboratively establish "SMART" therapy goals (Specific, Measurable, Achievable, Realistic, and Time-limited). Use motivational interviewing procedures.
- Model a style of thinking. Ask the patient, "Do you ever find yourself in your day-to-day experiences asking yourself the same kind of questions that we ask each other here in therapy?"
- Encourage the patient to self-monitor (collect data) so that he/she can better appreciate the interconnectedness between feelings, thoughts, behaviors, and resultant consequences, and perhaps, inadvertently, unwittingly, and unknowingly behave in ways that may maintain and exacerbate presenting problems (e.g. avoidance behaviors reinforce PTSD symptoms).
- Conduct a pros and cons analysis and help the patient to break the behavioral "vicious cycle."
- Address any therapy interfering behaviors and potential barriers. Solicit patient commitment statements. Play "devil's advocate."
- Provide intermediate summaries and a summary at the end of each session. Over the course of treatment, have the patient generate this treatment summary. Highlight how the present session follows from previous sessions and is related to achieving treatment goals. Be specific. Have the patient generate the reasons why he/she should undertake behavioral changes.
- Help patients generate alternative "healing" narratives that empower them to examine their dominant "trauma" story and develop and live personal accounts that contribute to posttraumatic growth.
- Solicit feedback from the patient each session on how therapy is progressing and ways to improve treatment. Convey that you, the therapist, are always trying to improve and tailor treatment to the needs and strengths of each specific patient. Monitor the relationship for any alliance strains. Accept part of the responsibility for any difficulties in the relationship.

- overgeneralized memories and a recall style that intensifies hopelessness and impairs problem solving;
- contra-factual thinking, repeatedly asking "why" and "only if" questions for which there are no readily acceptable answers;
- engage in "thinking traps" that reinforce hypervigilance, safety and emotionally distancing behaviors and that contribute to the avoidance of self-disclosing and help seeking;
- negative spiritual coping responses (having a "spiritual struggle," anger responses, moral injuries, complicated grief, guilt, shame, and the like).

The trauma patients tell others and themselves "stories" that lead them to become stuck. One central goal of trauma therapy, no matter what form it may take, is to help patients develop and live a "healing story." There is a need for patients to integrate the trauma events into a coherent autobiographical account, so the traumatic events are landmarks, but not the defining elements of their accounts. Trauma patients need to develop "redemptive" stories that bolster hope, strengthen self-confidence, and indicate that their efforts will bear fruit. Changes in story telling provide access to new solutions. The patient's ability to generate a coherent narrative helps to reduce distress and hypervigilance, increases a sense of control, reduces feelings of chaos and unpredictability, and helps the patient develop meaning. Narrative coherence conveys a sense of personal self-efficacy and helps the patient make sense of what happened and points a direction to the future. Trauma is only one part of an individual's life, rather than the determinant aspect. Effective trauma therapy helps the patient learn to let the "past be the past." Patients can learn to disentangle themselves from the influences and lingering impact of traumatic events. In trauma therapy, patients engage in a narrative healing process.

Trauma therapists, no matter which form of acronym therapy they employ, are in the business of helping traumatized patients become "story-tellers" who can evidence resilience, moving from the 20–30% group to the 70–80% resilient group. The therapeutic alliance is the framework whereby trauma patients can share their trauma accounts, as well as what they did to survive and cope in the past; bolster their courage to confront rather than avoid trauma-related situations and remembrances; develop and strengthen coping strategies that foster hope; undertake meaning-making missions and reengage life. Move from being a "victim," to a "survivor," to a "thriver."

In my consultative capacity, I train trauma therapists to become "exquisitive" listeners and help them become collaborators in their patient's journey to develop "healing stories." As Stephen Joseph (2011, p. 131) has observed: "Human beings are story tellers. We are immersed in stories." The role of the trauma therapist is to help traumatized patients move along this journey of collecting data (results of personal experiments) that will "unfreeze" their beliefs about themselves, others, the world and the future. The therapeutic alliance is the ground in which such growth develops and blossoms (Meichenbaum, 1996, 2007). Its importance to the change process needs to be highlighted, repeatedly.

## Conclusion

Much effort has been expended to develop evidence-based interventions with patients diagnosed with PTSD and comorbid disorders – what are called "Acronym Therapies."

Exposure-based interventions such as Direct Therapy Exposure and Cognitive Processing Therapy have been endorsed as being most effective. Meta-analytic studies of various so-called evidence-based therapies for PTSD patients versus bona-fide comparison groups that were intended to succeed have raised questions about the differential effectiveness of various treatments. Both dismantling and specificity-based studies have questioned the mechanisms of change on those interventions. Common to all these "Acronym Therapies" are a set of core psychotherapeutic tasks, with the most central being the nature and quality of the therapeutic relationship which accounts for the largest proportion of treatment outcome variance.

The impact of the therapeutic relationship on treatment outcome is strengthened when ongoing, real-time session-by-session feedback is solicited from patients and used by the psychotherapist to identify potential failures and dropout risk and to alter treatment accordingly. Other core psychotherapeutic tasks beside establishing, maintaining, and monitoring therapeutic alliance include psychoeducation, nurturing hope by means of collaborative goal-setting and bolstering resilience, teaching coping skills and building in generalization procedures. Key ingredients in the development of a therapeutic alliance include empathy, trust, respect and a caring attitude. Table 13.1 provides a list of psychotherapeutic methods to enhance the therapeutic alliance and treatment outcomes.

A constructive narrative perspective of the therapeutic relationship highlights how to help traumatized/victimized patients develop "healing stories" with redemptive endings that engender hope, self-efficacy and help move trauma patients (some 20–30% of victimized individuals) to the 70–80% of resilient individuals. The therapeutic relationship provides patients with an opportunity to share, reframe, and develop the courage to reexpose, reexperience, reengage and review their lives so traumatic events are incorporated into a coherent narrative and a personal account.

## Summary points

- Meta-analytic studies have raised questions about the differential effectiveness of various treatments.
- The nature and quality of the therapeutic alliance accounts for the largest proportion of treatment outcome variance.

- Core relationship tasks include empathy, trust, respect, and a caring attitude.
- A constructive narrative perspective of the therapeutic alliance highlights how to help traumatized/victimized patients develop "healing stories" with redemptive endings that engender hope and self-efficacy.

## Notes

1. DTE: Direct Therapy Exposure; VRE: Virtual Reality Exposure; CPT: Cognitive Processing Therapy; EMDR: Eye Movement Desensitization and Reprocessing; SIT: Stress Inoculation Training; AMT: Anxiety Management Training; MBSR: Mindfulness-Based Stress Reduction; MAGT: Mindfulness and Acceptance Group Therapy; ACT: Acceptance and Commitment Therapy; CR: Cognitive Restructuring; TF-CBT: Trauma-Focused Cognitive Behaviour Therapy; DBT: Dialectical Behaviour Therapy; CP: Counting Procedures; CMT: Compassion Mindfulness Training; IPT: Interpersonal Therapy; IRT: Imagery Rehearsal Therapy.
2. SS: Seeking Safety Treatment; TARGET: Trauma Adaptive Recovery Education and Therapy; STAIR MPE: Skills Training in Affective and Interpersonal Regulation Followed by Modified Prolonged Exposure.

## Suggested reading

Duncan, B. L., Miller, S. D., Wampold, B. E., & Hubble, M. A. (eds) (2009). *The Heart and Soul of Change: Delivering What Works in Therapy* (2nd edn). Washington, DC: American Psychological Association.

Meichenbaum, D. (2006). Resilience and posttraumatic growth: a constructive narrative perspective. In L. G. Calhoun & R. G. Tedeschi (eds), *Handbook of Posttraumatic Growth: Research and Practice* (pp. 355–68). Mahwah, NJ: Erlbaum Associates.

Wamplod, B. E., Imel, Z. E., Laska, K. M., Benish, S., Miller, S. D., Fluckiger, C., Del Re, A. C., Baardseth, T. P., & Budge, S. (2010). Determining that works on the treatment of PTSD. *Clinical Psychology Review*, 30, 923–33.

## References

Ackerman, S. J., & Hilsenroth, M. J. (2003). A review of therapist characteristics and techniques positively impacting the therapeutic alliance. *Clinical Psychology Review*, 23, 1–33.

Benish, S., Imel, Z. E., & Wampold, B. E. (2008). The relative efficacy of bona fide psychotherapies of post-traumatic stress disorder: a meta-analysis of direct comparisons. *Clinical Psychology Review*, 28, 746–58.

Bonanno, G. A. (2004). Loss, trauma and human resilience: how we understand the human capacity to thrive after extremely aversive events. *American Psychologist*, 59, 20–8.

Bordin, E. S. (1979). The generalizability of the psychoanalytic concept of the working alliance. *Psychotherapy: Theory, Research and Practice*, 16, 252–60.

Duncan, B. L., Miller, S. D., Wampold, B. E., & Hubble, M. A. (eds) (2009). *The Heart and Soul of Change: Delivering What Works in Therapy* (2nd edn). Washington, DC: American Psychological Association.

Ehlers, A., Bisson, J., Clark, D. M., Creamer, M., Pilling, S., & Richards, A. (2010). Do all psychological treatments really work the same in posttraumatic stress disorder. *Clinical Psychology Review*, 30, 269–76.

Elliot, B. (2008). Research on the client experiences of therapy: introduction to the special issue. *Psychotherapy Research*, 18, 239–42.

Escudero, V., Friedlander, M. L., & Heatherington, L. (2011). Using the e-SOFTA for video training and research on alliance-related behavior. *Psychotherapy*, 48, 138–47.

Frank, J. D., & Frank, J. B. (1991). *Persuasion and Healing: A Comparative Study of Psychotherapy* (3rd edn). Baltimore, MD: Johns Hopkins University Press.

Friedlander, M. L., Escadero, V., Heatherington, L., & Diamond, G. M. (2011) Alliance in couple and family therapy. *Psychotherapy*, 48, 25–33.

Hamilton, B., & Coates, J. (1993). Perceived helpfulness and use of professional services by abused women. *Journal of Family Violence*, 8, 313–24.

Horvath, A. G., & Bedi, R. P. (2002). The alliance. In J. C. Norcross (ed.), *Psychotherapy Relationships that Work: Therapist Contributions and Responsiveness to Patients* (pp. 37–69). New York: Oxford Press.

Horvath, A. G., Del Re, C., Fluckiger, C., & Symonds, D. (2011). Alliance in individual psychotherapy. *Psychotherapy*, 48, 9–16.

Imel, Z. E., Wampold, B. E., Miller, S. D., & Fleming R. R. (2008). Distinctions without a difference: direct comparisons of psychotherapies for alcohol use disorders. *Psychology of Addictive Behaviors*, 22, 533–43.

Institute of Medicine (2008). *Treatment of Posttraumatic Stress Disorder: An Assessment of Evidence*. Washington, DC: National Academic Press.

Joseph, S. (2011). *What Doesn't Kill Us: The New Psychology of Posttraumatic Growth*. New York: Basic Books.

Keijsers, G. P., Schaap, C., & Hoogduin, C. A. (2000). The impact of interpersonal patient therapists behavior on outcome in cognitive-behavior therapy: a review of empirical studies. *Behavior Modification*, 24, 264–97.

Lambert, M. J. (2010). *Prevention of Treatment Failure: The Art of Measurement, Monitoring and Feedback in Clinical Practice*. Washington, DC: American Psychological Association Press.

Lambert, M. J., Harmon, C., Slada, K., Whipple, J. L., & Hawkins, E. J. (2005). Providing feedback to psychotherapists in their patient's progress: clinical results and practice suggestions. *Journal of Clinical Psychology*, 61, 165–74.

McFarlane, A. C. (1994). Helping the victims of natural disasters. In J. R. Freedy & S. E. Hobfoll (eds), *Traumatic Stress: From Theory to Practice*. New York: Plenum.

McLeod, B. D. (2011). Relation of the alliance with outcomes in youth psychotherapy: a meta-analysis. *Clinical Psychology Review*, 31, 603–16.

Martin, D. J., Garske, J. P., & Davis, M. K. (2000). Relation of the therapeutic alliance with outcome and other variables: a meta-analytic review. *Journal of Consulting and Clinical Psychology*, 68, 438–50.

Meichenbaum, D. (1996). Forming alliances: rescripting the narrative of trauma. *Professional Counselor*, June, 61–3.

Meichenbaum, D. (2006). Resilience and posttraumatic growth: a constructive narrative perspective. In L. G. Calhoun & R. G. Tedeschi (eds), *Handbook of Posttraumatic Growth: Research and Practice* (pp. 355–68). Mahwah, NJ: Erlbaum Associates.

Meichenbaum, D. (2007). Stress inoculation training: a preventative and treatment approach. In P. M. Lehrer, R. L. Woolfolk, & W. E. Sirne (eds), *Principles and Practice of Stress Management* (pp. 497–518). New York: Guilford Press.

Meichenbaum, D. (2009). Core psychotherapeutic tasks with returning soldiers: a case conceptualization approach. In B. Morgillo Freeman, B. A. Moore, & A. Freeman (eds), *Living and Surviving in Harm's Way* (pp. 193–210). New York: Routledge.

Meichenbaum, D. (2011). Resilience building as a means to prevent PTSD and related adjustment problems in military personnel. In B. A. Moore & W. E. Penk (eds), *Treating PTSD in Military Personnel* (pp. 325–55). New York: Guilford Press.

Meichenbaum, D. (2012). *Roadmap to Resilience*. Clearwater, FL: Institute Press.

Messer, S. B., & Wampold, B. E. (2002). Let's face facts: common factors are more potent than specific therapy ingredients. *Clinical Psychology: Science and Practice*, 9, 21–5.

Miller, S. D., Duncan, B. L., & Wampold, B. E. (eds) (2010). The Heart and Soul of Change (2nd edn). Washington, DC: American Psychological Association.

Miller, S. D., Duncan, B. L., Brown, J., Sorrell, R., & Chalk, M. B. (2007). Using formal client feedback to improve outcome and retention. *Journal of Brief Therapy*, 5, 19–28.

Muran, J. C., & Barber, J. P. (2010). *The Therapeutic Alliance: An Evidence-Based Guide to Practice*. New York: Guilford Press.

Norcross, J. C. (ed.) (2002). *Psychotherapy Relationships that Work: Therapist Contributions and Responsiveness in Patients*. New York: Oxford University Press.

Norcross, J. (2009). The therapeutic relationship. In B. L. Duncan, S. D. Miller, B. E. Wampold, & M. A. Hubble (eds), *The Heart and Soul of Change: Delivering What Works in Therapy* (2nd edn, pp. 113–42). Washington, DC: American Psychological Association.

Powers, M. B., Halpern, J. M., Ferenschak, M. P., Gillihan, S. J., & Foa, E. B. (2010). A meta-analytic review of prolonged exposure for posttraumatic stress disorder. *Clinical Psychology Review*, 30, 635–41.

Rogers, C. R. (1957). The necessary and sufficient conditions of therapeutic personality change. *Journal of Consulting Psychology*, 21, 95–103.

Rosen, G. R., & Frueh, B. C. (2010). *Clinician's Guide to PTSD*. Hoboken, NJ: John Wiley & Sons.

Safran, J. D., & Muran, C. (2000). *Negotiating the Therapeutic*. New York: Guilford Press.

Sharf, J., Primavera, L. H., & Diener, M. J. (2010). Dropout and the therapeutic alliance. *Psychotherapy: Theory, Research and Practice*, 47, 637–45.

Shimokawa, K., Lambert, M. J., & Smart, D. W. (2010). Enhancing treatment outcome of patients at risk of treatment failure: meta-analytic and mega-analytic review of psychotherapy quality assurance system. *Journal of Consulting and Clinical Psychology*, 78, 298–311.

Walsh, R. (2011). Lifestyle and mental health. *American Psychologist*, 66, 579–92.

Wampold, B. E. (2001). *The Great Psychotherapy Debate: Models, Methods and Findings*. Mahwah, NJ: Erlbaum.

Wampold, B. E., Mondin, G. W., Moody, M., Stitch, F., Benson, K., & Ahn, H. (1997). A meta-analysis of outcome studies comparing bona-fide psychotherapies: empirically "All must have prizes." *Psychological Bulletin*, 122, 203–15.

Wampold, B. E., Imel, Z. E., Laska, K. M., Benish, S., Miller, S. D., Fluckiger, C., Del Re, A. C., Baardseth, T. P., & Budge, S. (2010). Determining what works on the treatment of PTSD. *Clinical Psychology Review*, 30, 923–33.

Webb, C. A., DeRubeis, R. J., & Barber, J. P. (2010). Therapist adherence/competence and treatment outcome: a meta-analytic review. *Journal of Consulting and Clinical Psychology*, 78, 200–11.

Yalom, I. (2002). *The Gift of Therapy*. New York: Harper Collins.

# PART VI

# Working with Suicidal Patients

## Lessons Learned

The most difficult and challenging clients are those who express suicidal thoughts and behaviors. As noted in the initial article in this part, the first client I saw as a graduate student at the Veteran's Administrative Hospital died by suicide. I immediately felt that I was responsible for his death. My fellow clinicians, and my clinical supervisor, tried to console me, but deep down I felt I somehow failed and questioned whether I should continue my training to become a clinical psychologist. But, I soon learned that clinical practice and client suicide go hand-in-hand, as summarized in Table VI.1.

Over the course of my 45 years, I have had a number of clinical situations where clients I have seen, or for whom I was a clinical supervisor, manifested suicidal behaviors. For instance, at one psychiatric hospital where I was consulting, a client died by suicide and I was asked to evaluate the degree to which their setting

**TABLE VI.1** Clinical practice and client suicide

| |
|---|
| 1 in 3 clinical graduate students will have a client who attempts suicide, and 1 in 6 will experience a client's suicide at some point in their career. |
| Full-time psychotherapists average five suicidal patients per month. |
| 1 in 3 psychiatrists and 1 in 7 psychologists report losing a patient to suicide. |
| 1 in 6 psychiatric patients who die by suicide, die while in active treatment with a psychotherapist. |
| Completed suicides often take place soon after individuals are treated by a mental health provider. |
| In about 25% of instances of client suicide, the client's family will sue the treating clinician and his/her clinic. |

Sources. Bongar, 1992, 2002; Hawton & Van Heeringen, 2000.

met the "gold standard of care" for suicidal clients. I put together a Checklist Report for them.When I was an Honorary President of the Canadian Psychological Association (CPA), I was invited to give a keynote address at the CPA conference. My paper "35 Years of Working with Suicidal Patients: Lessons Learned," which I have chosen to include in this part, is the paper I presented. While a clinician is unlikely to be held responsible for the death of a specific client, the clinician will be held responsible as to whether he/she met the "gold standard" of care and documented, documented, documented, on an ongoing basis, the treatment protocol. How many of these checklist items do you, as a clinician, routinely include in your work with suicidal clients?

The second chapter in this part, "Every Patient's Worst Nightmare," provides a dramatic and tragic case study of traumatic bereavement and a prolonged and complicated grief disorder. The clinical intervention I employed illustrates a Constructive Narrative treatment approach of ways to help suicidal clients to develop self-compassion, as she "re-authors" her life and learns to transform her guilt, emotional pain, and grief into meaning-making activities.

Further readings on the topic of suicide include the following, all of which can be viewed and downloaded at the web address given on page xii:

- 35 Years of Working with Suicidal Patients: Lessons Learned (An Update).
- Treatment of Individuals with Prolonged and Complicated Grief and Traumatic Bereavement.
- Child and Adolescent Depression and Suicide: Promising Hope and Facilitating Change.
- Ways to Bolster Resilience in LGBTQ (Lesbian, Gay, Bisexual, Transgender, Questioning) Youth.
- A Psychotherapist's View of Decision-Making: Implications for Peaceful Negotiations.

## References

Bongar, B. (1992). Guidelines for risk management in the care of the suicidal patient . In B. Bongar (ed.), *Suicide: Guidelines for Assessment, Management and Treatment.* New York: Oxford University Press.

Bongar, B. (2002). *The Suicidal Patient: Clinical and Legal Standards of Care,* 2nd edn. Washington, DC: American Psychological Association.

Hawton, K. & Van Heeringen, K. (eds) (2000). *International Handbook of Suicide and Attempted Suicide.* Chichester: Wiley & Sons.

# 14

# 35 YEARS OF WORKING WITH SUICIDAL PATIENTS

## Lessons learned

*Donald Meichenbaum*

## Abstract

Following a personal description of several patients who have committed suicide in my clinical practice and consultation, I summarize the literature on risk assessment for suicide. The form adopted is a set of specific questions that a knowledgeable clinical supervisor might use to help a clinical team examine their clinical decision-making and determine practical guidelines in caring for a suicidal patient. The factors covered include suicidal risk assessment, presence of comorbid and protective factors, immediate emergency interventions on both an outpatient and inpatient basis, and possible short-term and long-term interventions. The training and practical clinical implications of following these guidelines are considered. The checklist, in the form of probing questions, is not intended to foster an adversarial process, but rather to provide a framework in evaluating the assessment and care of suicidal individuals.

My professional journey began as a graduate student in clinical psychology at a Veteran's Administration hospital. H.B. was a 45-year-old Caucasian male who was diagnosed as schizophrenic and who had a history of parental neglect, as well as combat-related stress experiences. He was one of my first clinical patients and I had worked with him for several months. While under my care, he killed himself.

Over the course of the next 35 years of clinical work, I have been involved with three other psychiatric patients who have died by suicide. Another suicidal patient was being seen by a clinical graduate student whom I was supervising. He was her first patient and he killed himself over the Christmas holidays.

– Meichenbaum, D. (2005). 35 years of working with suicidal patients: lessons learned. *Canadian Psychology*, 46, 64–72. Permission to republish by Canadian Psychological Association.

In fact, patient suicide is not that unusual in the life of clinicians. As Bongar (2002) has observed, one in six psychology interns and one in three psychiatric residents experience the suicide of a patient at some point during their training. Moreover, with clinical experience the incidence of patient suicide does *not* greatly diminish. A practicing clinical psychologist will average five suicidal patients per month. One in two psychiatrists and one in six clinical psychologists will experience a patient's suicide in their professional careers (Chemtob *et al.*, 1989).

Two other recent clinical consultations are the occasion for the present reflections. I was asked to consult to a Canadian treatment team called the Society of Northern Renewal headed by Dr. William Foote. They were addressing the high suicide rate of Inuit people in the territory of Nunavut. As noted in Dr. Foote's government report (private communication), the Inuit people are twice as likely to commit suicide than other native populations and four times as likely to engage in self-destructive behaviors. A variety of factors, including economic dislocation and deprivation, social isolation, disruption of traditional cultural patterns, and demoralizing social problems (substandard living, overcrowding) and substance abuse contribute to such self-injurious behaviors (Meichenbaum, in press). On top of this array of stressors in the early 1980s in three Inuit communities, a subgroup of 85 male Inuit youth were sexually abused by a self-confessed male paedophile school teacher over a period of six years. One of the consequences of this victimization experience is the very high rate of suicide among the Inuit, especially among the cohort of abused young men. For instance, the suicide rate among Inuit females is 32 per 100,000, 119 per 100,000 for Inuit males, and for the cohort of abused young men ages 19 to 29, the suicide rate is 200 per 100,000 (Foote, 2004, private communication).

These suicidal numbers stand in stark contrast to the base rate of suicide of only 12 per 100,000 in the general population. The suicide rate rises to 60 per 100,000 in a psychiatric population (Bongar, 2002).

My last consultation where a patient committed suicide was at a psychiatric facility where an adolescent patient was hospitalized on Friday evening by his parents for substance abuse and erratic behaviors. On Monday when his parents came to visit, the youth was dead, having hung himself. When I met with the hospital staff afterwards, they were concerned that somehow they had been negligent. Somehow they had missed the warning signs, failed to take proper precautions. Moreover, administrative concerns about legal liability also arose.

This recent dialogue with the hospital staff triggered for me a flood of memories and accompanying anxiety that come with the territory of working with a clinical population. Consider that one-third of the general (nonclinical) population have suicidal thoughts at some point in their lives. Given this high base rate of suicidal ideation in the North American population, how shall clinical staff respond when a potentially suicidal patient arrives at the clinic? The hospital staff asked me to summarize the empirical literature on risk assessment for suicide, as well as glean from my 35 years of clinical experience, a set of practice guidelines that they can use with future potentially suicidal patients, as well as in their postmortem analysis of the death of this youth. The clinical staff wanted to make sure that they had left no stone unturned clinically speaking and that no broader system issues were involved. The practice guidelines that I put together are offered in the form of a checklist of probing, but supportive, questions that can be used to improve the quality of care. The remainder of this chapter is the list of questions that reflect my best judgment about preventative efforts clinicians should follow when working with suicidal patients. These are *not* the only questions or guide-posts, but rather they reflect a set of practice guidelines that I now use in my clinical decision-making and in my consultations to psychiatric facilities. They also represent the guidelines that we follow at the Miami-based Melissa Institute for Violence Prevention and Treatment of Victims of Violence, where I am the Research Director (see www.melissainstitute.org).

The intent of this comprehensive list of probing questions is *not* to overwhelm the clinician, but rather to provide a set of reminders that can guide clinical decision-making, especially when clinicians are working under highly stressful and anxiety-engendering circumstances of trying to help suicidal patients. In fact, various surveys indicate that suicidal patients constitute the single most stressful aspect of most psychotherapists' work (Deustch, 1984). Marsha Linehan (1999) captured this level of stress when she observed:

> Therapy with suicidal patients is similar to *walking a tightrope* stretched over the Grand Canyon. Bending one direction, the therapist must act to keep the patient alive in the present. Bending in the other direction, the therapist must be careful not to respond in a manner that increases the likelihood of future suicide. Complicating all of this are the fears almost all therapists have of falling off the tightrope with the patient and of being held responsible for a patient's death if a misstep is taken and balance is lost.
>
> *(Linehan, 1999, p. 115)*

The following list of probing questions (see Appendix) that I put together for the hospital staff represents my assimilation of the research of multiple suicidologists, including: Aaron Beck, Bruce Bongar, Tom Ellis, David Jobes, Thomas Joiner, Phil Kleespies, Anton Leenaars, Marsha Linehan, J. Maltsberger, R. Maris, M. David Rudd, Ed Shneidman and their colleagues (see Berk *et al.*, 2004; Bongar, 1992, 2002; Bongar *et al.*, 1992; Bongar *et al.*, 1993; Clark, 1998; Ellis, 1990; Fremouw *et al.*, 1990; Friedman, 1989, Hawton *et al.*, 1998a, 1998b; Jobes, 2000; Joiner *et al.*, 1999; Kleespies & Dettmer, 2000; Kleespies *et al.*, 1999, 1999; Leenaars, 2004; Linehan, 1997, 1999; Maltsberger 1986; Maltsberger & Buie, 1989; Maris, 1981; O'Carroll *et al.*, 1996; Ramsay, 1987; Range & Knott, 1997; Rudd, 2000; Rudd & Joiner, 1998a, 1998b; Rudd *et al.*, 1996, 2001; Schneidman, 1993, 1996; Silverman *et al.*, 1994; Spirito *et al.*, 2000; Weishaar & Beck, 1990). Also see the American Psychiatric Association Practice Guidelines for Assessing and Treating suicide (http://www.psych.org/cme/apacme/index/cfm) and the Guidelines for

Clinicians offered by Aeschi Working Group on Suicide (http://www.aeschiconference.unibe.ch/).

Imagine that a patient of yours committed suicide and you were going to reflect on your clinical efforts. How many of the following questions could you answer? Or, if you are not a clinician, imagine that a family member or a friend of yours has expressed suicidal thoughts and you refer him/her to a clinician. You want to ensure that your loved one will receive "state-of-the-art" care. How many of the following practice guidelines inherent in the series of questions will the clinician follow? In short, after 35 years of clinical experience, this is the list of guidelines I use when seeing a suicidal patient. Obviously, I cannot keep all of these comprehensive steps in mind when seeing a suicidal patient, but after a session with the patient or right before a future session, a quick review of the questions in the Appendix provides me with a set of reminders of the steps I need to consider.

The Appendix provides a set of practice guidelines for assessing and intervening with suicidal patients. This list can assist in clinical decision-making and in improving patient care. It is a checklist that I aspire to keep in mind when working with suicidal patients. When considering this list of practice guidelines, it is important for clinicians to heed the warnings offered by Ellis (2004), Hendin (1995) and Jobes (2000). They each cautioned clinicians to be attentive to their own attitudes toward the suicidal patient and to their own fears about possible legal liability. If clinicians use suicide management techniques such as threat of involuntary hospitalization that reflect a controlling posture, then such efforts may inadvertently result in the suicidal patient relinquishing the responsibility for staying alive to others and thus compromise the therapeutic alliance and treatment efficacy.

In considering the practice guidelines enumerated in the Appendix, there are several additional caveats to keep in mind. First, the list of questions and accompanying guidelines do not address all of the issues that might arise in the assessment and treatment of suicidal patients, but they do reflect the cumulative wisdom I have developed over 35 years of clinical experience. Research based on empirical prediction models have consistently failed to reliably predict suicide in any individual case. Such algorithmic equations have resulted in high false-positive and false-negative rates (Pokorny, 1993; Rudd et al., 1996). As Kleespies and Dettmer (2000) have reported in an estimated 60% to 70% of suicide completers they have no known history of prior attempts and they commit suicide on their first attempt.

While there are still limitations to the science of suicidology, there is an urgent need to ensure that our new clinical students have a working knowledge of assessment and treatment guidelines. In fact, a survey of clinical graduate programs in North America by Bongar and Harmatz (1991) indicated that only 40% of graduate programs in clinical psychology offer any formal training in the assessment and interventions with suicidal individuals. Perhaps, the rate of such clinical training have gone up since the Bongar and Harmatz initial survey. Hopefully, the present reflective article will be a catalyst for such additional training, given the widespread occurrence of suicide in the patients we see.

Finally, on a personal note, a colleague's spouse had attempted suicide. My colleague asked me what advice I had that she could pass along to the clinical treatment team for her husband. I gave her a copy of the Appendix. Hopefully, these practice guidelines will help save a life.

I am indebted to Dr. Tom Ellis for his helpful comments on this paper. Direct correspondence about this paper to dhmeich@aol.com.

## APPENDIX

Evaluation of Suicidal Patients: Risk Assessment and Practice Guidelines

## What are you doing to establish a therapeutic alliance with the suicidal patient?

- Before we examine how you are assessing ongoing risk, let me (the supportive clinical supervisor) ask some questions about how you (the clinician) are going about establishing a *therapeutic relationship* with your patient so he/she feels comfortable sharing his/her "story" and accompanying suicidal feelings, thoughts, and behaviors.
- Specifically, how are you connecting with your patient so you can understand the current and lifetime circumstances that led to the present suicidal behaviors?
- How are you going about establishing a supportive, collaborative, nonjudgmental therapeutic relationship?
- Have you asked your patient to tell his/her "story" of what happened that led up to the present suicidal behaviors? In what ways have you become a "fellow traveler" in understanding the developmental pathways, the inner experiences of pain and shame, and the goal-directed behaviors behind the present suicidal urges and acts? (See Maris, 1981; Michel & Valach, 1997).
- How are you *sharing decision-making responsibility* with the patient in order to foster a collaborative relationship? What are you doing to help nurture a collaborative "team" approach so you both work on an agreed-upon treatment plan, and both feel responsible for progress?
- How are you nurturing a collaborative "we" effort right from the outset of your contact?
- How are you monitoring the quality of this therapeutic relationship with the patient? Are you using any specific probes, Patient Therapy Alliance Scales, monitoring and recording patient active involvement?

*I ask these questions because the research evidence highlights the critical importance of a therapeutic alliance in the assessment and treatment process of suicidal patients. (See Chiles & Strosahl, 1995; Ellis, 2004; Hawton et al., 1998b.)*

## What assessment strategies are you using to determine ongoing risk of suicide?

- Having established such a therapeutic relationship with the patient, how are you systematically assessing for the patient's level of suicidality and ongoing risk of suicide?

- More specifically, has the patient evidenced suicidal verbalization, talk of death or dying, mood and behavioral changes? Are you assessing for the severity of the suicidal attempt in terms of intent, motives, precautions to prevent discovery, and premeditation?

- What specific assessment measures and interview questions are you using in formulating the level of suicide risk? (See Collaborative Assessment and Management of Suicidality, CAMS, Protocol developed by Jobes, 2000.)

- Have you explicitly assessed for:
  - your patient's history of all past suicidal behaviors, including suicidal ideation, plans or threats of such suicidal acts, even if no expressed intent to die, and patient's previous statements not to engage in suicidal behavior;
  - the degree of symptoms that Joiner and colleagues (Joiner *et al.*, 1997; Joiner *et al.*, 1999) describe as Resolved Plan and Preparation which include:
    - the intensity and duration of suicidal ideation (more important than the frequency of suicidal ideation);
    - specificity of the suicidal plan;
    - preparation for the suicidal attempt;
    - sense of courage and competence to make an attempt;
    - the likelihood of the patient acting impulsively and his/her sense of confidence and control to delay acting on impulses;
    - access and means to engage in self-injurious behaviors (availability of a weapon in the house, means to overdose).

- Have you conducted behavioral and cognitive chain analyses of the events that led up to the suicidal act?

- Have you assessed for the patient's Reasons for Living?

- Since over 90% of suicidal patients have an underlying psychiatric and substance abuse disorder, what DSM-IV diagnoses did your patient evidence at the time of your initial contact and over the course of his/her lifetime (i.e., lifetime comorbidity)?

- How often do you conduct re-evaluations of suicide risk? On an ongoing basis, have you assessed the patient's suicidal ideation, intent, and plans, access to lethal means, degree of hopelessness, acute dissociative and psychotic symptoms, drug and alcohol use, and the use of psychiatric medications? How do you choose the re-assessment times?

- Have you assessed for specific maladaptive cognitions and accompanying feelings such as hopelessness, helplessness, unworthiness, unloveability, and an inability to tolerate distress? Have you assessed for the patient's feelings of having been humiliated, estranged, emotionally numb, and the patient's beliefs that such feelings are both irreversible and unendurable?

• Have you assessed for the patient's tendencies to evidence rigid, dichotomous thinking concerning him/herself and others, poor problem-solving skills, and his/her view that suicide is a desirable, and the only, solution to his/her problems?

• Have you been able to determine what intra-and interpersonal problems suicide might solve for the patient (e.g., escape from self, avoid stressors and conflict, restore sense of control, hurt others, and the like)?

• Based on your assessment, what risk and protective factors (e.g., family or friends) have you determined to be present in this case? Have you asked the patient to recall times from the past when he/she was able to "tough it out" and cope with suicidal urges and various stressors?

## What background factors have been assessed?

• What background and developmental factors have you considered in formulating your appraisal of suicidal risk? Have you found any evidence of a history of physical and/or sexual abuse? How was this determined?

• Have you obtained a family history (use a Genogram) that tracks the incidence and seriousness of depression and suicidality in the patient's family and community?

## How have you assessed for comorbidity and determined level of suicidal risk?

• Have you found any evidence of any other comorbid psychiatric or medical disorders that could have increased the risk of suicide? How are you assessing for the presence of major affective disorders: anxiety disorder such as panic attacks, PTSD, schizophrenia, substance abuse, and Borderline Personality Disorder, angry, hostile and irritable behaviors?

• How would you characterize your patient's level of suicidal risk? Is the suicide risk nonexistent, mild, moderate, severe, or extreme?

• What is the patient's legal status? What steps have you taken to ensure that the legal guidelines for treating suicidal patients are followed?

• Given that your suicidal patient has been judged to be at high risk as evidenced by his/her multiple suicidal attempts, psychiatric history, and diagnostic comorbidity, and elevated level on the Resolve Plan and Preparation indicators, have you provided intensive follow-up care such as increasing the frequency of your treatment appointments, providing intensive case management, ongoing telephone calls, letter writing to the patient, and/or home visits?

- Have you considered psychiatric hospitalization (including involuntary hospitalization), especially for patients who are judged to be at severe and extreme risk of suicide as evidenced by a history of multiple suicidal attempts and a lifetime history of comorbid disorders? Is hospitalization available and accessible to the patient?

## What have you done explicitly to reduce the presence of risk factors?

- Have you ensured that all easily accessible means of committing suicide such as firearms and drugs are removed? What have you done to convince the patient to remove such lethal items? Have you informed family members (cohabiting individuals) of the existence of lethal items? Have you removed (or have someone removed) the potentially lethal items?
- How have you conveyed your availability to your suicidal patient? Have you scheduled the therapy sessions more frequently? Have you provided the patient with designated times to call in between sessions? Have you called the patient between sessions? When you are away, have you provided the patient with the name and telephone number of the backup therapist?
- Have you provided the patient with a wallet-size "crisis card" that includes names, telephone numbers of hospital emergency rooms, hotlines, and social supports?
- Have you generated contingency plans with the patient (and significant others) of how to handle emergencies? Have you encouraged the patient to seek services early in a crisis by calling an emergency number or by going to the emergency room?
- While there is some debate about the usefulness of a written and oral "Contract for Safety" with suicidal patients, have you employed such an intervention, as described by Fremouw *et al.* (1990) and Linehan (1993). If you have not used such a Contract for Safety, what is your rationale for omitting it?
- Have you been able to solicit from the patient a commitment to both refuse to act on suicidal urges and to inform the therapist, other staff members, family or friends before acting?
- Have you engaged the patient in a discussion of the relationship between depressed feelings and thoughts and suicidal behaviors? For example, have you conveyed to the patient: *"While suicide is an available option and given your view of your situation that is understandable, it is critical that you allow us some time to work on reducing your emotional pain. The depression that you are experiencing has a way of obscuring other possible solutions. Would you be willing to partner with me and hold off on the suicide option in order to allow yourself the time that is needed to address these issues? You are just plain wrong in your belief that suicide is the only or the best solution to your problems. I do not want you to make a permanent decision to what may be a temporary problem."* (See Ellis, 2004.)

- Have you directly treated the patient's suicidal behaviors (e.g., frequency and duration of suicidal ideation, level of hopelessness, improved the patient's adaptive coping efforts such as emotion-regulation skills, distress and frustration tolerance skills, problem-solving abilities) and the patient's ability to form and sustain supportive relationships?

## Have you involved family members and significant others?

- How will you decide if significant others (family members, friends) should be involved in assessment, treatment planning, and interventions? Are there any contra-indications to involve family members such as risk of (re)victimization, level of family members' psychopathology?
- How have you involved the patient's significant others (spouse, parents, caregivers) in the initial assessment, treatment planning, and ongoing risk assessment processes? How have you evaluated the significant others' ability to provide and maintain a safe, supportive environment for the patient? How have you assisted the significant others to develop communication skills with the patient and to address their own needs, stress, and psychopathology, if present?
- Have you helped the patient to establish and mobilize available and accessible social supports? What exactly have you done to accomplish these treatment goals?
- What have you done to communicate assessment and treatment information to the patient's significant others?
- What have you done to alert family members of the patient's suicidal risk? Have you worked out a plan with family members of risk indicators and instituted a suicide watch at home, if indicated? Have you provided a list of preventative interventions/options to help the family members decrease the risk of suicide?
- Have you notified significant others (if appropriate) of the treatment plan and enlisted them as allies in reducing ongoing stressors, and as facilitators of treatment adherence?
- How have you used community resources during the patient's suicidal crises, namely, the police, paramedics, crisis hot line team, the patient's physician, mental health team, and family members?

## How have you gone about determining the role of medication?

- How have you gone about assessing *all forms of medication* (prescribed psychotropic, over the counter and other forms of unprescribed medications) that he/she is using? How have you determined what illegal forms of substances the patient is using?

- In consultation with a psychiatrist, what specific psychotropic medications have been prescribed for symptomatic relief? What have you done to ensure that your patient takes the medications as prescribed?
- Given that medication was prescribed, what anticipatory adherence counseling, including a consideration of possible barriers to treatment compliance, have you addressed in treatment?

## What specific psychotherapeutic interventions did you provide?

- Let us begin with a question I raised at the outset of this inquiry. Given the critical importance of the *therapeutic relationship* to the assessment and treatment process, what have you done to enhance this relationship and to foster a collaborative working alliance? Have you collaborated with the patient in re-evaluating his/her treatment goals in order to nurture a self-help orientation? (See Ellis, 2004.)
- More specifically, based on your evaluation of the patient's suicidal risk, what specific assessment and treatment decisions and actions have you taken?
- Have you increased the frequency and/or duration of your clinical contacts with the patient?
- Have you conducted frequent assessments of suicide risk and documented these?
- Have you solicited at the outset of treatment in both verbal and written form the patient's informed consent concerning issues of confidentiality and safety?
- In addition, have you considered with the patient the treatment goals and the various treatment options (kind, time, costs, potential benefits) to achieve these goals?
- How have you gone about choosing a specific psychotherapeutic intervention with this patient? In choosing your interventions, where have the promising results on problem-solving therapy with suicidal patients fitted in (e.g., Clum & Lerner; 1990; Hawton & Van Heeringen, 2000; Townsend *et al.*, 2001; Salkovskis *et al.*, 1990) and cognitive therapy with suicidal patients (Beck *et al.*, 2004; Ellis, 2004; Freeman & Reinecke, 1993; Jacobs, 2000; Linehan, Armstrong, Suarez, Allman, & Heard, 1991; Meichenbaum, 1994, 2002; Reilly, 1998; Rudd, 1998; Rudd *et al.*, 1996, 2001).
- It has been recommended that the treatment for patients who are experiencing an acute suicidal crisis should consist of relatively short-term psychotherapy, that is, directive and crisis-focused, which emphasizes problem-solving and skills building. How have these recommendations, if at all, influenced your treatment decision-making?
- It has been recommended in the instance of chronic cases of suicidality that relatively long-term psychotherapy, in which relationship issues, interpersonal communication, and self-image issues, should be the focus of your

intervention. How have these recommendations, if at all, influenced your treatment decision-making?

- Have you addressed in treatment with the patient the identified stressors that contributed to suicidal risk? Has the patient experienced losses, reversal in status, changes in circumstances or health? How have these issues been addressed?

- Have you reframed the suicide attempt as a failure in problem-solving, and worked with your patient to increase options for dealing with life stressors and interpersonal conflicts?

- Have you helped the patient break what he/she perceives as his/her problems into smaller parts in order to deal with one aspect at a time? How have you helped the patient appreciate that the stressors he/she experiences are potentially solvable problems?

- What have you done over the course of therapy to remove or lessen the impact of ongoing stressors in the patient's life? How have you helped the patient to address the variety of factors that may have contributed to the initial suicidal attempt such as acute conflict with significant others, losses, history of victimization?

- Which of the following targeted-identified skills deficits that contributed to the suicidal behavior have you targeted for treatment, namely: emotional dysregulation, poor distress tolerance, impulsive behavioral style, anger management, interpersonal communication, cognitive distortions, poor problem-solving, self-image disturbances, and day-to-day functioning at home and at work? How have you helped the patient address each of these deficits?

- What have you done to help the patient extricate him/herself from such difficult situations? How have you helped the patient to address his/her sense of loneliness, feelings of unworthiness, and unloveability?

- What have you done to help the patient develop a life that is "worth" living? What specific therapeutic steps have you taken to help the patient improve his/her life? As Linehan (1999, p. 166) observed, "*Therapy must be more than a suicide prevention program. It must be a life improvement program.*"

- Have you given the patient anything to read concerning suicidal behavior? For example, bibliotherapy such as *Choosing to Live* (Ellis & Newman, 1996).

- Given the high rates of nonattendance of suicidal patients at aftercare follow-up, some 50%–60%, what explicitly have you done to increase the likelihood that your patient will indeed show up at your sessions? Have you set up a specific date and time for follow-up appointments; thoroughly explained the reasons for continuing with care; reviewed the likely goals and proposed length of therapy; reviewed with the client and, where appropriate, the client's family, their expectations and possible misconceptions about therapy; directly addressed any possible resistance and maintained ongoing contact with the patient; actively sought out the patient when he/she became less responsive and did not show up for treatment; and actively engaged the patient and significant others in a verbal agreement to engage in at least six brief therapy sessions and, based on the progress during this time period, to consider extending treatment (see Moller, 1990; Rudd & Joiner, 1998a).

- Have you increased the number of outpatient visits and/or increased the number of telephone contacts?
- How have you evaluated the relative effectiveness of your interventions in reducing the patient's suicidal ideation and self-injurious behaviors (e.g., frequency, intensity, duration, specificity) and accompanying comorbidity and correlates (e.g., attributional style, ruminative behavior, problem-solving ability)? Have you also assessed for changes in protective factors such as an increase in social supports?
- On an ongoing basis, what patient changes have influenced the assessment and treatment decisions you made?
- If you are referring your patient to others, have you called ahead to verify that the patient could be seen, as advised? Have you followed up to ensure that the patient has in fact attended the sessions and is continuing treatment?
- Have you kept both accurate records and progress notes concerning the patient and have you shared this information and consulted with a colleague?

## INPATIENT STATUS

**When the suicidal patient has been seen on an inpatient basis, the following questions must be addressed**

- If the suicidal patient is an *inpatient*, are you providing constant surveillance in a secure ward? Have you informed the attending staff members of the patient's suicide risk?
- Have you put the patient on a suicide watch?
- Have you used physical and/or chemical restraints?
- Have you used oral or intravenous medications? How are you monitoring their effectiveness?
- Have you conducted a careful, systematic search of the patient and a careful review of the environment to remove all potential items that could be used in suicidal attempts?
- Have you trained your staff to identify suicide risk factors? Please describe this training and how you provide ongoing evaluation of the staff's skills.
- Do you have a rapid intervention team in your hospital setting to respond to suicidal attempts?
- Do you confer with professional colleagues about the suicidal risk assessment of this patient and document the formal consultation in the patient's record?
- Do you document in your progress notes the level of suicidal risk and attendant decisions and actions you take?

# References

Baumeister, R. F. (1990). Suicide as escape from self. *Psychological Review*, 97, 90–113.

Beck, M. S., Henriques, G. R., Warman, D. M., Brown, G. K., & Beck, A. T. (2004). A cognitive therapy intervention for suicide attempters: an overview of the treatment and case examples. *Cognitive and Behavioral Practice*, 11, 265–77.

Bongar, B. (1992). Guidelines for risk management in the care of the suicidal patient. In B. Bongar (ed.), *Suicide: Guidelines for Assessment, Management, and Treatment* (pp. 268–82). New York: Oxford University Press.

Bongar, B. (2002). *The Suicidal Patient: Clinical and Legal Standards of Care* (2nd edn). Washington, DC: American Psychological Association.

Bongar, B., & Harmatz, M. (1991). Clinical psychology graduate education in the study of suicide: availability, resources and importance. *Suicide and Life-Threatening Behavior*, 21, 231–44.

Bongar, B., Maris, R. W., Berman, A. L., & Litman, R. (1992). Outpatient standards of care and the suicidal patient. *Suicide and Life-Threatening Behavior*, 22, 453–78.

Bongar, B., Maris, R. W., Berman, A. L., Litman, R., & Silverman, M. (1993). Inpatient standards of care and the suicidal patients. Part 1. *Suicide and Life-Threatening Behavior*, 23, 245–56.

Chemtob, C. M., Bauer, G. B., Hamada, R. S., Pelowski., S. R., & Muraoka, M. Y. (1989). Patient suicide: occupational hazard for psychologists and psychiatrists. *Professional Psychology: Research and Practice*, 20, 294–300.

Chiles, J. A., & Strosahl, K. D. (1995). *The Suicidal Patients: Principles of Assessment, Treatment and Case Management*. Washington, DC: American Psychiatric Press.

Clark, D. C. (1998). The evaluation and management of the suicidal patients. In P. Kleespies (ed.), *Emergencies in Mental Health Practice* (pp. 75–94). New York: Guilford Press.

Clum, G. A., & Lerner, M. (1990). A problem-solving approach to treating individuals at risk for suicide. In D. Lester (ed.), *Current Concepts of Suicide*. Philadelphia, PA: Charles Press.

Deutsch, C. J. (1984). Self-reported sources of stress among psychotherapists. *Professional Psychology*, 15, 833–45.

Ellis, T. E. (1990). Strategies for helping suicidal clients, Part 1: Crisis management. In W. F. Fremouw, M. dePerczel, & T. E. Ellis (eds), *Suicide Risk: Assessment and Response Guidelines* (pp. 98–129). New York: Allyn & Bacon.

Ellis, T. E. (2004). Collaboration and self-help orientation in therapy with suicidal clients. *Journal of Contemporary Psychotherapy*, 34, 41–57.

Ellis, T. E. (in press). *Cognition and Suicide: Theory, Research and Practice*. Washington, DC: American Psychological Association.

Ellis, T. E., & Newman, C. F. (1996). *Choosing to Live: How to Defeat Suicide Through Cognitive Therapy*. Oakland, CA: New Harbinger Publications.

Freeman, A., & Reneicke, M. A. (1993). *Cognitive Therapy of Suicidal Behavior: A Manual for Treatment*. New York: Springer.

Fremouw, W. J., dePerczel, M., & Ellis, T. (1990). *Suicide Risk: Assessment and Response Guidelines*. New York: Pergamon Press.

Friedman, R. S. (1989). Hospital treatment of the suicidal patients. In D. G. Jacobs & H. N. Brown (eds), *Suicide: Understanding and Rresponding* (pp. 379–402). Madison, CT: International University Press.

Haw, C., Hawton, K., Houston, K., & Townsend, E. (2001). Psychiatric and personality disorders in deliberate self-harm patients, *British Journal of Psychiatry*, 178, 48–54.

Hawton, K., & van Heeringen, K. (eds) (2000). *International Handbook of Suicide and Attempted Suicide*. Chichester: Wiley & Sons.

Hawton, K., Townsend, E., Arensman, E., Gunnell, D., Hazell, P., House, A., van Heeringen, K. (1998a). *Deliberate Self-harm: The Efficacy of Psychosocial and Pharmacological Treatment*, Cochrane Review. Oxford: Cochrane Library.

Hawton, K., Arensman, E., Townsend, E., Bremner, P., Feldman, E., Goldney, R., et al., (1998b). Deliberate self-harm: Systematic review of efficacy of psychological and pharmacological treatment in preventing repetition. *British Medical Journal*, 317, 441–7.

Hendin, H. (1995). *Suicide in America: New and Expanded Edition*. New York: Norton.

Jacobs, D. G. (ed.) (2000). *The Harvard Medical School Guide to Suicide Assessment and Intervention*. New York: Wiley.

Jobes, D. A. (2000). Collaborating to prevent suicide: a clinical research perspective. *Suicide and Life-Threatening Behavior*, 30, 8–17.

Joiner, T. E., Rudd, M. D., & Rajab, M. H. (1997). The Modified Scale for Suicidal Ideation: factors of suicidality and their relation to clinical and diagnostic variables. *Journal of Abnormal Psychology*, 106, 260–5.

Joiner, T. E., Walker, R. L., Rudd, M. D., & Jobes, D. A. (1999). Scientizing and routinizing the assessment of suicidality in out-patient practice. *Professional Psychology: Research and Practice*, 30, 447–453.

Kleespies, P. M., & Dettmer, E. L. (2000). An evidence-based approach to evaluating and managing suicidal emergencies. *Journal of Clinical Psychology*, 56, 1109–30.

Kleespies, P. M., Deleppo, J. D., Gallagher, P., & Niles, B. (1999). Managing suicidal emergencies: recommendations for the practitioner. *Professional Psychology: Research and Practice*, 30, 454–63.

Kleespies, P. M., Deleppo, J. D., Mori, D. L., & Niles, B. L. (1998). The emergency interview. In P. Kleespies (ed.), *Emergencies in Mental Health Practice: Evaluation and Management*. New York: Guilford Press.

Leenaars, A. (2004). *Psychotherapy with Suicidal Patients*. Chichester: John Wiley & Sons.

Linehan, M. M. (1993). *Cognitive-Behavioral Treatment of Borderline Personality Disorder*. New York: Guilford.

Linehan, M. M. (1997). Behavioral treatment of suicidal behaviors. In D. M. Stoff & J. J. Mann (eds), *Behavioral Treatment of Suicidal Behaviors: Neurobiology of Suicide*. New York: Annals of New Academy of Suicide.

Linehan, M. M. (1999). Standard protocol for assessing and treating suicidal behaviors for patients in treatment. In D. G. Jacobs (ed.), *The Harvard Medical School Guide to Suicide Assessment and Intervention* (pp. 146–87). San Francisco, CA: Jossey-Bass.

Linehan, M. M., Armstrong, H. E., Suarez, A., Allman, D., & Heard, H. L. (1991). Cognitive-behavioral treatment of chronically parasuicidal borderline patients. *Archives of General Psychiatry*, 48, 1060–4.

Maltsberger, J. T. (1986). *Suicide Risk: The Formulation of Clinical Judgment*. New York: New York University Press.

Maltsberger, J. T., & Buie, D. H. (1989). Common errors in the management of suicidal patients. In D. Jacobs & H. N. Brown (eds), *Suicide: Understanding Responding*. Madison, CT: International University Press.

Maris, R. W. (1981). *Pathways to Suicide: A Survey of Self-Destructive Behaviors*. Baltimore, MD: Johns Hopkins University Press.

Meichenbaum, D. (1994). *Treating Adults with PTSD*. Clearwater, FL: Institute Press.

Meichenbaum, D. (2002). *Treatment of Individuals with Anger-Control Problems and Aggressive Behaviors: A Clinical Handbook*. Clearwater, FL: Institute Press.

Meichenbaum, D. (in press). Trauma and suicide: a constructive narrative perspective. In T. Ellis (ed.), *Cognition and Suicide: Theory, Research and Practice*. Washington, DC: American Psychological Association.

Michel, K., & Valach, L. (1997). Suicide as goal-directed behavior. *Archives of Suicide Research*, 3, 213–21.

Michel, K., Maltsberger, J. T., Jobes, D. A., Leenaars, A. A., Orbach, L., Stadler, R., *et al.* (2002). Discovering the truth in attempted suicide. *American Journal of Psychotherapy*, 56, 424–37.

Moller, H. J. (1990). Evaluation of aftercare strategies. In G. Ferrari, M. Bellini & P. Crepet (eds), *Suicidal Behavior and Risk Factors* (pp. 39–44). Bologna: Monduzzi Editore.

O'Carroll, P., Berman, A., Maris, R., Moscicki, E., Tanney, B., & Silverman, M. (1996). Beyond the Tower of Babel: a nomenclature for suicidology. *Suicide and Life Threatening Behavior*, 26, 237–59.

Pokorny, A. D. (1993). Prediction of suicide in psychiatric patients. In R. W. Maris, A. L. Berman, J. T. Maltsberger, & R. I. Yulit (eds), *Assessment and Prediction of Suicide*. New York: Guilford.

Ramsay, R. F. (1987). *A Suicide Prevention Training Program: Trainer's Handbook* (3rd edn). Calgary, AB: Ramsay, Tanney, Tierney & Long.

Range, L. M., & Knott, E. C. (1997). Twenty suicide assessment instruments: evaluation and recommendations. *Death Studies*, 21, 25–8.

Reilly, C. E. (1998). Cognitive therapy for the suicidal patient: a case study. *Perspectives in Psychiatric Care*, 34, 26–31.

Rudd, M. D. (1998). An integrative conceptual and organization approach to treating suicidality. *Psychotherapy*, 335, 346–60.

Rudd, M. D. (2000). Integrating science into practice of clinical suicidology. In R. W. Maris, S. S. Connetto, J. L. McIntosh, & M. M. Silverman (eds), *Review of Suicidology, 2000* (pp. 47–83). New York: Guilford Press.

Rudd, M. D., & Joiner, T. E. (1998a). The assessment, management and treatment of suicidality: towards clinically informed and balanced standards of care. *Clinical Psychology: Science and Practice*, 5, 135–50.

Rudd, M. D., & Joiner, T. E. (1998b). An integrative conceptual framework for assessing and treating suicidal behavior in adolescents. *Journal of Adolescence*, 21, 489–98.

Rudd, M. D., Joiner, T. E., & Rajab, M. H. (2001). *Treating Suicidal Behavior: An Effective, Time-Limited Approach*. New York: Guilford Press.

Rudd, M. D., Rajah, M. H., Orman, D. T., Studman, D. A., Joiner, T., & Dixon, W. (1996). Effectiveness of an outpatient intervention targeting suicidal young adults: preliminary results. *Journal of Consulting and Clinical Psychology*, 64, 179–90.

Salkovskis, P., Atha, C., & Storer, D. (1990) Cognitive-behavioral problem-solving in the treatment of patients who repeatedly attempt suicide: a controlled trial. *British Journal of Psychiatry*, 157, 871–6.

Schneidman, E. S. (1993). *Suicide a Psychache: A Clinical Approach to Self-Destructive Behavior*. Northwale, NJ: Jason Aronson.

Schneidman, E. S. (1996). *The Suicidal Mind*. New York: Oxford University Press.

Silverman, M., Berman, A., Bongar, B., Litman, R. E., & Maris, R. (1994). Inpatient standards of care and the suicidal patient. Part II. *Suicide and Life-Threatening Behavior*, 24, 152–69.

Spirito, A., Boergers, J., & Donaldson, D. (2000). Adolescent suicide attempters: post-attempt course and implications for treatment. *Clinical Psychology and Psychotherapy*, 7, 161–73.

Townsend, E., Hawton, K., Altman, D. G., & Arensman, E. (2001). The efficacy of problem-solving treatment after deliberate self-harm: meta-analysis of randomized controlled trials with respect to depression, helplessness and improvements in problems. *Psychological Medicine*, 31, 979–88.

Weishaar, M., & Beck, A. T. (1990). Cognitive approaches to understanding and treating suicidal behavior. In S. Blumenthal & D. Kupfer (eds), *Suicide Over the Life Cycle*. Washington, DC: American Psychiatric Press.

Werth, J. L. (1996). *Rational Suicide? Implications for Mental Health Professionals*. Washington, DC: Taylor & Francis.

# 15

## EVERY PARENT'S WORST NIGHTMARE

*Donald Meichenbaum*

Monica had all of the characteristics that predict a favorable prognosis. She was a prototypical "YAVIS" – Young, Attractive, Verbal, Intelligent, and Successful. Monica was a thirty-six-year-old mother and teacher, married to a successful businessman. Although her husband, Bruce, traveled frequently as part of his work, they had a solid marriage and an excellent relationship with their eleven-year-old daughter, Vickie. They lived in a comfortable suburban area where they felt insulated from the dangers of urban living.

Although Monica was fortunate to live a "privileged life," as she described it, she entered the therapy office depressed to the point of contemplating suicide. Distraught, listless, and fearful, her life had turned around on a dime. Meichenbaum wondered to himself what events could have so affected an individual that her life had changed so quickly and profoundly. He invited Monica to tell her story.

### The home invasion

Monica spent a great deal of time at home with her daughter. With her husband traveling so much, Monica and Vickie enjoyed an even closer than usual mother–daughter relationship. Vickie was a bright and precocious girl, "wise beyond her years," as her mother described her, which allowed them to relate to one another on many different levels. It had been their custom to talk about their lives and share intimacies, catching one another up on their respective days before they would prepare themselves for bed.

– Meichenbaum, D. (2003). Every parents' worst nightmare. In J. A. Kotler & J. Carlson (eds), *The Mummy at the Dining Room Table*. San Francisco, CA: Jossey Bass (pp. 299–304). © Jossey Bass. Reproduced with permission from Wiley.

It was late one evening while her husband was out of town when Monica was suddenly awakened in the middle of a very deep sleep. She listened carefully for a minute or two, drifting back to sleep, when the noise repeated itself. She bolted upright in bed, now convinced that there was somebody else in the house. Their home had been invaded by burglars.

Monica could distinctly hear the footsteps of people rummaging downstairs. They didn't even seem to be trying to cover the sounds of their work downstairs. Utterly terrified, Monica's first thought was for Vickie. Somehow she had to protect her. After dialing 911 to call for help, she carefully crept into her daughter's room to wake her. They hid in the closet until the burglars left.

## Protective action

Fortunately, the burglars never did come upstairs. They took the stuff they wanted and left before the police arrived. Both Vickie and Monica were severely shaken by the experience, but came away relatively unscathed.

As one would suspect after such as event, the family engaged in a number of protective acts, including changing the locks and having an alarm system installed. As a last resort, Bruce convinced Monica to purchase a handgun.

Although these protective measures made Bruce feel more secure, Monica continued to live in fear that her house could be attacked again. She was also afraid of the ugly-looking handgun in her night-stand, reluctant even to look at it, much less touch it. When her neighbors reassured her that they too kept firearms in case of robbery, she felt a little better about the situation but still apprehensive.

Several months went by and routines in the house had returned to normal. Bruce was again on the road, leaving his daughter and wife alone. It was a stormy night. The wind was howling, and the rain was beating heavily against the roof and windows. The trees were making whistling sounds. The shutters were pounding against the side of the house.

A strange noise awakened Monica, different from those of the storm. Where was the sound coming from? Could it be that the burglars were back? Was it the harsh rain, the whistling trees, the clamoring shutters? Monica concentrated more and more; it was obvious that someone was in the house once again. Yet that couldn't possibly be so! How could they get past the new locks and the alarm system? She tried to remember if she had indeed set the alarm.

Monica sat up in bed, terrified, straining to discern the sounds from below. She thought she heard footsteps. Could she be dreaming? No, it was someone. Thank God, Monica thought, I have the gun.

She bolted for the nightstand, ripped open the drawer, lifted out the handgun. It was heavier than she remembered, not at all easy to hold in her trembling hand.

With her heart pounding and fear overwhelming her, she took the gun in hand and headed for Vickie's room, where they could hide once again. Now she felt protected by the gun.

The next part happened very quickly. The next thing Monica knew was that her bedroom door was suddenly thrown open and she heard the sound of a deafening boom. It was her gun. The gun had gone off when the bedroom door hit her hand.

There was a body lying on the floor, wedged in the doorway. A spreading pool of blood flowed from underneath the head. Monica, stunned and disoriented, looked down to see her daughter Vickie lying crumpled on the floor. Her brain matter, bits of bone, and blood were splattered across the opposite wall.

Monica was found twenty-four hours later by her husband, upon his return from his business trip. Monica was sitting on the floor in a catatonic state, with Vickie's body in her lap.

## Healing the trauma

When Meichenbaum heard Monica's story, he found that he could barely listen without being moved to tears. With four children of his own, he could not imagine what Monica went through in losing her daughter in such a tragic manner. No wonder she was depressed and suicidal.

The challenges were immense. How could he help Monica stay alive and continue functioning? Her daughter was gone. Her husband, who felt responsible for the tragedy, had left. Her life was in ruins. She could no longer work. She was totally without hope.

Friends and family had tried to console Monica. She was reassured repeatedly that what happened was not her fault. Doctors had prescribed antidepressants, but her sense of loss and feelings of guilt and hopelessness were unremitting.

"As every day passed," Monica observed, "I realized more fully that I had not only lost my daughter and my husband, I had lost the very purpose and shape of my life. Depression is winning and I am losing." On that tragic night, Monica lost not only her family but also her basic assumptions about the world, herself, and the future. Prior to the tragedy, Monica had a sense of a "story-book life," as she described it. The present, the past, and the future were bright.

In a situation like this, there are no words that can heal the pain or cure the aftermath of trauma, so the first task of Monica's therapy was to establish a therapeutic relationship in which she could tell her story, at her own pace, in as much detail as she wished. Meichenbaum noted that the goals of treatment were not only to help Monica with the bereavement process and to help her address her feelings of responsibility and guilt but also to help her find meaning in the experience of loss, allowing her, one would hope, to come to see herself as a survivor and not merely as a victim.

In order to avoid becoming overwhelmingly dispirited, Meichenbaum reminded himself that the stories of those who had been exposed to traumatic events and loss, whether the Holocaust or the ravages of war and terrorist attacks, are tales of resilience and courage. Where and how do they find the courage, the will to go on, to create a new way of making a life for themselves?

Meichenbaum's strategy was to encourage Monica to talk more fully about her pain and loss, but to do so in a way that would permit and encourage her to get "unstuck" from the moment that the gun went off and the immediate next twenty-four hours of despair. He asked Monica to do something that would be very difficult – and she should feel free to say no: Would she consider bringing into the next session a picture album of Vickie? Meichenbaum has found that reviewing such photo albums is a useful way to help those who grieve to broaden their memories from the moment of a tragedy, to that of a consideration of a full life.

Although it was very painful for Monica to review the lifetime of family pictures involving Vickie, the reflective process also provided her with the occasion to observe that one of the things that impressed her most was that Vickie was "wise beyond her years."

"If Vickie was here right now," Meichenbaum said to Monica, "if she could curl up into those loving arms and look into your caring eyes, what advice, if any, would Vickie, who was 'wise beyond her years,' as you describe her, have to offer? Moreover, Monica, if you kill yourself as you are considering, what will happen to the memory of Vickie? Those memories will die with you. Is that what Vickie would want?"

Meichenbaum was trying to accomplish two things simultaneously. First, he was honoring Vickie's memory, holding a sacred ceremony of reviewing their lives together. Second, he was helping Monica find reason to go on. He used the "absent other" of Vickie as a way to help Monica collaborate in generating coping efforts.

"Before this," Meichenbaum observed, "Monica had tried to suppress thinking about Vickie. The more she would suppress, the more she would have intrusive disturbing thoughts and feelings." So rather than hiding from the painful memories, Monica needed to transform her memories. The absent Vickie was transformed into a "consultant," a co-therapist in the healing process.

Under the guise of soliciting what advice Vickie might offer, Meichenbaum guided and supported Monica in collaboratively developing a variety of coping efforts. These included ways Monica could address her overwhelming feelings of guilt and her penchant to continually engage in "what if" forms of contrafactual thinking; her tendency to avoid social contacts and ways to re-enter life; and ways she could find meaning and develop a purpose in life. As Monica observed, "There are only so many if-onlies left. The only thing I can change is what I do now."

Meichenbaum helped Monica transform her pain and find meaning in her suffering. Monica concluded that if she could help prevent one more innocent child from dying from guns, then perhaps Vickie would not have died in vain. Monica decided to share her tragic story with anyone who would listen, including parent-teacher associations and church groups. She found meaning by highlighting the dangers of keeping guns in the house and the value of using gun safety locks.

## So the story continues

Monica continues to struggle with grief and depression, especially on the anniversary of her daughter's death. But her work on behalf of parent education groups in her effort to prevent similar tragedies in other households gives purpose to her life. She and her husband remain friends, but they decided to divorce. She went back to teaching in order to give to others.

One loose end that you might be wondering about: Were there really burglars in the house that fateful night that Vickie died?

Indeed there were. Somehow they managed to break into the house even with the new safety system in place. They had been downstairs when they heard the gun go off and had taken off right afterwards. Monica found some consolation in that, knowing that the sounds she had heard that night were not all in her head. She had enough to live with already.

# PART VII

# A Look to the Future

I mentioned at the outset that I am now retired and I spend the winters in Clearwater, Florida walking the beaches looking for dolphins to swim by. In addition, I while away the hours contemplating how to give "psychology away." For instance, consider how the world might be different if each President and Prime Minister included in his/her cabinet a cognitive behavior therapist, or someone who is an "expert" on decision-making? As described in the chapter in this part, could political leaders be made aware of the decision-making errors and improve their negotiation skills? I have enumerated the "dirty dozen" errors that contribute to dangerous aggression-engendering decisions.

Several papers reflect my beach-related musings. The following can be viewed and downloaded at the web address on page xii:

- How to Engage Members of the NRA in a Discussion to Change Gun Regulations.
- A Look into the Future of Psychotherapy: The Possible Role of Computer Technology.
- Self-Care for Trauma Psychotherapists and Care Givers: Individual, Social and Organizational Interventions.

Thank you for accompanying me on my journey. May you continue this venture.

# 16

# WAYS TO IMPROVE POLITICAL DECISION-MAKING

## Negotiating errors to be avoided

*Donald Meichenbaum*

## Foreword

I have been nurturing a "fantasy" for over a decade, and it is now time to go public with this preoccupation. I am sure some readers will characterize this "fantasy" as nothing more than an unrealistic "fairy tale" that would never ever come true. But as the popular entertainer Frank Sinatra used to sing, "Fairy tales can come true if you are young at heart," and I would add optimistic and practical. By the end of this chapter, you can determine if there is any basis for my hopefulness. Perhaps, my "fantasy" will inspire other young-at-heart dreamers.

## Origins of the fantasy

In order to understand the roots of this "pipe dream" it is relevant to describe how I spend my professional time. For the last 35 years I have been conducting research on the development of cognitive-behavior therapy, and in particular, I have been studying the thinking processes of an array of clinical populations. In fact, I have characterized myself as a "cognitive ethologist" who studies how individuals make decisions, especially under conditions of uncertainty and stress. Like the behavioral ethologist who is an astute and informed observer of animal behaviors, I am an observer (perhaps, even a voyeur) of how individuals tell "stories" to themselves and to others, and the implications this has for how they behave. In turn, I am eager to see how they behave and the resultant consequences, and the subsequent impact on their story-telling behaviors.

– Meichenbaum, D. (2011). Ways to improve political decision-making: negotiation errors to be avoided. In F. Aquilar & M. Galluccio (eds). *Psychological and Political Strategies for Peace Negotiations: A Cognitive Approach*. New York: Springer (pp. 87–98). Permission to republish granted by Springer.

For instance, with colleagues we have studied how individuals who have experienced traumatic events construe such events and construct "stories" that they tell themselves and others and what are their accompanying coping behaviors. What factors will determine if they will develop post traumatic stress disorder (Meichenbaum 2000), or whether they will evidence post traumatic growth and evidence resilience (Meichenbaum 2006a). I have also explored the heuristic value of adopting such a constructive narrative perspective in analyzing the thinking processes that contribute to such behaviors as becoming angry and aggressive (Meichenbaum 2002), attempting suicide (Meichenbaum 2006b), and not complying with medical procedures and engaging in treatment non-adherence (Meichenbaum and Fong 1993).

In short, I work with varied psychiatric and medical clients to develop a supportive, nonjudgmental, compassionate therapeutic alliance so they can better appreciate how they make decisions that impact their lives and the lives of others. I help them learn how to conduct cognitive, affective, and behavioral chain analyses and how to consider the motivational, developmental, functional, and consequential aspects of their decision-making processes. During the course of therapy with individuals, couples, families, and groups, I try to help educate them by means of the "art of questioning," discovery-based procedures, guided instruction, generalization and relapse prevention procedures, on how they construct their "realities" and make decisions. I help them learn how they can use feedback to make more informed and adaptive decisions in the future. I work to have my clients "take my voice with them." I ask them the following question:

> "Do you ever find yourself, out there, in your day-to-day experiences, asking yourself the questions that we ask each other right here in our sessions?"

A major objective of my work with clients is to establish a trusting, supportive, confidential relationship where they can collaboratively develop behavioral, achievable, and measurable, short-term, intermediate, and long-term goals that can help nurture "hope," and that can lead to behavioral changes (See Meichenbaum (1994, 2002, 2007) for examples of how to conduct such psychotherapeutic interventions.)

## My fantasy

Here is my fantasy. Could one provide a similar supportive service to politicians who make critical decisions that have widespread impact such as going to war, or decisions that impact the nation's economic well-being, or that impact global ecological concerns? Imagine for a moment, *what would happen if* every political leader included a cognitive-behavior therapist as an integral member of his or her closest advisory team. I told you this was a "fairy tale."

But hold on! There is a research literature on decision-making that could be brought to bear. In the same way that behavioral economics has emerged as a field, as reflected in the research program of Nobel Prize winner Daniel Kahneman and his colleagues (Kahneman *et al.* 1987) and in the recent book by Akerlof and Shiller (2009) on how "irrational exuberance" and misperceptions drive economic decision-making, could we develop a similar discipline called behavioral politics? In fact, some fine examples of this approach are already evident (see George 1980; Houghton 2008; Iyengar and McGuire 1993: Janis 1982; Jervis 1976; Staub 2007).

Just how far-fetched are these ideas? Appointed commissions, historians, and journalists often analyze after-the-fact (post-hoc), the decision-making processes of politicians that contribute to their decisions to go to war. They highlight how these politicians framed questions, selectively attended to certain aspects of data, held confirmatory beliefs (the drunkard's search), engaged in a wide range of cognitive and motivational errors, engaged in impulsive cognitive shortcuts, employed mental heuristics (or habits of thought) and stereotypes, used analogical and metaphorical thinking that distorted and compromised problem-solving efficiency, and used wishful thinking and "denial" procedures that contribute to their failure to both consider the credibility of the sources of information and the long-term consequences of the decisions to be taken. In addition, misperception-induced failures to empathize and perspective-take and group-think processes as well as "gaming the system" procedures may also undermine decision-making efficiency. See Tables 16.1 and 16.2 for examples of these cognitive errors and distortions that need to be avoided.

**TABLE 16.1** List of motivational and cognitive errors in decision-making "What to watch out for"

---

**I. *Use of cognitive shortcuts***

1. Tendency to use the most *salient* or most *readily available examples* and the tendency to take them as being most *representative* of a whole class of events. Such "mental heuristics" (habits of thought) may be emotionally charged and be selectively retrieved in a mood-congruent fashion (Tversky and Kahneman 1974, 1981, 1986).

2. Tendency to use *stereotypes* and *black-white prejudicial dichotomous thinking* in formulating decisions (Kahneman *et al.* 1987).

3. Tendency to use *metaphors* and *analogies* that may oversimplify and misrepresent the complexity of the present situation. Tendency to draw on experience that is familiar from a historical analysis, but that *distorts the present situation* (Dodge 2008; Dyson and Preston 2008; Khong 1992: Lakoff and Johnson 1980).

4. Tendency to reason by *historical analogies* by turning to history to justify policies that have already been settled on by misreading historical parallels and engaging in "rhetorical jujitsu." As Lakoff and Johnson (1980) observe, "Frames trump facts."

**II. *Desire for cognitive consistency***

5. Tendency to employ a *confirmatory bias* and seek information that is only consistent with prior views or existing hypotheses. This is also known as the "drunkard's search" to characterize someone who looks for his key at night time under the lamp post because the light is best there, even though he has lost his key in the alleyway. The directive to seek information that "fits" what you are looking for, or to only ask those who concur with your opinion for their views illustrates this confirmatory bias (Houghton 2008).

---

*(Continued)*

**TABLE 16.1** (Continued)

6. Tendency to *stubbornly hold a mind-set* and to "cherry pick" for consistent data and to manipulate information to fit pre-existing notions that may be anchored to faulty suppositions. Desire to hear what one wants to hear and disregard incompatible information and to view non-agreeing participants as not being part of "the team" (Suskind 2004).

### III. *Cognitive deficits and distortions*

7. Tendency to engage in informational processes that *fail to* consider how the questions or situations *were framed* (posed); *fail to* consider multiple non-violent options or alternatives; and *fail to* consider the full range of possible consequences; not think through the "aftermath" of decisions; and *fail to* calculate which course of action is in your and others' best interests and that are most consistent with your values (Brooks 2008; Dodge *et al.* 1990; Jervis 1976; Tversky and Kahneman 1986).

8. Tendency to hold *a hostile attributional bias* whereby you readily view each perceived provocation as a sign of "intentionality," which contributes to aggressive counter reactions. Tendency to misperceive and misinterpret interpersonal cues and *fail to* consider *alternative interpretations* (Dodge 2008).

9. Tendency to *fail to demonstrate empathy* with one's adversary and *fail to* perspective-take on what may contribute to the decision-making processes of others. Putting oneself in the shoes of another in order to better understand his/her actions can contribute to conflict avoidance and conflict resolution (Houghton 2008; White 1968).

10. Tendency to engage in *impulsive* and *snap decisions* when handling complex problems, thus failing to adequately weigh consequences (Gladwell 2005; Houghton 2008). As the adage goes, "If there is a simple solution to a complex problem, it is usually wrong."

11. Tendency to make the *fundamental attribution error* of overestimating the extent to which *one's actions* are viewed as the result of situational factors, while someone else's actions are viewed as being the result of their disposition. This attribution error can lead to over- and under-estimation of behavioral responsibility and lead to misconceptions of how alterable an individual's or a group's behavior may be (Fiske and Taylor 1984; Ross and Nisbett 1991).

12. Tendency to engage in *stereotyped fallacies* in their thinking. Decision-makers may make unwise decisions because they believe they are so smart, so powerful, and so invincible. Out of "fear," "hubris," and "irrational exuberance," this can lead to tunnel vision and immoral choices (Sternberg 2002, 2007).

13. Tendency to make *schema-related errors* or the tendency to make decisions based on personal and developmental issues ("hidden agenda") that go well beyond the demands of the present situation (e.g., prove one's manhood, not appear weak, win an election, improve popularity, a distraction procedure) (Houghton 2008; Iyengar and McGuire 1993; George 1980).

14. Tendency to *lack curiosity*, avoiding debates and confrontations among advisers, engaging in denial, and engaging in wishful thinking, reflecting a failure in question posing (Woodward 2006).

15. Tendency to *reason defensively* when failure occurs (blame others, or extraneous events, or chance), rather than evidence the emotional maturity to ask the anxiety-arousing challenging questions (e.g., about the validity of deeply held assumptions or about personal flaws in diagnosis or execution). Leaders need support and guidance on how to learn from errors and failure (Hackman and Wageman 2007).

**TABLE 16.1** (Continued)

16. Tendency to depend on *group think processes* that strive for unanimity and high group cohesiveness and that contribute to group homogeneity and solidarity and feelings of correctness and invulnerability. The insulation of the decision-making group contributes to self-censorship, collective rationalization, and self-reinforcing self-analysis, as some group members act as "guardians" of decision-makers. These processes are exacerbated when decisions have to be made under time pressure. Such group-think processes can lead group members to proceed along a path that in retrospect was obviously wrong-headed. Group-think tends to be closed to outside ideas and decision-makers and fails to ask or encourage difficult and challenging questions. Group-think can skew and close down the decision-making process (Brown and Paulus 2002; Janis 1982; Stroebe and Diehl 1994).

17. Tendency to use *gaming the system procedures* whereby advisors intentionally and strategically decide to avoid, bypass, misrepresent, and selectively distort other advisors' opinions and positions in order to manipulate the decision outcome. This type of "bureaucratic combat" may take the form of using back channels and proxies that can undermine the decision-making process.

**TABLE 16.2** Examples of "thinking errors"

| Type of error | Definition | Examples |
|---|---|---|
| 1. Use thinking shortcuts | Tendency to use well-worn "mental habits." Pick out most readily available other past examples and take them as a general representative example. | It is the same as … just like … |
| 2. Thinking by historical analogy | Tendency to seek historical analogies that misrepresent and do not fit present circumstances or situations. | Watch out for "like a" statements. This is like Lord Chamberlain giving into Nazism. |
| 3. Drunkard's search, use of "confirmatory bias" | Tendency to seek information that is only consistent with prior views. Seek information that "fits" what you are looking for. | Looks for keys at night under the lamp post because the light is best there, although he had lost his keys in alleyway. |
| 4. Mindset that leads to tunnel vision | Tendency to stubbornly hold firm beliefs that lead to selecting and manipulating data to "fit" what one wants to hear and believe. | "Cherry pick" the data. Frames always trump facts. How one frames questions influences decision-making. |
| 5. Lack of consequential thinking | Tendency to fail to consider short-term, intermediate and long-term consequences of one's actions. | Little or no planning and forethought. "State of Denial." |
| 6. Make snap decisions | Tendency to engage in impulsive decision-making. | "If there is a simple solution to a complex problem, it is usually wrong." |

*(Continued)*

**TABLE 16.2** (Continued)

| Type of error | Definition | Examples |
|---|---|---|
| 7. Use black-white thinking | Tendency to be prejudiced in your judgement. | "You are with us or against us.""You did it "on purpose" without checking this out. |
| 8. "Arrogance" | Exaggerated pride, wins "irrational exuberance." and unquestioned self-confidence | Know-it-all. No need to check with others. |
| 9. Reason defensively | Tendency to blame others, events, chance. | Failure to learn from errors or failures. Use "psychobabble" to explain failures. |
| 10. Lack of curiosity | Avoid debate, minimize confrontation, not question the accuracy of the data. | "What we have here is a failure to communicate and question." |
| 11. Use group-think processes | Strive for unanimity and high group cohesiveness, focus on group solidarity, homogeneity of decision. | Self-censorship, closed to outside ideas, close down decision-making process. |
| 12. Game the system | Strategically bypass, and misrepresent other advisors' positions. | Jumping chain of command. |

My fantasy is why wait until *after* such decisions have been made to write post-hoc analyses. Imagine what would be the impact if a politician had someone in his or her cabinet who could observe the group decision-making process in action and in a non-threatening, supportive, and confidential manner could provide in situ feedback on the possible impact of cognitive distortions and cognitive errors. For a moment, think through how this could be done both on a preventative basis and on an ongoing feedback basis.

## Preventative interventions

Since I have done a good deal of work on stress-inoculation training (Meichenbaum 2007), I fantasize how political decision-makers (as well as military decision-makers) can be encouraged to invite psychological researchers who have expertise in decision-making, as well as presidential historians and journalists to present the lessons to be learned from such events as the Cuban Missile Crisis, the Bay of Pigs invasion, and the invasion of Iraq. The examples need *not* be limited to U.S. historical episodes. One could find similar examples from many international conflicts. For example, consider the failure of U.N. members to act to prevent genocide in Rwanda (see Dallaire 2003). In fact, what would be the impact of such ongoing workshops, seminars, invited address for world leaders at the United Nations? What would be the impact if all key advisers (members of the "kitchen cabinet") to the president had to take a course in decision-making? Surely, this fantasy is getting out of hand.

Two immediate sets of questions emerge. What should be the content of such presentations? What do we know about decision-making under conditions of uncertainty and stress that could inform world leaders and politicians? Could one generate a "decisional checklist" for politicians and their advisors so they could self-monitor the efficacy of their decision-making efforts? The second set of questions concerns whether world leaders and their advisors and politicians would be interested and open to such feedback. Is this a naïve proposal?

As a clinician, I can attest to the fact that I am quite often confronted with unmotivated clients, and even mandated clients, who are uninterested in changing their behavior. Fortunately, there is a good deal of research on how to work effectively with such unmotivated clientele, subsumed under the research heading of motivational interviewing (Miller and Rollnick 2002). There are a number of intervention strategies that can be used and evaluated in an effort to teach decision-making procedures to politicians. The research field on instruction has learned a great deal about how to teach decision-making and problem-solving procedures to all types of professionals such as doctors, researchers, students, and negotiators (see Kelman 2008; Kirschner *et al.* 2006). Can we bring this research literature to bear in training politicians on decision-making? Perhaps there is some basis to this fantasy?

## Translating a "fantasy" into a practical intervention

What does the research indicate are the major motivational and cognitive errors that contribute to faulty decision-making? Table 16.1 provides a summary of many of these decisional errors. In working with policy decision-makers there would be a need to provide multiple case examples of each error, and moreover, there is a need to have participants, in any workshop, generate their own examples of each of these errors. They can then develop strategies and skills to counter each motivational and cognitive error. The first step in changing behavior is to increase awareness. The second step is to teach strategies and skills in effective decision-making using a combination of guidance-directive exercises and experiential training trials (Kirschner *et al.* 2006). Kelman (2000, 2008) describes a way to use integrative problem-solving as a means to nurture negotiation, mediational, and communicative decision-making skills. Brooks (2008), George (1980) and Thaler and Sunstein (2008) highlight that training in effective decision-making should include:

- A search and analysis of the presenting situation or problems and a careful consideration of how questions are being framed.
- A consideration of the major goals, values and interests that will be affected by the proposed decisions.

- A generation of a wide range of options and alternatives and a consideration of the likely and unlikely consequences of each – namely, the ability to ask critical questions and "think through" the problem and decision-making processes.
- A careful consideration of the problems and potential barriers that may arise during the implementation and the back-up plans should these be needed.
- A built-in evaluative and corrective feedback process and a willingness to change course, if necessary.

There is a difference between having policy-makers be able to articulate these decision-making steps and their actually using them on a regular basis while under pressure. This is when the cognitive behavior trainer comes into play. Like a good coach who is present during a game, the trainer or decision-making consultant can act like a supportive coach or "cognitive ethologist" and provide feedback in private about the decision-making process. For example, a conversation with a President might go like this:

> I noticed something and I wonder if you noticed this as well?
> How did you judge the credibility of the information that was presented? Whom else did you rely on for advice?
> Do you think it would be useful to solicit any other opinions of how you should proceed? Whom else do you think you should hear from?
> I noticed that in today's Press Conference you stated that "One of the lessons we learned from … (historical analogy) was …" I wonder if we could take a moment and examine the exact similarities that you were referring to and whether there are any important differences between the present situation and the historical example you offered? (e.g., Chamberlain in 1938) Moreover, if these important differences do indeed exist what are the implications for the decisions you are now considering?
> With regard to possible options, what are the pros and cons of taking such actions, both the short-term and the long-term consequences, including the historical consequences of the chosen option?
> What potential barriers or obstacles might arise and what will be the back-up plans that you should have in place?
> How did you come to the decision to do X? Could you take me through the decisional steps you took to come to this decision?
> What were your goals in this situation and how will undertaking these steps help you achieve your goals? How will you know if you are making progress?
> How do you feel about our chatting like this about the decision-making process? Do you believe this is helpful? Whom else in your cabinet would you like me to see next?

The need for such an ongoing consultation on the decision-making process was highlighted by Barton Gellman, who in his 2008 Pulitzer prize winning book on the Vice Presidency of Dick Cheney in the United States, describes in detail how decisions are made at the highest levels of government. One critical feature that he highlights is the way politicians "game the system" by selectively manipulating the type of information that is input into the decision-making process and how this information is framed (Gellman 2008). Gellman describes how politicians would intentionally and strategically avoid, bypass, and misrepresent the views of other advisors whose opinions may differ. Such actions can clearly undermine and bias the decision-making process.

Such "gaming the system" behaviors may arise out of a desire to exert influence, pursue a "hidden agenda" policy position, or avoid admitting a mistake. Whatever the motivational origins of such behaviors, the end result can be quite catastrophic, as Gellman documents.

How can the decision-making consultant help a president avoid such "traps"? The President can be encouraged to ask each of his or her advisors such questions as:

> *I appreciate your advice and input, but I am wondering if you have 'gamed the system' in presenting your position? Can you tell me which other advisors (members of our team) you have intentionally avoided discussing your views with?*
> *How would their views differ from your position? What steps, if any, have you already taken to implement your position?*

By the way, note that most of the questions asked by the decision-making consultant are "How" and "What" questions and not "Why" questions. The consultant wants to help decision-makers become more aware and knowledgeable about possible motivational and cognitive errors and cognitive distortions that can undermine the decision-making process. Tables 16.1 and 16.2 provide examples of the kind of motivational and cognitive errors that have been identified in the research literature that can be incorporated in any training program or consultative session. Such training would have to include concrete historical examples of each type of error and have participants offer their own examples of each type of error and strategies of ways to notice and change them in the future.

## A touch of reality testing

No "fairy tale" would be complete without an element of reality testing. Some readers may find this "fairy tale" as being too far-fetched. Consider some possible objections.

1. The decision-making processes are not as rational and linear as being depicted in this fantasy. Decision-makers often make emotionally charged, impulsive, intuitive, "gut" decisions based on incomplete information.
2. Decision-makers are often selecting options based on implicit (perhaps, unconscious) influences that act as "hidden agendas," guiding their decision-making processes.

3. Decision-makers often do not have the luxury of time to engage in such a reflective analysis.

4. There are too many critical decisions to be made in a short time and there is little or no time and little interest in analyzing how decisions are being made.

5. Decision-makers believe they already engage in such steps and are thus unlikely to be open, nor ready, to invite such ongoing probing and feedback. They may feel that they already have such decision-making skills in their repertoire or they would not have been chosen to be political leaders.

6. Decision-makers may be uninterested, feel embarrassed and threatened, and closed to receiving feedback on their decision-making processes. Their job is already very stressful. Why add more stress by receiving such feedback on a regular basis? Moreover, they do not want to be accused of being a "flip-flopper."

7. "Saving face" may be viewed as a critical feature and promoting a self-enhancing image may be considered as being central to political leadership. Such ongoing decisional feedback may compromise one's self-esteem and undermine self-confidence. Which political leader would want to learn that his or her cognitive errors and cognitive distortions contributed to the loss of life, economic downturns, or ecological endangerment? Political leaders have the ability to cognitively reframe events so they do not have to admit errors: "History will prove me correct!"

8. This reflective process involves a level of trust that would allow the observer (psychologist) to be "embedded" with decision-makers. The observer needs to focus on the integrity of the decision-making process and be neutral and dispassionate and not have "hidden agendas." Similarly, a life-time commitment to confidentiality is essential to gain such trust.

Any intervention to improve political decision-making would have to anticipate and address each of these potential barriers. How to anticipate and address these likely obstacles can constitute the basis for yet another fantasy for the young-at-heart. But such barriers are addressed on a day-to-day basis by cognitive-behavior therapists and their clients, with some success. Could the same intervention procedures be employed with world leaders and politicians? Dream on!

# References

Akerlof, G. A., & Shiller, R. J. (2009). *Animal Spirits: How Human Psychology Drives the Economy and Why It Matters for Global Capitalism*. Princeton, NJ: Princeton University Press.

Brooks, D. (2008, October 28). The behavioral revolution. *New York Times*, p. A23.

Brown, V. R., & Paulus, P. B. (2002). Making group brainstorming more effective: recommendations from an associative memory perspective. *Current Directions in Psychological Science*, 11, 208–12.

Dallaire, R. (2003). *Shake Hands with the Devil: The Failure of Humanity in Rwanda*. Toronto: Random House Canada. (Also see DVD at www.microfilmsinc.com.)

Dodge, K. A. (2008). Framing public policy and prevention of chronic violence in American youth. *American Psychologist, 63*, 573–90.

Dodge, K. A., Bates, J. E., & Petit, G. S. (1990). Mechanism in the cycle of violence. *Science, 250*, 1678–83.

Dyson, S., & Preston, T. (2006). Individual distractions of political leaders and the use of analogy in foreign policy decision making. *Political Psychology, 27*, 265–88.

Fiske, S., & Taylor, S. (1984). *Social Cognition.* Reading: Addison-Wesley.

Gellman, B. (2008). *Angler: The Cheney Vice Presidency.* New York: Penguin.

George, A. (1980). *Presidential Decision Making in Foreign Policy: The Effective Use of Information and Advice.* Boulder, CO: Westview.

Gladwell, M. (2005). *Blink: The Power of Thinking Without Thinking.* New York: Little, Brown.

Hackman, J., & Wageman, R. (2007). Asking the right questions about leadership: discussion and conclusions. *American Psychologist, 62*, 43–7.

Houghton, D. (2008). Invading and occupying Iraq. Some insights from political psychology. *Peace and Conflict, 14*, 169–92.

Iyengar, S., & McGuire, W. (eds) (1993). *Explorations in Political Psychology.* Durham, NC: Duke University Press.

Janis, I. L. (1982). *Group Think: Psychological Studies of Policy Decisions and Fiascoes* (2nd edn). Boston: Houghton Mifflin.

Jervis, R. (1976). *Perception and Misperception in International Policies.* Princeton, NJ: Princeton University Press.

Kahneman, D., Slovic, P., & Tversky, A. (eds) (1987). *Judgment Under Uncertainty: Heuristics and Biases.* Cambridge: Cambridge University Press.

Kelman, H. C. (2000). The role of the scholar-practitioner in international conflict resolution. *International Studies Perspectives, 1*, 273–88.

Kelman, H. C. (2008). Evaluating the contributions of interactive problem solving to the resolution of ethnonational conflict. *Peace and Conflict, 14*, 28–59.

Khong, Y. (1992). *Analogies at War: Korea, Munich, Dien Bien Plu and the Vietnam Decisions.* Princeton, NJ: Princeton University Press.

Kirschner, P. A., Sweller, J., & Clark, R. E. (2006). Why minimal guidance during instruction does not work: an analysis of the failure of constructivist, discovery, problem-based, experiential and inquiry-based teaching. *Educational Psychologist, 41*, 75–86.

Lakoff, G., & Johnson, M. (1980). *Metaphors We Live By.* Chicago: University of Chicago Press.

Meichenbaum, D. (1994). *Treatment of Adults with Posttraumatic Stress Disorder: A Clinical Handbook.* Clearwater, FL: Institute Press.

Meichenbaum, D. (2000). Treating patients with PTSD: a constructive narrative perspective. *NC-PTSD Clinical Quarterly, 9*, 55–9.

Meichenbaum, D. (2002). *Treatment of Individuals with Anger-Control Problems and Aggressive Behavior.* Clearwater, FL: Institute Press.

Meichenbaum, D. (2006a). Resilience and posttraumatic growth: a constructive narrative perspective. In L. G. Calhoun & R. G. Tedeschi (eds). *Handbook of Posttraumatic Growth* (pp. 355–68). Mahwah, NJ: Lawrence Erlbaum.

Meichenbaum, D. (2006b). Trauma and suicide: a constructive narrative perspective. In T. Ellis (ed.), *Cognition and Suicide: Theory Research and Practice* (pp. 333–54). Washington, DC: American Psychological Association.

Meichenbaum, D. (2007). Stress inoculation training: a preventative and treatment approach. In P. M. Lehrer, R. I. Woolfolk, & W. E. Sime (eds), *Principles and Practice of Stress Management* (pp. 497–518). New York: Guilford.

Meichenbaum, D., & Fong, G. (1993). How individuals control their own minds: a constructive narrative perspective. In D. M. Wegner & J. W. Pennebaker (eds). *Handbook on Mental Control*. New York: Prentice Hall.

Miller, W. R., & Rollnick, S. (2002). *Motivational Interviewing: Preparing People for Change* (2nd edn). New York: Guilford. (Also see www.motivationalinterview.org.)

Ross, L., & Nisbett, R. E. (1991). *The Person and the Situation*. New York: McGraw-Hill.

Staub, E. (2007). Preventing violence and terrorism and promoting positive relations between Dutch and Muslim communities in Amsterdam. *Peace and Conflict*, 113, 333–60.

Sternberg, R. J. (ed.) (2002). *Why Smart People Can Be So Stupid*. New Haven, CT: Yale University Press.

Sternberg, R. J. (ed.) (2007). A systems model of leadership: WICS. *American Psychologist*, 62, 34–42.

Stroebe, W., & Diehl, M. (1994). Why groups are less effective than their members: on productivity losses in idea-generating groups. In W. Stroebe & M. Hewstone (eds), *European Review of Social Psychology* (Vol. 5. pp. 271–303). Chichester: Wiley.

Suskind, R. (2004). *The Price of Loyalty: George W. Bush, the While House and the Education of Paul O'Neil*. New York: Simon & Shuster.

Thaler, R. H., & Sunstein, C. R. (2008). *Improving Decisions about Health, Wealth and Happiness*. New Haven, CT: Yale University Press.

Tversky, A., & Kahneman, D. (1974). Judgment under uncertainty: heuristics and biases. *Science*, 221, 453–8.

Tversky, A., & Kahneman, D. (1981). The framing of decisions and the psychology of choice. *Science*, 211, 453–8.

Tversky, A., & Kahneman, D. (1986). Rational choice and the framing of decisions. *Journal of Business*, 59, 251–78.

White, R. K. (1968). *Nobody Wanted War: Misperception in Vietnam and Other Wars*. Garden City, NY: Doubleday.

Woodward, B. (2006). *State of Denial: Bush at War. Part III*. New York: Simon & Shuster.

# INDEX